Prisoners—
— of Hope

Prisoners— —of Hope

111 INSPIRING STORIES

Jerald Borgie

Mill City Press, Inc.
322 First Avenue N, 5th floor
Minneapolis, MN 55401
612.455.2293
www.millcitypublishing.com

ISBN-13: 978-1-63505-321-0
LCCN: 2016913496

Cover Design by
Typeset by Jim Arneson, JAAD ~ Book Design

Printed in the United States of America

CONTENTS

Preface

In Dante's classic *Inferno*, the inscription over the gates of Hell declares: "Abandon all hope, you who enter here." We are in the midst of a society desperately seeking hope. I recently reread some of the inspirational stories in the *Chicken Soup for the Soul* series; it was amazing how popular these brief tales of ordinary people had become. So, I thought, why not write a book of short stories of hope based on Bible passages?

Prisoners of Hope: 111 Inspiring Stories actually had its impetus several decades ago. It was then that I, an ordained minister, rediscovered the meaning of Matthew 13:34: "Jesus spoke all these things to the crowd in parables; He did not say anything to them without using a parable." Jesus was a master storyteller.

Since then, I've made every effort to share the good news of the gospel through stories. These accounts are based on personal experiences, events in the lives of family and friends, articles, narratives, and legends that I have read.

Over one hundred stories of encouragement have now been penned. Some are humorous, others may bring tears; all, I trust, are inspiring. The message I want all readers to discover, however, is found in the biblical promise that for all God's children the best is yet to be.

Acknowledgments

W riting *Prisoners of Hope: 111 Inspiring Stories* would have certainly been a hopeless cause without the prayers, inspiration, and support of some very special people:

- To Samantha Edwards, my superb editor, a young lady I first met years ago when she was a student in our preschool.

- To David Cowen, my tech expert who took over whenever my computer-challenged brain failed me.

- To Ken Blanchard and Richard Swenson, renowned authors and personal friends who offered me ongoing words of encouragement

- To Marcia Borgie, my wife, who for the past 48 years has shared with me all that the years have brought including making sense out of my handwritten notes before the stories went to the editor.

- To you who are reading this book, may Jesus bless you with the gift of hope.

Sola Deo Gloria

"Your sin will find you out."

Numbers 32:23

It is said that King Charles III of Spain paid a visit to a prison in Barcelona, where he had several one-on-one conversations with some of the inmates. To each one he asked, "Why are you here?" One after another offered excuses, all trying to assure His Majesty that they were innocent victims of injustice and had done nothing wrong. One claimed that the judge had been bribed; another proclaimed that the witness against him was a liar; one more complained he had been framed; yet another insisted it was a case of mistaken identity.

The monarch was concluding his visit when he asked this question of a young convict. "I'm here because I stole some jewelry from an old lady." The king was astonished at this man's honest confession and declared, "You are much too bad to remain in the presence of all these innocent men. Surely your presence will corrupt them. Therefore, I am going to grant you a pardon and set you free."

One of my high school teachers often stated, "Honest confession is good for the soul." She was right. Our sins are not nearly as well-hidden as we might think they are. A burly National Football League lineman frequently stayed out late despite his team's curfew. He would often pile items under his blankets to make it appear as if he was in bed. At one hotel, however, he couldn't find enough things to stuff in his bed, so he picked up a floor lamp, stuck it under the covers, and out the door he went. When an assistant coach made the bed check rounds that night, he snapped on the light switch, and the whole bed lit up. Be sure, the Scriptures declare, "your sins will find you out."

We kid ourselves when we think they can remain hidden. Even more dangerous is the attitude that they are not all that important. "Surely God must have more important things to do than to worry about my petty vices." Not so, says the cross; sin matters. Some years ago there was a popular book on the *New York Times* Best Seller list titled *I'm OK-You're OK*. However, a very perceptive young Christian pondered, "If I'm OK and you're OK, what is Jesus doing on the cross?"

Whether we want to admit it or not, all of us are sinners. All of us—no exceptions—fall short and that creates a dilemma for God. He loves us but he cannot accept our sin. Transgression of His will for us brings brokenness and death. A child can be punished whenever he or she does wrong, but punishment in and of itself will not turn the child into a good and loving person. One cannot be punished into the kingdom of God. God's dilemma: He hates the sin but loves the sinner.

In Jesus Christ we see a God who is somewhat like the father in the following story. A father made it very clear to his belligerent young son that his conduct would have to change or punishment would follow. The boy tested the boundaries and disobeyed. As discipline, he was ordered to leave the dinner table and spend the night in the unlit attic. The fearful child made his way slowly up the steps, opened the seldom-used door, peered into the darkness and, with much apprehension, moved inside. The father sat at the dinner table. He had lost his appetite as he thought of his frightened child alone up in the cold, dismal attic.

"I know what you are thinking," his wife warned, "but you can't go back on your word. He will lose all respect for you."

"You are quite right. But it's so hard. I love that little guy and I know he is hurting and scared."

That night the father climbed the stairs with a biscuit and a glass of milk. He entered the pitch black room and sat down beside his boy. When the grateful child finished his snack, he peacefully fell asleep with his father's arm serving as his pillow. I believe our God is like that father.

"His works are perfect."

Deuteronomy 32:4

P astor James Lindvall was minister of a church that held a Christmas pageant for forty-seven consecutive years, always using the same director. The Christmas play ran like clockwork: perfect lighting, perfect pacing, just about everything was perfect. The director's commitment to perfection, however, was greater than her commitment to the children. She felt that when there were too many children there was no control. One year that policy was changed by the education committee, which included three mothers of last year's rejected shepherds, angels, wisemen, Mary and Joseph. They passed a resolution which stated that all children who wished to be in the Christmas pageant may do so. The longtime director resigned in disgust.

According to the Rev. Lindvall, the drama didn't fall flat with the director's resignation, but it was quite different. There must have been fifteen shepherds, twenty angels (without a doubt a heavenly host), and two dozen or more sheep. And, as you might have guessed, some of the lambs were wandering all over the church. Mary then entered the stage at a slow pace with her Joseph walking in all seriousness by her side. The narrator was supposed to read the biblical account that "Joseph went to Bethlehem to be taxed with Mary his espoused wife, who was great with child." However, the young mother who was reading the Scriptures was concerned that the children wouldn't understand the archaic language in the old King James Version, so she spontaneously switched to a more modern translation. She read, "Joseph went with Mary to register for the census. She was pregnant." As that last word echoed through the PA system little Joseph froze in his tracks. He gave Mary an astonished look, held his hands up and asked, "Pregnant? What do you mean pregnant?"

Needless to say, this really brought the house down. The pastor's wife was laughing out loud, leaned over to her husband and whispered, "You know that may well be what Joseph actually said." The former director glanced around with a look that seemed to say "See, I told you this would flop." During "Silent Night," some sheep meandered down the aisle and sat around the one-time director who had excluded them from previous pageants. Suddenly it all became very, very quiet. Even the sheep ceased moving about. Then Minnie McDonnel, a charter member, hard of hearing and always speaking too loudly, broke the spell when she exclaimed to her husband in a voice all could hear, "Perfect! It was just perfect!" And it was. It wasn't perfect in the way previous children's programs had been perfect, but it was perfect in the way our Lord makes things perfect, the manner in which He accepts our fumbling attempts at love and fairness and covers them with grace.

Have you ever known anyone who was a perfectionist? He or she would certainly be very hard to live with. In the British Museum in London rests the final draft of Thomas Gray's popular "Elegy Written In A Country Churchyard." Lovers of English literature marvel how each word seems to have been marked by painstakung effort. That is exactly what happened. Gray wasn't satisfied with his first draft so he rewrote it. Then he rewrote it again. This he continued to do for eight years. No matter what he did he was never satisfied. The museum has seventy-five drafts each carefully penned by hand.

Perfectionists are personalities who strain toward impossible goals and measure their self-worth only by their achievements. As a result, according to Stanford psychiatrist David Burns, they are terrified by the prospect of failure. They feel so driven but at the same time so unrewarded by their accomplishments. They are usually very unhappy individuals. Contrary to popular belief, Christians are not perfect. An old bumper sticker sums it up well: "Christians are not perfect, only forgiven."

Have you ever tried to keep a perfect house when a baby is in residence? Of course not. When an infant is there, we tend to forget about perfection and just think about love. That is the heart of Christmas; it is about a God who keeps His promises in ways beyond which we could possibly understand.

I read about a woman who was busy buying Christmas gifts and preparing delicious meals for her family's celebrations. Suddenly she realized that she had forgotten to send Christmas cards to her relatives and friends.

She dashed off to Target, chose a couple boxes of cards with a picture that she liked, hurried home to address the envelopes, made a special trip to the post office, and once and for all sighed with relief that the task had been completed. Imagine her shock the next day when she was glancing at the few cards that remained and read the message inside: "This card comes just to say that a little gift is on its way." Think of all those disappointed friends who are still waiting for the promised gift. Fortunately it wasn't like that with God's promised gift. The prophets continued to remind us that a gift was on the way, and what a gift it was! Not what we expected but way beyond our expectations. It was the perfect gift.

*"Choose for yourselves this day
whom you will serve..."*

Joshua 24:15

A Sunday school teacher was telling the story of the rich man and Lazarus: There sat Lazarus outside the wealthy homeowner's gate covered with sores and begging for food. The rich man passed by and paid no attention to him. Then they both died and Lazarus went to heaven, while the fellow with so much money found himself in far less desirable circumstances, which the teacher graphically described. When she had finished telling the story, she asked the children, "Now which would you rather be, old moneybags or Lazarus?" One little boy responded, "I would like to be the rich man until I died and then Lazarus afterwards." He expressed the desire of most of us: We want it both ways. We want our cake and we want to eat it too. The time comes for all of us, however, when we must make a choice. Most people are fortunate enough to have that option; pity the poor person who has no choice.

A young man was trying to convince his sweetheart to marry him, but she continued to resist him. Filled with anxiety, he asked, "Honey, is there someone else?"

She replied with a note of desperation, "There must be." She thought without a doubt she could do better. It is important for us to believe that we do have a choice.

In the 17th century Thomas Hobson rented out horses in Cambridge, England. He had a rule that any person renting one of his horses must take the one standing closest to the stable door. No matter who the person was, that was the rule. Soon people were using the expression "Hobson's choice," which really meant no choice at all. Sometimes life does throw us into "Hobson's choice" situations; certain circumstances can limit our options.

Maybe you will be able to identify with the owner of a small off-road motel. A recent business school graduate was staying one night in that motel. Eager to show off his new knowledge, he asked the owner, "So how's your business?"

The tired landlord shrugged his shoulders and muttered, "Not very good."

"Well, that's too bad. So what are your next steps? What do you plan to do to rectify this unhappy situation?"

The innkeeper scratched his head. "I don't know. I've never made enough in this business to stick with it. On the other hand, I've never lost enough to get out of it. I'm hoping to do one or the other this year."

Does his plight strike a responsive chord with you? Yankees legend Yogi Berra once pontificated: "When you come to a fork in the road, take it." It may be that even now you're standing at a fork in the road. Bearing the cross is not the same thing as wearing a cross.

There is a fascinating tale about a tourist who, on a trip to China, bought an old medallion which she liked so well that she had it dangling from her neck on numerous occasions. Its bizarre and striking design always gave rise to interested conversation; the lady became so fond of it that she adopted it as her own personal good luck charm.

The day came when she was a guest at a diplomatic dinner in the nation's capitol. She noticed that the Chinese ambassador was observing her medallion with a faint smile on his lips. "Have you seen one of these before, Mr. Ambassador?" the dignified woman inquired.

He admitted that he had, but then soon changed the subject.

"Please, sir, would you be so kind as to translate the inscription on it?"

The diplomat shook his head somewhat from side to side and politely responded that he would rather not.

"Oh please," she pleaded, "I'd be ever so grateful."

He took a deep breath and, with much reluctance, read: "Licensed Prostitute, City of Shanghai."

Talk about embarrassment. She had been proudly showing off that medallion with no hint or understanding of what it signified. How many people wear a cross on their lapel or on a necklace with no more of an idea of what it means than did that proud lady with her Chinese medallion?

In case you think I am overstating the matter, note the following item from *Leadership Magazine*. It seems a Denver woman shared with her pastor a recent experience that she felt was indicative of the times in which we live. She was a customer in a jewelry store looking for a necklace and explained to the clerk, "I'd like a gold cross." The employee behind the counter looked over the display case and then inquired, "Do you want a plain one or one with the little man on it?" If that doesn't make you laugh it will make you cry. Bearing a cross is not the same thing as wearing a cross. Most of us are like the little boy in Sunday school; we'd like to be the rich man until we die, then we want to be Lazarus. We can't have it both ways. The choice is ours. It is a decision that no one can make for us.

"Everyone did as he saw fit."

Judges 21:25

In 1985, Leo Rosten wrote a story about Yuri Smolenski, a Jewish engineer in the former Soviet Union. Yuri had been ordered to move to a minor position in a faraway Siberian outpost. His parents, in tears, were watching him pack. "I'll write every week," promised Yuri. "But the censorship," wailed his mother, "They will watch every word." The young man's father had an idea: "Anything you write in black we'll know is true. But anything you write in red ink we will know is nonsense."

A month passed, then from Siberia came a long letter–all in black ink! "Dear Mama and Papa," the missive reported, "I can't wait to tell you how happy I am here. It is a worker's paradise. We are treated like kings. I live in a fine apartment. The local butcher has fresh meat every day! There are many concerts and movies–all free. There is not even a tiny bit of antisemitism. Love your son, Yuri. P.S. There is only one thing we can't find here–red ink!"

It seems like it is getting more and more difficult to know what is true in today's world. To most Americans, truth is relative. According to author and pollster

George Barna, in an August 2005 survey, nearly three-fourths of all citizens of the U.S. believe that there is no such thing as absolute truth. The Bible is considered to be little more than an ancient book of inspiring stories and helpful suggestions.

Think of the moral crisis that we are in. Without absolute moral truth, there can be no right or wrong. Without right or wrong, there is no such thing as sin. Without sin, there is no judgment or condemnation. If there is no condemnation, then there is no need for a Savior. Consequently, the suffering, death, and resurrection of Jesus has no meaning and no eternal consequences. If we reject absolute moral truth as the Bible teaches, then Christians have nothing to offer our decaying culture beyond some mere buildings and some interesting or entertaining programs.

Dr. Vern Moreland, longtime professor at the University of Vermont, was strolling across the campus when he came upon one of his students sitting at a small table, reading a book and listening to music coming from a compact stereo. The friendly student invited Moreland to take a seat at his table, and the professor accepted. Very soon they found themselves engaged in thoughtful conversation. Eventually, the student commented, "Dr. Moreland, what you are saying is true for you but it's not true for me." He went on to insist that all truth is relative. As Moreland got up to leave, he reached over and picked up the stereo and started to walk away. "Hey! What are you doing?"

"I'm taking your stereo."

"What do you mean you're taking my stereo? You can't do that."

"Why not? I like it and I plan to listen to some inspirational music. Since everything is relative, you have no right to force me to accept your belief that it is wrong for me to take your stereo." He concluded, "My friend, are you absolutely certain that there is no absolute truth?"

If it is absolute truth, it is true for all people, in all places, for all time. Eighty times Jesus declared, "I tell you the truth..." It is in the Holy Scripture that truth is found. Jesus said it is knowing the truth that sets us free. We need to heed the truth, otherwise we become like the widow who was talked into a major house repair by a shady contractor. She lost nearly $50,000 of her life's savings. She called the Better Business Bureau and filed a complaint.

The BBB representative said, "It sounded a bit fishy right from the beginning, didn't it? Why didn't you call us before you invested your money?"

"Oh," she confessed, "I was afraid if I called you, you'd advise me not to do it."

We shake our heads at such a foolish approach to the truth but most of us have to admit there were times when we just closed our eyes or ears because we really didn't want to see or hear. "If you continue in my word," Jesus said, "You will know the truth..."

"For their prayer reached heaven..."

II Chronicles 30:27

Karen Hansen is a member of Praying Compatriots, an online prayer cell. People from across the nation share with each other joys, sorrows, pains, and victories. They join together in offering to God their petitions, intercessions, and words of thanksgiving.

Carol, a coed from Texas Lutheran University, e-mailed the group with an amazing story of answered prayer. She had gone home for the summer and had spent many hours one Friday visiting with some friends. The evening had been a wonderful time of reminiscing and sharing. It was quite late when she said goodnight, and headed for home, which was only about a ten minute walk. She lived in a small town where just about everybody knew each other. Carol prayed a quick prayer that God would keep her safe and escort her on her brief journey.

She approached a darkened alley, hesitated a moment, then decided to take it as a short cut. Carol had gone about halfway when she saw a man standing at the end, as though he was waiting for her. This was a bit frightening and her heart started pounding as she asked God to protect her. She soon felt a comforting feeling of quietness and security. It was almost as if someone was walking with her. When she reached the end of the alley, the stranger stepped aside and she walked right past him and was soon in the safety of her own home.

The following morning she heard on the local radio newscast that a young lady had been attacked and raped in the same alley just twenty minutes after she had been there. Deeply troubled by this tragedy and the fact that it could have been her, sent tears cascading down her cheeks.

Thanking the Lord again for her safety, Carol decided to report to the police what she had experienced. She was certain that she could recognize the man. The officers asked if she would be willing to look at a lineup to see if indeed she could identify him. Carol agreed and without a moment's hesitation, pointed out the man she had seen in the alley. The rapist, knowing that he had been caught, broke down and confessed.

The police congratulated her for her bravery and, as a way of expressing their appreciation, asked if there was anything they could do for her. She requested that they ask the man one question. She was curious as to why he had not attacked her. He answered, "Because she wasn't alone. She had a big guy walking right beside her."

In 1946, PFC Bruce Borden returned home from World War II and found his mother desperately ill with kidney problems. She needed an immediate blood transfusion to save her life. Barring a miracle, this would be impossible. Her blood type was AB negative and no one in the family shared this. It was so rare that less than one percent of the population had AB negative blood and nation-wide blood banks did not exist in those days. Her loved ones pleaded with the Lord to heal her but she grew weaker and weaker.

Bruce decided to gather his family together and offer a final farewell to his mother. As he was driving home from the hospital, he stopped to pick up a young soldier who was hitchhiking. The traveler thanked him for stopping and introduced himself and added that he was headed home and with good luck he would reach his destination before nightfall.

They engaged in small talk for a while, when the perceptive young soldier observed, "You're hurting, aren't you?" Through his tears, Bruce blurted out his story of his dying mother who would soon perish because it was not possible to match her blood type. The hitchhiker suggested that the driver pull over to the side of the road. Then, in silence, he removed his dog tags from around his neck and handed them to Bruce. Imprinted on the tags was the soldier's name, his social security number, his religious preference, and his blood type—which was the very rare *AB negative*. The critically ill patient received the blood transfusion a few hours later. She recovered fully and lived another forty-seven years.

Coincidence? I don't think so. The GI and his family were 100 percent convinced that this was no accident—the hitchhiker had been sent by God. All we know is that these so-called coincidences happen quite often to people of faith who believe in the power of prayer. Only the Lord Himself knows how many have been blessed with emotional, spiritual, and sometimes physical healing through the fervent prayers that have reached heaven. Alfred Lord Tennyson, Poet Laureate of Great Britain during the reign of Queen Victoria, wrote, "More things are wrought by prayer than this world dreams of."

"I will dwell in the house of the Lord forever."

Psalm 23:6

Mandy was a brand-new Christian and expressed her deep concern for a good friend who was in the final stages of her battle with terminal cancer. She knew that her beloved neighbor had never had any room for God in her life. Even so, she was bold enough to ask her if she would be open to a visit from her pastor. Out of respect for her devoted friend, the dying woman agreed. I visited her in her home where she was living out her final days. A note taped to the front door had my name on it along with the invitation to come in. I entered her room and introduced myself, adding, "Your friend, Mandy, told me you might be open to some heart-to-heart conversation."

"That's right. I let her know that would be fine."

I paused, then asked, "What's going on in your life?"

In a very matter-of-fact fashion she stated, "I'm dying. I'm a bit surprised that I've lived this long. Cancer can be found in every part of my body. Everyone is amazed that I'm still around but I'm sure it won't be much longer."

"May I read to you the Twenty-third Psalm? It's in the heart of the Bible."

"I don't know what that is. Go ahead if you like."

I opened the Bible to its middle pages and she heard the well-known Psalm for the first time. With a puzzled expression, she inquired, "What does it mean? My eyes are closed but I'm listening and want to understand."

For the next twenty minutes, her bedroom became akin to that of a kindergarten Sunday school class. Her sense of wonderment was like that of a small child, desiring to hear more about the Good Shepherd. I could tell that she was tiring and didn't want to overstay my visit, so I asked her if we could conclude with prayer. She responded, "You do the praying. I don't know how."

I offered up prayers for insight and mercy. "Shall we continue our conversation next week?"

"Thank you, pastor. Yes, I would like that."

I returned the following Tuesday, and spoke with her husband out on the porch. He said, "All her life she has claimed to be an atheist, yet this morning she confessed that maybe she'd been wrong. Maybe there is a God. Possibly there could be an afterlife."

She was much weaker that day. "Thanks for coming. I'm having trouble talking today, so you do the talking and I promise to listen." We went back to square one, starting with John 3:16. "How is it that I have never heard those words before?" Then she answered her own question, "I guess I never bothered to listen."

"I'm going to pray a prayer and when I finish, if you can honestly say, 'Yes, that's my prayer,' then declare 'AMEN'. Here we go: Lord, have mercy on me, a sinner. Thank you for loving me even though I've ignored you all these years. Forgive me, remember me, save me for Jesus' sake."

She confessed, "That is my prayer, my prayer...my prayer. Have mercy on me." With tears streaming down her cheeks, she added, "Amen." She lived three more days. Only the Lord knows for sure what was happening in her heart, but we trust that her prayers for mercy and forgiveness were received with rejoicing in heaven.

Since the beginning of time, all people have found themselves in a world where they are only temporary visitors. It is never a question of if we will die–the only question is when it will happen. We don't know how long our road through this life will be, but we do know where it ends. The grave is waiting.

Human beings of every race have hoped that there was more beyond the burial place. Egyptians placed a supply of food next to the dead in order for them to have nourishment as they traveled into the unknown. Scandinavians provided weapons for the Viking warriors to accompany them on their journey to Valhalla. Some African tribes buried wives with their husbands for companionship. Even American Indians held a belief in a tomorrow that would lead to the happy hunting ground.

Nearly every tribe, creed, and culture hoped that there would be an answer to what lies beyond this life, but there was only silence until the Word of God was made flesh and dwelt among us and conquered the grave. This answer was forever made plain through the empty tomb. Every child of God could have engraved on his/her tombstone: "To be continued. The best is yet to be."

Before Christopher Columbus discovered the New World, the coat of arms of Spain bore the motto: "Ne Plus Ultra," which means there is nothing beyond. But Columbus had a vision of unknown worlds that would be revealed to an adventurer. With his discoveries, the "Ne" was dropped from the Spanish insignia, leaving the "Plus Ultra"–there is more beyond. Before Jesus came into the world and removed the sting of death with his victory over the grave, "Ne Plus Ultra" remained the motto of most of humanity. Now the burial sites of all His children proclaim, "Plus Ultra." There is more beyond. How much more? Saint Paul, through the power of the Holy Spirit, gave us this observation: "No eye has seen, no ear has heard, no mind has conceived what God has prepared for those who love Him."

"As a father has compassion..."

Psalm 103:13

A pastor was quizzing a dozen seated boys and girls during the children's sermon about the influences in their lives. "Who taught you to count?" he inquired.

Tommy piped up and responded, "My dad taught me to count."

"Great, Tommy," commented the preacher, "What comes after 8?"

"9," Tommy answered with confidence.

"And what comes after 9?"

"10!" he boldly declared.

"And what comes after 10?"

"A jack!" the boy shouted triumphantly.

We learn many things from our fathers, don't we?

During a special time of remembrance at his father's funeral, a man named Jeremy Dye shared the following childhood memory. The circus had arrived in their town and the children's excitement was at fever pitch. He and his father stood in line at the entrance to the Ringling Bros., waiting to buy their tickets. Standing patiently in front of them was a husband and wife with six children, all under the age of twelve. They were remarkably well-behaved and most certainly thrilled with the anticipation of this dream coming true.

It became clear to Jeremy and his dad that this was a family of modest means. When the father of the family was informed of the entrance fees, his face filled with disappointment. He didn't have enough money to purchase tickets for his whole family. Mr. Dye took a twenty- dollar bill out of his pocket and dropped it on the ground. He then bent down, picked it up and tapped the gentleman on the shoulder. "I found this on the ground. It must be yours." Jeremy watched in silence and awe as the grateful father of six accepted the cash and bought tickets for his happy family. Jeremy did not see the circus that day, but he did see a glimpse of the Heavenly Father in his own father's selfless act.

There is nothing more important that a father can do for his children than to provide them with a good example. A young dad was romping around with his three-year-old son when the child firmly placed both his hands on his father's face-to make sure that he was listening. Then, in all seriousness, he promised, "Daddy, when I grow up I'm going to be just like you." The stunned parent later stated that his son's words caused both exhilaration and fear. He confessed that he was driven to his knees with the heartfelt prayer that he would always be a worthy example for his boy.

One of the most distinct childhood memories I have is learning how to ride a bike. Dad was my instructor, calmly explaining and demonstrating how to mount, stop, and pedal. Then it was my turn: the Schwinn wobbled and almost fell but Dad steadied it as he ran alongside me. Then he let go. I fell. We tried again, over and over. I was a slow learner, but at long last I got it! Away I went, leaving him in the distance shouting words of encouragement as I disappeared around the corner.

The years flashed by and suddenly I found myself demonstrating for my own six-year- old son how to ride a bicycle. I ran beside the Roadmaster, sometimes hundreds of yards, my heart beating and my tongue hanging out. I struggled to help him keep his balance. Then, to my surprise and his delight, there he went. I shouted words of encouragement as he got farther and farther away. I sensed that I was being left behind. The cycle of life continues and although I have some regrets about things I wish I had done, I'm glad I was there when my son was learning to ride a bike. Life goes by so swiftly and that day will never come again. I must make the most of it.

Fred Rogers, whose TV show *Mister Rogers' Neighborhood* was popular with children for over a quarter of a century, once passionately declared, "My dad has shown me that if I take care of the present, I take care of the forever at the same time." That is most certainly true. The time to love is now, and in the lives of most children, love is spelled T-I-M-E. For over twenty years our family table prayer was: "Bless our home, Father, that we cherish the bread before there is none, discover each other before we leave, and enjoy each other for what we are while we have time." The clay may be soft and pliable today, but all too quickly it will harden and good intentions will be to no avail. Tomorrow may very well be too late.

All parents would do well to heed the inspired words of the apostle Paul when, in his letter to the Ephesians, he reminds fathers that they have been instructed by their Heavenly Father to teach their children the way they should go. The very best teaching is always, without exception, by example.

"Hope in His unfailing love."

Psalm 147:11

It was a very cold and windy evening in Houston in early December of 1989. The Holiday Inn had rented less than a third of its rooms that day. The banquet hall, though, was at full capacity, the bar was hopping, and the dining room packed. One of the hotel guests thought he heard a baby crying. He looked out into the hallway where he spotted a plain cardboard box. His heart beat with excitement when the startled man discovered a baby in the box. He ran to the front desk shouting, "Come quick! There's a newborn baby out here!"

The manager hurried after the guest down the corridor and there they found a tiny baby in a blood stained towel lying in a box. The hotel executive snatched the box with its precious cargo and raced to the assistant manager's office. This take-charge lady placed her jacket over the baby and coddled it next to her body in an attempt to keep it warm. A 911 call was placed and soon police and an ambulance arrived. The newborn's condition was critical. An emergency team of physicians worked through the night in a monumental effort to save the infant's life. At last the baby was stabilized. The police made a room-to-room search of the hotel looking for clues that might lead them to the baby's mother. They found nothing and concluded that the birth had taken place elsewhere and that the newborn had been brought to the hotel and abandoned there.

The next day, Houston newspapers were telling the incredible story. Hotel guests, Holiday Inn employees, and others who heard the account brought gifts, clothing, and money for the local hotel's youngest unregistered guest: newly named Holly Lynn. Within a few months, a loving adoptive home had been found for the little girl. For many years the parents brought Holly Lynn and her brothers to visit the Holiday Inn where she was found.

As I reflected on that wonderful news, I wondered if Mary and Joseph ever took Jesus back to the stable in Bethlehem. It would have been so interesting to hear what they told him about the innkeeper, the shepherds, and the arrival of the wise men. Somewhere along the way, Mary must have told the boy Jesus about her miraculous conception and described for him her innermost feelings, fears, anxieties, and hopes as she prepared to give birth to God's own Son.

Where do you turn when you are desperate for hope? When you need some assurance that God is still in your life? Some fifteen years ago, Lisa Ford shared a very personal story of hope found in a bird's nest. One day she discovered a bird's nest under the roof of her porch. She watched daily as the large-tailed fowl and his mate created a home for their anticipated brood. Lisa carried in her heart a wish that she and her husband, Wayne, would be doing the same thing. They had been hoping and praying for years for a family but it had not happened. In May, the swallows laid their eggs and Lisa watched with great interest to see when they would hatch. Her vigil kept her from dwelling on her own unrealized hopes to start her own family. The incubation period is usually less than a month but her calendar now announced it was June and still no baby swallows. This delay could be evidence of a problem. Lisa hoped this was not the case. By now she had an emotional investment in this special swallow family.

Two more weeks came and went and no eggs hatched. Bird experts were very pessimistic, informing her they would never hatch this far beyond their due date. Her own hopes for a family had been tied up in seeing the little fowl's eggs hatch. She was literally ill over the turn of events.

One Friday evening Lisa and Wayne went to a high school banquet at which the choir sang "His Eye is on the Sparrow," a song of reassurance. It was a beautiful rendition about a trusting and loving God who cares for even the smallest creatures. A calmness came over her as she somehow sensed that she could trust God's timing in all things. She just could not give up after all this time.

Ten weeks after the eggs first appeared in the nest, they hatched. Five precious little creatures filled the nest. The experts were all wrong. They said this couldn't happen. Lisa gazed at the wide-mouthed newly hatched babies and started to cry. This seemed to be proof that God can work all things out in His own time and His own way. Today Lisa is even more sure of this truth. She and Wayne are reminded of it every day as they look at their own two little sons, the children they were finally able to conceive.

Some who read this story will put it all down as a nice coincidence. But it is interesting how often such coincidences happen in the lives of those who trust in the Lord. Laura Pedersen, in her book *Best Bet*, summarized this very well when she penned: "Coincidence is often God's way of remaining anonymous."

"A wise son brings joy to his father..."

Proverbs 10:1

Hanoch was just a small boy when his world was turned upside down. His parents had divorced and he and his mother and brother moved out of their nice house into a small apartment in a rough section of town. At night Hanoch would lie afraid in his bed, dreaming about having a big tough father who could protect him from all those things that go bump in the night. A few years later, his mother began dating a police officer named Frank McCarty. In the boy's mind this was perfect; Frank was exactly the sort of dad he wanted.

Frank was a great cop but had no experience in parenting. He had been raised by a stern and strict father, and so that is how he treated Hanoch and his brother. Hanoch fiercely resisted discipline and often got into a battle of wills with his stepfather. He seemed to ignore Frank's good traits: how he took the boys to ball games, brought them to work, spent time helping them with their homework, gave them common sense fatherly advice, and he even hugged them and let them know that they were loved. This was not enough, because Hanoch still consciously sought to distance himself from his stepdad.

In Hanoch's senior year in college, he began reflecting on his life and the estranged relationship between himself and his mother's husband. He started to remember the many good things Frank had done and how difficult it must have been for him to carve out a place in a ready-made family. Hanoch vowed that he would do something to atone for his ingratitude. As he pondered this, he remembered Frank expressing his regrets that he had no child of his own to carry on the family name. He was the last of his family and the McCarty name would end when he went to the grave. Hanoch smiled. He knew what he had to do. He contacted an attorney and made arrangements to change his last name. He came home for Frank's birthday and presented him with a court certificate declaring that he had legally changed his name to Hanoch McCarty. As this tough cop read the document, he started to cry. It is never too late to restore a relationship.

Susan Kidd is a registered nurse as well as an inspirational writer and speaker. She shared the following personal experience: She was assigned the evening shift one particular week and, upon her arrival at work, noted that she would be caring for a Mr. Williams in room 412. He had suffered a slight heart attack but seemed to be doing well. The polite gentleman that he was he asked Susan if she would be so kind as to call his daughter and let her know where he was. Then he also asked for a piece of paper and something to write with. She found him a writing utensil and a notepad, then went back to the nurses' station to call his daughter.

She was startled at the daughter's panicked response: "No. No. Don't let him die! Oh, please, don't let him die!" Susan thought it was a strange reaction and assured her that her father's condition was stable and there was no reason to believe that he was near death. The daughter went on to explain, "We had a terrible argument on my twenty-first birthday. I stomped out of the house screaming, 'I hate you!' I haven't seen him since then. Please tell him I'm on my way. I'll be there as soon as I can."

Susan returned to his room with that message and discovered something was radically wrong. The patient seemed to have no pulse. She cried out, "Code 99!" and in a flash a medical team started feverishly working to resuscitate him. They were having no success. "Oh, no, please," Susan prayed, "Please Lord, not like this. His daughter is coming." But there was no response. He was dead. Badly shaken, Susan went out into the hallway just as the man's daughter was getting off the elevator. She took her hands and said, "Janie, I'm so sorry. Janie, it's too late."

Janie went into her father's room and flung herself on his bed with deep, deep sobs. Susan stood there feeling ever so helpless. Then she noticed a scrap of paper on the floor with handwriting on it. She glanced at it and handed it to the grieving woman. It read: "My dearest Janie. I forgive you and pray you will forgive me. I know you really didn't mean it. I know that we have never stopped loving each other! Dad." Susan saw Janie clutching that lifeline to her heart as she thanked God. A few minutes later, Susan made a phone call to her own dad, "Dad, I just called to say I love you."

"A generous man will himself be blessed..."

Proverbs 22:9

For many years, John Brodie was the All-Pro quarterback for the San Francisco 49ers football team. He was also the ball holder for extra points and field goal attempts. A sports writer once interviewed Brodie and asked why a million dollar player accepted the humble task of holding the ball for the kicker. His simple response was, "If I didn't, it would fall over." In all humility, he recognized that his value to the team was being there and doing whatever he could to help them succeed. And, of course, that is how one becomes a winner in the eyes of the Lord.

God-honoring conquerors are those willing to pay a price few others are willing to pay. The ceiling of the Sistine Chapel in Vatican City was painted by Michelangelo. This required lying horizontally, but that posed a problem for the artist since he had a bad back. If he laid on his back for any length of time, he suffered intense pain. Moreover, he had some kind of nasal problem which cut off some of his air supply when he lay on his back. And yet, he did this almost every day for four years. The result was one of the greatest masterpieces of all time. This is the key to being a winner: total commitment.

After Carl Lewis won four gold medals in the 1984 Olympics, he was asked how many years he had spent developing his tremendous track skills. He replied, "The day I stopped crawling I took up running…" Winning comes by paying the price. Jesus asked, "Are you willing to pay the price?" Victors are willing to make the hard choices that few are ready to make. Dr. Rufus Broadway, MD, tells of a heartbreaking decision he once had to make. This was when the government was just starting to look at kidney dialysis cases. Some pilot projects had been set up and committees appointed to determine which patients would be treated. Dr. Broadway was on that committee.

Monday evening, the committee met to choose between two patients because they knew that they could only treat one of them. One was a young husband and father of three children. The other was a lovely sixteen-year-old girl, a gifted musician. One would live, the other would die. It was up to them to decide. Dr. Broadway resigned the next morning because, as he put it, "I didn't want to play God." We can appreciate his agony while confessing that the decision makers are the ones who make their mark in this world.

In Dante's *Inferno*, a group of lost souls sigh and moan as they whirl about aimlessly in the air. These wretched creatures are termed by Dante as "the nearly soulless." They were cautious people, fearing to make decisions, always striving to be neutral. Never actually bad but never really good either. Worthy of neither blame or praise. Now they hang forever suspended between a heaven that will not accept them and a hell that has contempt for them. Never again will their names be mentioned. "Look," said the guide, "and then quickly pass on."

Winners in the eyes of the Lord are always willing to give more than they expect to receive. U.S. President Calvin Coolidge once put it like this: "No person was ever honored for what he received. Honor has been the reward for what he gave." Jesus declared, "It is more blessed to give than to receive."

A monk once found a beautiful and expensive precious stone. One day he met a traveler, and as he opened his bag to share his bread, the stranger saw the sparkling jewel. He asked the monk if he would give it to him. The friar did so. The recipient left overjoyed with the unexpected gift. A few days later, though, he came back looking for the generous giver. He found him, gave back the priceless birthstone, and made a request: "Please give me something of far greater value than this precious gem. Please give me that which enables you to freely give the treasure to me..." The suddenly wise traveler was certainly correct; the ability to freely give is far greater than the ability to obtain. Winners in the eyes of the Lord give more than they receive and they recognize that there is never a wrong time to do the right thing.

"He who has a wise son delights in him."

Proverbs 23:24

"Jenny," her father said tenderly, "I want you to know how special you are to Mom and me. We prayed for you for years, and now that you're here and growing up to be such a wonderful girl, we couldn't be more proud of you." Once he had said this, he stopped talking and reached over for his fork to begin eating, but he never got the fork to his mouth. His daughter stretched out her little hand and laid it on top of his hand. His eyes met hers, and in a soft voice she begged, "Longer, Daddy...longer." We never get tired of that, do we? No matter our age, such words warm our hearts. It was always one of my life goals to make my parents proud of me.

In a recent *USA Today* article, Neil Chethik shared a memory from the time his grandfather passed away. As he and his dad were going through some of his grandfather's effects, Neil looked over at his dad who was starting to cry. The son was stunned. He had never seen his father shed a single tear and now they were flowing. He just stood in silence, feeling very uncomfortable, not sure what to do. His father finally explained, "I'm sobbing not only for my father but also for me. His death means I'll never hear the words I've always wanted to hear from him: that he was proud of me, of my family, and of the life that I have lived." Then he turned to his firstborn and, with gentleness in his voice, stated: "So you'll never have to feel this way," he paused, placing a hand on his son's shoulder, "I want you to know right now how proud I am of you." As I read the article I thought, oh yes, I remember hearing those special words from my father and how they sent my spirits soaring.

Years ago one of our sons had received accolades and affirmations from a number of sources for his academic abilities as well as athletic accomplishments, but something he did one day, I've already forgotten what it was, had disappointed me and I told him so. There was a long period of silence and then, with quivering lips, this fine young man made eye contact and solemnly stated: "Dad, more than just about anything else, I want you to be proud of me."

Dads, please pay attention to this. Others may sing the praises of your children but nothing will touch their hearts more than when it comes from your lips. An article in *Focus on the Family* described a young preacher who had given his Father's Day sermon, in which he spelled out the traits of a godly father. He had proclaimed as a fact that such a dad prays for his children, loves them no matter what, and lets them know how glad he is to be their father. That Sunday afternoon, he was having lunch with family and talking with his wife about his sermon when he was interrupted by his six-year-old son and received the stab of his life. His boy, with a quizzical look on his face, asked, "Have I ever seen a dad like that?"

In like manner Johnny Carson said his young son, Richard, gave him a paper which read: "To the man who has inspired me with his fatherly wisdom."

Carson smiled and said to his son, "I'm truly touched. What a wonderful message to receive."

"Uh, um, ah, actually Dad I was hoping that you would fax that to Bill Cosby."

From the "Sayings of the Wise" in the book of Proverbs we read: "The father of a righteous man has great joy; he who has a wise son delights in him. May your father and mother be glad; may she who gave you birth rejoice!"

"He will swallow up death forever."

Isaiah 25:8

Just fourteen hours before her death, I had the sacred privilege of visiting with Joyce, a forty-seven-year-old mother of three daughters. She was emaciated, her face covered with shingles, propped up in a bed in the family room. She was positioned in such a way that she would have a good view of her backyard. She had always enjoyed gardening and this was one of her favorite sights. She thanked me for coming and asked if I could help her move to the hammock near several bushes ablaze with yellow roses. We sat down side by side and in slow tempo started rocking. She took my hand and we rocked in silence. "Joyce, what are you thinking?"

She thoughtfully replied, "I know death is just around the corner but I'm not afraid. I've had some interesting dreams in which I've been on a surfboard although I've never been a surfer. I'm going so fast that I'm out of control and heading straight for me is a huge ship. We're on a collision course and then I woke up. Last night, as the same big boat came closer, I saw a smiley face on it. Then it slowed down, circled me and started to nudge me from behind. I was surprised how pleasant and comforting it was. Do you believe there is meaning in dreams?"

"Of course," I replied. "A number of times in the Scriptures we read of God speaking to people through dreams. Sometimes a warning, other times giving directions, most often offering pictures of comfort and hope." It was quiet and peaceful as we swayed. A pair of doves were drinking out of her bird bath.

The silence was broken when Joyce mused, "I am really curious about what lies beyond the grave; what tomorrow will bring."

I smiled, and squeezed her hand. "It is beyond our wildest imagination. In 1 Corinthians, the apostle writes, 'No eye has seen, no ear has heard, no mind has conceived what God has planned for those who love Him.' "

Then I told her this story: Some years ago, Billy Graham was a guest on *The Phil Donahue Show*. Somehow the conversation got around to heaven, which Donahue said sounded boring to him: spending eternity floating around on clouds while playing a harp. Graham laughed at that description and agreed that would surely be a boring existence. The surprised host asked, "So what will heaven be like?"

I believe Billy Graham had Paul's passage from I Corinthians in mind when he painted this picture: "After spending a thousand years rejoicing with the saints, I'll approach the Lord this way: 'While I was on earth you called me to be an evangelist, and this I did to the best of my ability, but if I had a second choice I would have wanted to be an astronaut.' God will nod and announce, 'So be it Billy. I've got untold worlds that need exploring. You're my man. Go do it.' " Donahue stared at Graham in amazement. The evangelist's point was this: heaven is thrills and joys, excitement and dreams, beyond our wildest imagination.

"I like that," Joyce whispered. She let out a deep sigh and then asked: "Some say that at the moment of death you feel like you are being sucked through a tunnel with a dazzling bright light at the other end. What do you think?"

"I don't know, but I like better what I read in Matthew 24, where we are told a trumpet will sound and then God will send forth His angels to escort His children home."

"Oh, I love that. I have always believed in angels. I hope at my special service everyone will sing a hymn about angels." (Even though it was the month of May, we sang "Angels We Have Heard on High" at the celebration of her life).

Our hammock was swinging at a gentle pace. "Do you think I'll still be able to pray for my girls when I'm in heaven?"

"That I don't know, but I am certain that the prayers you are praying right now will still be circling around the throne of heaven like sweet perfume long after you are gone." Her eyes were closed with an expression of contentment on her face. Minutes went by.

"Joyce, how do you pray now?"

"For a long time I prayed that the cancer would go away that God would do a miracle and restore my health. Now I humbly ask that the Lord will have mercy on me."

"Joyce, that is such a powerful prayer. Remember what happened when a roadside beggar cried out to Jesus, 'Lord, have mercy!' The next verse states, 'And Jesus stopped.' So we pray, 'Lord, have mercy' and leave it up to God to decide what mercy is at this time and place. Joyce, what was the first Bible passage you memorized?"

A faint smile crossed her face as she remembered John 3:16. "I followed your suggestion and circled the word 'world' and made it personal by inserting my name. Now it reads, 'For God so loved Joyce...' I've asked my girls to make sure that everyone sings 'Jesus Loves Me' at my service. 'Jesus loves me this I know for the Bible tells me so, little ones to him belong; they are weak but He is strong. Jesus loves me He who died, heaven's gates to open wide; He will wash away my sin and let His little child come in...' Whenever doubts come to mind about His love for me, I just look to the cross," she affirmed.

The hammock continued its gentle rocking. "Joyce, how would you like to be remembered?"

She pondered and then responded, "I'm not sure."

"Here is how I see you: she fought the good fight, she kept the faith and is now wearing the crown of life."

"Oh, yes, yes. That's the way I want to be remembered."

"Anything else we should share?"

"Thank you. I'm getting very tired. I am ready to meet Jesus. Please help me back to my bed."

Fourteen hours later, this child of God heard the trumpets sound and was escorted by angels to her heavenly home. The pain is gone, tears wiped away, and ultimate healing taken place. Death is swallowed up in victory. We are more than conquerors through Him who loved us.

*"I have summoned you by
name; you are mine."*

Isaiah 43:1

Let's think for a few minutes about names. They often reflect our heritage. They may also say something about our parents. Do you know how former Attorney General Janet Reno got her name? She was born with the Danish name of Rasmussen, but when her father immigrated to this country he thought that name was too difficult to spell so he decided to choose a simpler one. He selected the name by closing his eyes and pointing to a map of the U.S. His finger came down on Reno, Nevada. I guess he should be thankful that it didn't land on Jackson Hole, Wyoming or Thief River Falls, Minnesota.

Names are important. Everyone has one. Sometimes people are embarrassed by their names and look for nicknames or choose to be known only by their initials. Dale Carnegie convinced us many years ago that the sweetest word a person can hear is the sound of their own name. Our names have special significance for us. Hannah Wallstein, a Methodist minister, recalled that when she was six years old her mother was expecting another baby. Her grandmother came for a visit and brought a book listing names and their meanings. There, seated on her grandmother's lap, she was told what her name meant: "God has favored me." She said she inhaled that message like a bear to honey; it lodged deep within her mind and the sweet aroma of it has never left her. "Because of that small unexpected event," Hannah stated, "I've always felt graced by God. It has left a lasting impression."

Not many four–year–olds are quoted in a national news magazine, but after the tragic events of September 11, *Newsweek* featured a suggestion by four–year–old Laura Kulbacki on how to deal with terrorists who hate a country full of people they don't even know. Laura asked, "Why don't we just tell them our names?"

Did you ever wonder what a terrorist is thinking as he is waiting to board a plane in the gate area, knowing that he intends to kill all these innocents? I am certain that he is not interested in knowing the names of those he plans to murder. As long as he can think about the plane's passengers in group terms, such as infidels, enemies, or agents of the Great Satan, he is able to follow through on his insane proposal. I can imagine that if a four–year–old got talkative in the waiting area, the last thing a terrorist would ask is, "Little girl, what's you name?" He wouldn't want to know. This was one of the chief reasons why there was such opposition to desegregation of America's schools in many parts of our country. Once we get to know names it challenges racial bias, because we can no longer view people as a group who all look and think alike. Even four–year–old Laura knew that.

In the New Testament book of Acts we see John and Peter standing before the temple leaders who had arrested them for healing a disabled beggar. They were asked by what power they had performed this unauthorized act. Their response was crystal-clear: "By the name of Jesus Christ of Nazareth whom you crucified but whom God raised from the dead this man is standing before you. There is no other name given under heaven by which we must be saved."

Helen Keller was only nineteen months old when she was stricken with an illness that left her both blind and deaf. Upon learning the Gospel story of Jesus for the first time, it is reported that she cried out, "I already knew that such a God existed. I simply did not know His name." Is that not the world's complaint? There is a hunger in every heart for the unconditional love of God. Our task is to link a name to that hunger.

*"Why spend and labor for that
which does not satisfy?"*

Isaiah 55:2

Anne Morrow Lindbergh wrote a delightful little book, *Gift from the Sea,* about her alone time at her beach cottage while on vacation. Her life in the suburbs involved food, shelter, planning, bills, doctors, dentists, school conferences, carpools, traffic jams, laundry, tutoring, cleaning, vacuuming, phone calls, fax machines, computers, Scouts, and so on. Lindbergh writes that life in our society is based on the premise of ever–widening demands, personal, family, community, church, national and international concerns. Our life just reels sometimes. If we are not careful we can get sucked into the bottomless pit and destroy our own soul.

But Anne received a gift from the sea: simplicity. The ocean and her tiny beach cottage taught her the art of sharing the good that she had received. She learned how little one can get along with and how much one can get along without. She discovered that she had no need for a closet full of clothes; one suitcase is enough. She couldn't bring her vacation back, of course, but the sea shell on her desk reminded her of simplified life.

I meet so many people whose lives are so compli-
cated. I wonder how they are able to keep track of all
the conflicting schedules. Everyone seems to be running
in different directions, with no time to eat together,
no time to talk, no time to even be alone. I recall a
woman in our church who was one of those overcom-
mitted types, always too busy. Unable to say no, she was
hardly able to catch her breath. One day she was asked:
"How do you ever expect God to get hold of you if you
never stand still?" The questioner was only met with a
blank stare.

I remember attending a graduate school class over
thirty years ago where the professor predicted that one
of the problems facing the next generation would be the
abundant amount of spare time. A twenty-four-hour
work week would be the norm, and workers would
start retiring at age forty. I thought about his prediction
when I read the results of a recent Harris Poll which
indicated that in the past twenty-five years, the average
American's workload jumped from forty-one hours a
week to forty-seven (including commuting time). What
has happened? Do we really need to be this busy? The
profit-driven media attack us with daily propaganda
that suggests what we must have is just a little bit more
and we'll find happiness. It is unfortunate how millions
buy into that lie.

I very much enjoyed hearing the story of an Iowa
farmer who entered a drawing at the county fair and
won a week-long, all-expense-paid vacation for two to
New York City. He and his wife stayed in ritzy hotels,

ate at exotic restaurants, and had orchestra seats at a Broadway show. Every day a new adventure had been planned for them. For a full week they took in all the sights and sounds of the nation's largest city. When they returned to their Iowa farm the lucky winners were interviewed by the editor of their local weekly newspaper. One of the farmer's observations was so very powerful: "I saw so many things that I didn't need." May God bless all of us with that same type of vision.

Matilde was an honest, honorable person in a family with very limited means. One day, she and her husband received a surprising invitation to attend a super elegant, formal event. She was delighted, and borrowed a necklace from a wealthy friend to wear to the gala. Her striking piece of jewelry elicited several compliments from other guests. The next day, however, Matilde found herself in the worst possible situation: she had lost the necklace.

Panic-stricken, she and her husband borrowed $36,000 and bought a necklace that looked just like the one she had worn. She then returned the prized accessory to her friend, telling her nothing about what had happened. For five agonizing years, the desperate couple slaved and toiled to pay back the money that they had borrowed. They sold their modest home and moved into a rental. Matilde even took on a second job in an effort to raise the necessary funds.

More than half a decade after the necklace had been lost, the debts were finally paid off. Matilde saw her friend one day and confessed what she had done. She revealed the hardship that she and her husband had gone through in paying for the replacement. The well-to-do woman stared at her with a stunned expression on her face. She explained to Matilde that what she had borrowed was a pretty piece of costume jewelry. It was made mostly of paste, worth fifty dollars at the very most, and maybe quite a bit less.

Isn't that a parable of contemporary life? People give their time, energy, resources, their very life, for that which, in the end, turns out to be only paste.

Eugene Peterson, author of *The Message*, paraphrases Jesus' words from Matthew chapter six. "Don't hoard treasure down here where it gets eaten by moths and corroded by rust or—worse!—stolen by burglars. Stockpile treasure in heaven, where it is safe from moth and rust and burglars. It's obvious, isn't it? The place where your treasure is, is the place you will most want to be, and end up being."

"Arise, shine, for your light has come..."

Isaiah 60:1

According to Greek legend, a woman went down to the river Styx to be ferried across to the Region of the Departed Spirits. Charon, the celebrated ferryman, reminded her that it was her privilege to drink the waters of the Lethe river and thus forget the life she was leaving. She said eagerly, "I will forget my failure."

The sage added, "And also your victories."

She continued, "I will forget how I have been despised."

"And," Charon reminded her, "how you have been loved."

She paused to consider the whole matter and finally left the water of the Lethe untasted, preferring to retain the memory of sorrow and failure rather than give up the memory of life's loves and joys.

This week you and I will cross into a new year. For most of us, the past year was a mixture of the bitter and the sweet, the joyful and the sorrowful. For all of us, however, as our calendar turns to January it promises us a fresh start. Isaiah has some good news for us as we begin a new year. This prophet of God declared, "Arise, shine for your light has come." This is surely a great way to launch a new year. Our light has come, darkness vanishes. His light shines first of all into our puzzled minds.

I wish that life was as easily explained as that great philosopher of the comic strips, Charlie Brown, once decided that it was. Lucy said to him, "Life is a mystery, Charlie Brown. Do you know the answer?" Charlie Brown responded, "Be kind. Don't smoke. Be on time. Smile. Eat sensibly. Avoid cavities. Mark your ballot carefully. Avoid too much sun. Send overseas packages early. Love all creatures above and below. Insure your belongings. Always try to keep the ball low." Before he could utter another platitude, Lucy interrupted. "Hold real still," she said, "because I am going to hit you right in the nose." We can surely appreciate her frustration, can't we?

It reminds me of a cartoon by Mike Maslin which showed a middle-aged man, in a middle-class living room watching a middle-class TV set. On the screen was a large pot and a voice behind it said, "How much would you pay for all the secrets of the universe? Wait, don't answer yet. You also get this six quart covered combination spaghetti pot and clam steamer. Now, how much would you pay?"

We need to acknowledge—as the Scriptures do—that life is a mystery, but also in the midst of the darkness, there is a light shining. And that light is Jesus Christ. I had a philosophy professor who once asked us how we could prove we were alive. It stimulated some wild and crazy answers, but a more important question, it seems to me, is whether the life we are living has any real meaning. St. Paul wrote that now we see only in a glass dimly but that there is a divine purpose to it all.

In the famed motion picture *The Wizard of Oz*, a young Judy Garland sang and popularized a song which deeply touched the hearts of millions who greatly admired her rendition of "Somewhere Over the Rainbow." The song expresses a longing to escape to some faraway place where problems melt like lemon drops. It tells of a distant Shangri-La where bluebirds fly over the rainbow and asks, "Why, oh why, can't I?" Did Judy ever find what the heart yearns for: significance, purpose, meaning and spiritual satisfaction? I don't think so. She later took her own life.

There are times when all of us know what it is like to dream of happiness somewhere over the rainbow. At some point all of us travel through some dark valleys. How we need to see that light shining at the end of the tunnel.

I once read a story about a despondent poor old lady who was waiting on an eviction notice because she was so far behind on her rent payment. Her bills had piled up and her utilities had been cut off. There was a knock on the door. She trembled in absolute silence. Her door was locked and her drapes were drawn. Breathlessly, she stood shaking in fear. She was certain that it was the authorities coming to evict her. At last, determined to face the inevitable, she opened the door, and there stood her smiling pastor. Through the goodness and generosity of many friends, he had accumulated enough money to pay the rent, utilities and the rest of her bills.

That should be a reminder to us as we wrap up the old year and move into the new. There is a friend knocking at the door of your life. There is a light shining in the darkness.

*"...The Lord has anointed me to
preach good news to the poor."*

Isaiah 61:1

Every Easter for the past couple of decades the parable of the caterpillar who morphs into a butterfly has been the focus of the children's sermon. It is a powerful symbol of the resurrection. As a visual aid I use a large cloth caterpillar that, when turned inside out, becomes a butterfly. This exotic bug traveled with me on my first mission trip to India. The Indian evangelist, who also served as our interpreter, had made contact with a band of Gypsies living as squatters in a remote section of Uttar Pradesh. They had recently heard the Good News of the Gospel for the first time and they pleaded with the young Christian to return and tell them more.

Gypsies are on the absolute bottom of the socio–economic pyramid. Most live in dire conditions, are undernourished and illiterate, with a life expectancy of around 50 years. They are even a notch below the Untouchables, who at least have some minimal rights granted by the Indian government. Gypsies are also a very superstitious people, with their own language and customs which only adds to their isolation.

As we approached the compound, we were met by their leader, a bare chested man with a gray beard, a red turban on his head, no shoes, and wearing toga-like garb. He was followed by 30-35 curious but friendly men, women and children. They had no houses, only small dugouts with branches, box covers, or whatever they could scavenge to provide some shelter. In one of the makeshift hovels, I noticed a mother pig with her newborn piglets sharing living quarters with a woman and her children. Nearby was an unclothed infant, lying on the ground shaded by a huge banana leaf. When I expressed my concern, I was informed this was common practice; they believed it was good for a newborn to be coddled by Mother Earth.

How do they survive in the midst of such wretched poverty? It was explained to me that they made bracelets and necklaces out of whatever they could find and sold them to celebrants at the many Hindu festivals. When they ran out of customers, they would change occupations and produce broomsticks or various other working tools. But, sooner or later (usually sooner), they would be on the road again, heading for somewhere else in search of a livelihood.

While our translator was in conversation with the chief, a small boy snuck up behind me, touched my back, and then sped away with a grin on his face. His friends applauded his playful boldness. After all, none had ever seen a white person before, much less actually touched one.

The village elder encouraged all his people to listen with both ears to the words that the missionaries were about to share with them. Our leader focused on John 3:16 and made it very clear that God loved them. He reminded them that Jesus was crucified, put to death, and his body placed in a tomb. The next morning the tomb was empty and Jesus was gone. His disciples were crying and filled with despair, but that was not the end. On that Sunday morning, the greatest news ever heard was announced by angels: "He is risen!" He had conquered death and all his children would share in his victory. The Gypsies' response was hard to define. Bewildered? Perplexed? Uncertain? How could this be? They exchanged uneasy glances with one another.

With my cloth caterpillar in hand and a prayer on my lips, I got down on the ground. "Life for a caterpillar can be very difficult," I began, "each day is a struggle to find food. Some nights they go to bed hungry because they have found nothing to eat. Other times are happier, for a peach leaf has been found and makes a delicious meal." I pushed the fuzzy worm through the dirt as I continued on. " For the most part caterpillar life is not easy, roaming around in the mud of the earth, each new morning a battle of survival."

They listened intently. "One day a family of caterpillars noticed that an older member of their tribe was really slowing down," I said, moving my caterpillar more slowly. "There was hardly any life at all. This was strange and disturbing. They were very worried but had high hopes that tomorrow would be a better day. The next morning they were up early to check on their friend. To their horror, he wasn't moving at all. Nothing remained but an empty shell." The caterpillar is prodded and poked, picked up and turned over but remains motionless. "All were certain that something terrible had happened to him. They gathered around the empty shell, weeping big, sorrowful tears. Grief-stricken and heads bowed, they continued to wail.

Oh, how sad were those foolish caterpillars. They should have looked up," I exclaimed as I picked up the caterpillar and, with wonder and excitement, instantly turned him inside out. The result, of course, was the sudden appearance of a golden butterfly with big, beautiful wings. "Had they raised their eyes, they would have seen high above them, soaring joyfully and free, their loved one now transformed into a radiant butterfly, celebrating a life so much better than they could ever imagine."

I have told this story numerous times but never had a response like this: Nearly everyone, no matter what age, started clapping their hands, cheering and dancing. Some rushed over to kiss the butterfly. Others reverently rubbed their cheeks on the butterfly's wings. No one could better identify with the caterpillar than these desperate Gypsies. The words of Jesus in Luke 6:20, "Blessed are you who are poor, for yours is the Kingdom of God."

Alittle boy came home from church looking visibly upset. His mother asked what was wrong. "We learned a silly song in Sunday school today."

"What was the song?

"It's all about Jesus wanting me to be a sunbeam."

"A sunbeam? What's so silly about that?"

"Because," the young fellow fumed, "I don't want to be a sunbeam. I want to be a truck driver."

Don't buy into the idea that serving God is an either/or situation. You can be a truck driver and Jesus' sunbeam at the same time. No matter where you are in life, God has given you a blessed purpose for living. Jeremiah the prophet, spokesman for God, declared, "Before I formed you in the womb I knew you, before you were born I set you apart..." You are unique, special, and have a purpose. You might ask: "Who am I and why am I here?" God knows and will make it known to all who sincerely ask him.

Some time ago I read about a man in Ocean Springs, Mississippi whose last name is Unknown. It is going to sound like the old Abbott and Costello routine, "Who's on First?" This man's last name really is Unknown. His full name is Nikone Unknown. He acquired that name when he came to this country in 1979. His last name was so hard to pronounce that the immigration officials simply listed it as "unknown." His wife is Ratchanee Unknown and his son is Nick Unknown. The world is filled with people that think they are unknown.

I remember hearing an interesting account of how, centuries ago, sailing ships would record the names of their passengers according to their social order. Royalty and government officials were on the very top of the roster, acknowledging their status. At the bottom of the list, all lumped together, appeared the remaining number of persons and the notation: "Persons of No Importance." There are a lot of people that sense that this is where their names would be found in the grand scheme of things. Persons of no importance. Name unknown.

Karen Mays, inspirational Christian author, writes that when one of her children was small and misbehaving, the little boy found himself at the end of a stern lecture. "What are we going to do with you?" asked his exasperated mother. Sadly, the dejected child suggested, "Why don't we jest fro me in the garbage." Karen confides that this has now become a signature statement when any member of the family is frustrated with themselves: "Maybe you should jest fro me in the garbage."

This is where some people see themselves. No real value, no potential, no purpose. But what does God our Father declare? "Even before you were born I knew you." We are not unknown to Him. We are not persons of no importance. We are not garbage to be thrown out. We are His children. Who am I? There is our answer: I'm a child of God.

Why am I here? John W. Gardner, founding chairman of *Common Cause,* a citizens advocacy group, helps us to answer that question when he tells about a cheerful old man who asks a specific question of just about every person he meets. Somewhere in the conversation he will inquire, "What have you done that you believe in and that you are proud of?" He never asks a common question like "What do you do for a living?" It's always "What have you done that you believe in and that you are proud of?" Gardner concludes that it's an uncomfortable question for those who have built their self–esteem on their bank account or their job title. He was delighted by a woman who answered, "I think I'm doing a good job raising my children." He also liked the response of a carpenter who declared, "I'm a craftsman and I practice good workmanship every day." Gardner said, "I really don't care how people answer that question. I just want to put the thought in their minds that they should live their lives in such a way that they have a good answer. Oh, not one that is good for me but one that is good for themselves and their Creator." None of us can ever be really happy and satisfied until we know who we are and why we are here.

"Plans to give you hope and a future."

Jeremiah 29:11

Pastor Tim Zingale of St. Olaf Lutheran church in Fort Dodge, Iowa, told this moving story of hope that he was able to experience:

A little girl about six years old had been shopping with her mother at Walmart. It was pouring down rain outside–the kind that gushes over water spouts. A group of shoppers stood there huddled under the awning of the superstore waiting for the storm to let up. Some were content to wait patiently. Others were becoming quite irritated.

The voice of a child broke the silence, "Mom, let's run through the rain."

"What?"

She repeated, "Let's run through the rain."

"No, no. no. We will wait until it slows down a tad."

The freckle-faced little girl waited a minute or two before exclaiming, "Let's go now."

"We can't do that. We'll get soaked."

"No we won't. That's not what you said this morning."

"What do you mean? When did I ever say we could run through the rain and not get wet?"

"Mother, don't you remember? When you were talking to Daddy about his cancer you said, 'If God can get us through this, He can get us through anything.'"

The entire crowd stopped in dead silence. Nothing could be heard for the next couple of minutes except for the falling rain. The little one's mother was struggling to figure out what to say next. Some might think that what she decided to do was silly, but it was a time when innocent trust could be nurtured. "Honey, you are absolutely right. Let's run through the rain and if God lets us get wet it'll be because we need washing." Off they ran, getting soaked but laughing all the way. Tim looked at the others, clapped his hands in excitement, and with joyous laughter, ran out into the drenching rain. He added, "I was most certainly in need of a good washing."

Jesus said that He will never leave nor forsake us. There will even be times when we will run through the rain together. Our Lord's favorite way of being with us is through the presence of other Christians. We've been called to be little Christs, His Spirit working through us.

Douglas Mauer, a young teenager from a small town in Missouri, had been feeling ill for several days. His temperature was stuck at 103 degrees and he was suffering from flu-like symptoms. His parents finally took him to a hospital where blood tests revealed one of the most agonizing reports that any parent can receive: Douglas had leukemia.

During the subsequent forty-eight hours, the youngster endured blood transfusions, spinal and bone marrow tests, and chemotherapy. His mother stayed at his bedside for five days. His doctor was quite frank: The young man's condition was very serious. He would need chemotherapy treatments for the next two years. Side effects would cause him to lose all his hair and his body would be bloated. As you might expect, distraught Douglas began to slip into a deep depression.

A friend stopped by the Brix Flower Shop in St. Louis to purchase a unique floral arrangement for Douglas. "I want it to be extra special," she stated. "It's for a young friend who has leukemia."

"OK," promised the florist, "I'll make it as bright as I can."

When it arrived, it was beautiful to behold. Douglas opened the card from his well-wisher, read it, and offered a polite word of thanks. Then his eyes spotted a second envelope. Where did it come from? He carefully opened it and read: "Douglas, I work at Brix Flower Shop. I took your order. I had leukemia when I was seven years old. I am now twenty-two. My heart goes out to you. God bless you. Laura."

The youth's face lit up. His mother declared, "For the first time since he started his treatment, he has received some hope." A simple card from someone he'd never met gave him a ray of hope that he, too, could win the battle. Often it is the little extra things we do that make such a difference: loving actions, encouraging words, a note of hope.

"I prayed to the Lord..."

Daniel 9:4

An old Swedish couple had been married for nearly fifty years, but they had never really been happy with each other. Both were often finding fault, fighting and quarreling. Finally, Inga had a proposal for her husband: "Sven, this thing is not working. We've been hitched for nearly half a century. We tried just about everything yet our bickering never ends. Why don't we pray to the Good Lord to call one of us home and then I'll go live with my sister."

Isn't it remarkable how many of the requests we make of God are for our own purposes? Do you think we truly must have some of the things we bombard heaven for? Five-year-old Jessica slipped into bed one night without saying her prayers. Her mother asked her if she'd forgotten to talk to God that evening. "No," she explained to her mother, she had not forgotten, "there are some nights when I just don't want anything." Her childish honesty reminds us of the sad practice of too many grown-ups.

There is an old song that admonishes us to "count your many blessings, name them one by one...and it will surprise you what the Lord has done." There are times when I start daily devotions and then find myself at a loss as to what to pray. Has that ever happened to you? I'm sure it has. A nurse–whose name I cannot remember– shared what she calls her "five finger prayer." It is a wonderful help when you are having trouble getting started.

Here is what she does: She puts her hands together in front of her heart, so that the nearest finger is her thumb. This digit reminds her to pray for those that are closest to her: her spouse, her children, her parents, her brothers and sisters, her grandparents, and others that she dearly loves. She thanks God for them and seeks His blessing on them.

The next digit is your index finger. It is used for pointing– a reminder to thank God for all those who have pointed you in the right direction and set for you an example of godly living. This could include Sunday school teachers, pastors, authors of inspirational books and stories, and friends who are Jesus' followers.

The third digit is the tallest of all your fingers. It is symbolic of our leaders, thus a remembrance to intercede with the Lord for the president of our country, our Congress, and our local mayor. This could also include world leaders and all God-fearing people, wherever they may be, who are in positions of leadership.

What comes next is the ring finger. Ask anyone who plays the piano and they all agree that this is the weakest finger. It is certainly God's plan that we remember the weak: widows, orphans, sick, homeless, those who have no advocate, and perhaps saddest of all, those who have no one who loves them.

The final digit is at the end of your hand—your little finger. Our Lord made it very clear: "If anyone wants to be first, he must be the very least." So your prayer concludes with a humble petition for yourself that you will always be the person He wants you to be. Next time you're ready to talk to God but can't think of anything to say, let the five finger prayer be your guide.

This additional thought: God does not always answer our prayers as we had hoped but He will give us what we really need. The following was prayed by an unknown Confederate soldier:

"He was a Christian and he prayed. He asked for strength to do great things; he was given infirmity that he might do better things. He asked for riches that he might be happy; he was given poverty that he might be wise. He asked for power that he might have the praise of others; he was given weakness that he might feel the need of God. He had received nothing that he asked for, all that he hoped for; his prayer seems unanswered, but he is most blessed."

"My heart is changed..."

Hosea 11:8

Jim Burns, now an executive with Campus Crusade for Christ, also known as Cru, relates an unforgettable experience as a senior in high school. A girl named Marie had been in his class since grade school. To his knowledge, he had never even once spoken to her. She was a good student, quite intelligent, but shy and not very attractive. The young lady was pretty much ignored by just about everyone. Her house was right around the corner from Jim's but they never once walked home together. In fact, the young leader confessed with embarrassment, there were times when he would cross the street lest anyone see him with her.

During his senior year, some major changes took place in his life as he was maturing in his faith and it dawned on him that he needed to be more kind and caring to others—even people like Marie. It was lunch time and Jim was on his way to his usual spot where he would meet his clique of friends. The trip took him past Marie. Something compelled him to stop and ask her a question. The look she gave him was so startling it was as if she was saying, "After all these years of going out of your way to ignore me why are you talking to me now?" The next day he brought several of his friends, both male and female, to have lunch with Marie. They did this for a week, then invited her to a Cru meeting. She accepted the invitation. Sometime later he drove her home after a meeting. As they reached her house, she stopped dead in her tracks and stared at him. "Why are you and your friends being so nice to me?" He stuttered and stammered and muttered something about his conviction that this is what Jesus would want them to do. Then she blurted out, "The last time anyone ate lunch with me was when I was in the seventh grade until you and your friends sat with me last month." Jim was stunned. He could not imagine how a person could eat lunch alone for five years. He couldn't remember *ever* eating lunch by himself.

Eight years later, Jim was speaking at a Campus Crusade Bible camp. After he finished his presentation, one of the camp counsellors came up to him accompanied by around fifteen high school girls and asked, "Do you remember me?"

"You look like a girl I knew in high school."

"That's me," she smiled, "I'm Marie, newly appointed regional director of Campus Crusade for Christ. Thanks for having lunch with me way back then."

What happened next? Jim cried. Maria Robinson, teacher and poet, is credited with this profound observation: "Nobody can go back and start a new beginning, but anyone can start today and make a new ending."

The year was 1941. He was a young married man and father of a five-year-old daughter. Work was scarce and finances were very limited. Christmas was near and they were down to their last ten dollars. The invitation had come to spend Christmas Day with his wife's parents, an offer which was gratefully accepted. She had gone shopping with the ten dollar bill purchasing inexpensive but thoughtful gifts for her family. Nevertheless, her stressed out husband berated her for buying a dollar's worth of fancy gift wrap. He told her in no uncertain terms how foolish this was.

Husband and wife were in the basement looking for boxes for the presents when he called on Tina, his only child, to go upstairs and get the gold wrapping paper. Ten minutes passed and she had not returned. Exasperated, he climbed the stairs to see what was taking her so long. In anger and disbelief, he stared at what she had done: the little girl had taken all the decorative paper to wrap a small box and, not only that, she had used up an entire roll of Scotch tape. That was the last straw. Furious he yanked her up by one arm and slapped her. When his wife arrived on the scene and tried to intervene, he brushed her aside shouting, "She deserved that! There was no excuse for what she did!"

The next day as the three of them were preparing to depart for his in-laws' home, they decided that each would open one gift before departing. The child, her eyes filled with excitement, approached her father with the gold-wrapped box and proudly announced, "Daddy, I made this for you." He picked it up–it was very light–carefully opened it up, and was shocked to discover it was empty. He looked at her with disgust, shook his head, and said, "Not only did you waste a whole dollar's worth of Christmas paper, but all you did was decorate a silly old useless box." Tears filled her eyes and her lips trembled as she explained, "Daddy, it's not a silly, useless box. I filled it with love and kisses just for you." His eyes focused on that precious little person and his heart broke. Right then and there he begged her to forgive him and made the same request of the Lord. For the next fifty years, Tina's daddy had on his shelf a "priceless little box," symbol of a daughter's love and a father's changed heart.

"Your young men will see visions..."

Joel 2:28

S ometime during the late 90s I attended a WordAlone conference in Roseville, Minnesota. The gathering consisted of hundreds of Lutheran pastors and lay leaders with the goal of bringing reform and renewal to our denomination. Representatives from various mission endeavors were present and had set up information booths in an effort to solicit support for their specific mission concerns. Enthusiastic leaders from the newly formed Eastern European Mission Network were present. Their focus of concern was former Soviet Bloc countries: Estonia, Latvia, and Lithuania. The priorities were evangelism and rebuilding the Body of Christ in these countries that had been recently freed from the atheistic occupation of the former Soviet Union. It was at this time that I was introduced to Guntis Dislers, a bright, young pastor from Latvia with a vision and dream for his country. Little did I know the impact this encounter would have on my life.

I listened as this zealous Latvian man of God passionately shared his vision of building a Christian university which would produce Latvia's future leaders, men and woman under the lordship of Jesus who would all take part in the rebuilding of his beloved country. A group of people who shared his dream had pooled their resources and purchased an abandoned building once occupied by Russian troops. Classes were underway, and conditional accreditation had been granted in theology, social work, and church art. They had been blessed with encouragement, advice, and financial assistance from Christian groups in Finland and Sweden and now hoped that there would be similar interest on the part of some American Christians.

We shared a meal that evening and I learned that this pastor had been removed from his church during the occupation and drafted into the Russian Army. He was fluent in Latvian, Russian, German, and English; he also could read some Swedish, Greek, and Hebrew. The Soviets needed his translating skills.

So what was life like for him under communism? His church had been closed and converted into a warehouse. A few token church buildings were open on Sunday mornings but most soon became theaters, reception halls, gymnasiums, museums, or in one case, a planetarium. Eighty percent of the pastors had gone into exile or had been sent to Siberia or placed in prison. A handful—mainly older priests—were allowed to retain their pastoral positions. The few congregations that remained open were attended almost exclusively by the elderly, whom the Russians viewed as harmless. Even so, some pastors had been coerced to spy on their parishioners.

Bibles were banned in all Soviet-occupied countries. Possession of a Bible could result in a prison sentence and no confessing Christian would ever be able to hold any responsible job or position of influence. Janis Vanags, later to become archbishop of the Evangelical Lutheran Church of Latvia, was a chemistry teacher when he gradually came to the conclusion that Christianity was true. Before long the authorities became aware of his belief in God and dismissed him from the teaching position, and since they had no one to replace him, they cancelled the chemistry class. This brilliant young man was given a new assignment: washing windows.

I was convinced that the Lord wanted us to support this ministry. I promised prayer and financial assistance. I also suggested that we start a type of internship program for students at the Latvian Christian Academy who were planning on full-time positions in church work. The academy would select the students and we would cover all expenses. He wasn't as enthusiastic about my offer as I expected him to be. One of his first graduates had been invited to intern in a congregation in Colorado. She left Latvia and never returned. He said, "We are training our students to be God-fearing leaders in Latvia. Nevertheless, I believe your suggestion is a good one that could bring great blessings. We'll just have to be more careful in our selection process."

Our congregational leaders happily endorsed the plan. The Latvian Christian Academy became part of our mission budget, the prayer team placed them on the prayer list, and we prepared to host a Latvian intern.

Eventually we received word that two young ladies who would soon graduate from the academy and who spoke very good English had been selected to join us and share in our ministry. With excitement and joy, we welcomed them to our little section of America. Liva and Dace were true Latvians: modestly dressed, dark hair, and blue eyes.

How did they become Christians while being raised in a place where atheism was the only accepted philosophy of life? Liva's parents accepted communist teachings without a second thought, however, her grandmother never gave up her faith and shared Bible stories with her grandchildren. Those seeds, faithfully sown, took root.

Dace was born into a family where no one ever spoke of Jesus. So how did she meet Jesus? She loved to read and spent many hours in the library. One day while in the philosophy section, she came across a book called the Bible. "I was reading in the gospel of John and read about a God who loved me. It gave me much hope. It was such good news. Many times I returned to the library and continued to read the Bible. I asked Jesus to come into my heart. And He did."

Both young ladies started and ended each day with prayer and thanksgiving. This was a lesson they taught us. Dace and Liva returned to their native land to live and serve. Liva, a wife and mother, is the center of a godly home. Dace earned her doctorate, married the man of her dreams, and now is a professor at the Latvian Christian Academy. The school has become a bright and shining star in helping to bring many people to Jesus and is producing some of Latvia's future leaders as this long persecuted people joyfully rebuild their nation.

In 2011 I was invited to return to campus, which now is thriving with a dedicated faculty of thirty full-time and part-time leaders and full accreditation throughout Europe. In a very heartwarming ceremony, I received the Doctor Honoris Causa degree.

The following morning was the Lord's Day and I was invited by Guntis to be the guest preacher at the historic Church of the Cross in Riga. For over fifty years the building had been shuttered and used as a warehouse for Russian military supplies. Restoration was underway and beauty was returning. The church doors were opened and a dozen senior citizens reverently entered and prepared for worship. Pastor Guntis and I went into his office for a time of prayer. We were ready to begin the sacred service and opened the sanctuary door. I was startled by what I saw. Over one hundred people were present—most under the age of thirty! Guntis smiled, and said, "They have been spiritually starving. Here they are fed." What a privilege and joy to share with Guntis his God-given vision.

"But Jonah ran away from the Lord..."

Jonah 1:3

Every once in a while you run across a story that is very strange but nevertheless believable. Here is one from a newspaper in Kentucky: A youth pastor was charged with calling in a bomb threat to a church in the western part of the state where he was scheduled to preach that night. The young minister said he made that call on Sunday evening because he was unprepared to lead the service. He told the police he called 911 from the church about six-thirty and told the dispatchers there was a bomb in the church. When questioned, "He was very cooperative," the police chief said, "The church was evacuated and a thorough search revealed no bomb." However, the 7:00 p.m. service was cancelled.

When I read that article my reaction was: He did what? He called in a bomb threat because he had not been able to prepare a sermon? I guess every preacher has been tempted at some time or another to do something drastic like that. My guess is so has every teacher, every attorney, and every sales person who has a presentation to make for which he or she feels unprepared. Sometimes when we are not prepared or something just doesn't feel right or we just don't want to do it, we will go to desperate measures to avoid it.

In the well-known Bible story of Jonah, we read of a prophet who without question thought of calling in a "bomb threat." Perhaps the only reason he didn't was because he didn't have a phone. I guess no bomb either. Times were simpler then but problems were much the same. Jonah's dilemma was he didn't want to do what God wanted him to do. God called him to go preach to the people of Ninevah. As far as he was concerned, they were no-good, rotten sinners and he didn't want to be anywhere near them. I'm convinced that all of us, at one time or another, sense God wanting us to do something that we are reluctant to do. There are all too many who complain, "Oh, if I only knew what God's will was I would..." I would what? Not knowing God's will is usually not the issue. The key is actually doing God's will as it has been clearly revealed to us through His Word.

Woodrow Bradley Seals, a former U.S. District Court Judge, founded what is known as the Society of St. Stephen in the Methodist church. It became a nationwide program with the sole purpose of helping people in need. One day, a church invited the distinguished judge to their congregation to explain how they could begin a Society of St. Stephen in their location. The assumed agenda was that their guest would inform them about the various options for ministry followed by refreshments and discussion.

While people were gathering in their places, the host pastor provided a warm and welcoming introduction for their esteemed speaker. The special invitee sampled some cookies and poured himself a cup of coffee. He walked over to the piano, put his coffee cup on top of it, reached into his coat pocket, and took out a slip of paper. He adjusted his glasses and started to read what was on that little note. There was a name of a mother and four children, including their ages and their clothing sizes. He mentioned several other needs that the family had and then added that their address was on the paper. He placed it on top of the piano. Judge Seals concluded, "If you want to start a Society of St. Stephen, you should contact this woman by noon tomorrow and get help for her by evening."

He thanked them for the gracious invitation, the fresh-brewed coffee, and homemade cookies and was on his way. His entire presentation had taken less than five minutes. Judge Seal wasn't content to sit around twiddling his thumbs waiting for God to give more specific direction. He knew what God wanted done. The problem is seldom lack of knowledge, but rather lack of action.

I can tell you right now that if you are a married person, God's plan for you is to be a loving, forgiving and supportive spouse. If you have children, God wants you to be a parent who prays for your children, loves them, sets an example, and spends time with each one. I can tell you for certain that God's will is for you to share your faith and do unto others as you would have them do to you. It is His will that you use your talents, abilities, and finances in ways that will help others and honor Him. Most of us understand what God's will is for us; the problem is surrendering ourselves to do what we know our Father wants us to do.

Jonah knew what God wanted him to do. He wanted him to go to Ninevah and conduct revival services. It was crystal clear what God's will was. He had not a hint of doubt what the Lord desired of him. That was not his problem. It almost never is. *Doing* His will is the problem. When we finally pray from the heart, "Thy will be done," healing, purpose, and hope will flood our hearts and action will follow.

"He cares for those who trust in Him."

Nahum 1:7

James Tedder told the following story about picking up lost pennies: Once a friend of his and his friend's wife were invited to spend a wonderful evening with his employer and his spouse. The boss was a very wealthy man. He was also quite generous and took this young couple to a Broadway show where they had excellent orchestra seats in the second row. It was something that they never would have been able to do on their own because it was way too expensive.

After the play was over, they got into their host's brand-new Lexus and headed for a very exclusive dining experience. The valet parked their car and they started walking toward the restaurant when, quite suddenly, their friend stopped and looked at something on the pavement near the curb. The employer saw something that the others couldn't see—or so they thought. After all, there was nothing there except some paper litter and an old penny. Silently, he reached down and picked up the penny. He held it up and, with a contented look on his face, put it in his pocket as if he'd found some great treasure. How strange. Why would this rich man take the time to stop and pick up a penny?

Throughout the entire dinner, the young lady could not stop thinking about that scene. Finally, she could stand it no longer so she politely asked him if he had found a coin of some value. With a smile on his face, as he reached into his pocket to retrieve the coin. He held it out for her to examine. She had seen many pennies in her lifetime. What was the point of this?

"Look at it," he encouraged, "read what it says."

She did as she was told and read, "United States of America."

"No, not that. Please keep reading."

"One cent."

"No, not that either. Keep reading."

"In God we trust."

"Yes! You see, if I trust in God, the name of God is holy even on a penny. Whenever I find a U.S. coin I see the inscription. It is written on all coins minted in America. God drops a message right in front of me reminding me to trust Him. Who am I to pass it by? I pick up the coin in response to God; yes, I do trust Him. I think it is His way of starting a conversation with me. I am so thankful that God is patient and pennies are plentiful."

There are times when all of us just need to slow down, stop our busy lives, and feel God's presence. Sometimes we need a little reminder, like a penny lying on the ground. It is such a simple device. A few words printed on a nearly worthless coin can be a powerful reminder that Jesus is near. May each of us pick up a penny soon.

In 1854 a cavalry officer named Jeb Stuart graduated from West Point and was sent to his first assignment in Texas. He boarded a steamboat in New Orleans and in no time at all found himself in the middle of a storm on the Gulf of Mexico. Poor Stuart was violently ill and lay defenseless suffering in a bunk while the ship pitched and rolled. When at last he managed to raise his head from his bed, he discovered that the boat was docked and had been for some time. While he feared he would die from his seasickness, he could have walked a few feet to land at any time during the previous twelve hours. Our penny reminds us to trust in God. He is close and He is there to help us, whether we take advantage of it or not.

The great preacher of years past, Charles Spurgeon recalled one evening when he came home tired, depressed, and feeling helpless. It had not been a good day. Before retiring, he opened his Bible and read, "Trust in the Lord with all your heart..." There he paused and reflected, closed his Bible and reopened it. This time he heard the Lord's promise, "My grace is sufficient for you." *I should think so,* he thought and started to laugh. It was holy laughter that made his lack of trust and his helplessness seem absurd. "It was as if a little fish, being very thirsty, was troubled about drinking the river dry, but the mighty river declares, 'Drink on, little fish, my stream is sufficient for you.' "

John H. Sammis penned the following words which were later put to music by Daniel Towner: "Not a burden we bear, not a sorrow we share, but our toil He doth richly repay; not a grief or a loss, not a frown or a cross, but is blest if we trust and obey. Trust and obey, for there's no other way to be happy in Jesus, but to trust and obey."

A staid, conservative old congregation in rural Ohio was left without anyone to lead their Easter morning worship after their pastor had moved to another state. They called the Lutheran School of Theology and made arrangements for a student to be there on Resurrection Sunday. This was to be the first Easter service this seminarian had ever led and he wanted it to be something special, so he invited three of his classmates to come with him—all of whom were trumpet players. The celebration started with a magnificent fanfare of trumpets sounding forth from the balcony. This startling innovation was not received, however, with unanimous approval. In fact, one elderly lady complained: "Young man, I expected some changes in our Easter worship since I know you are only a student. But those awful noisy trumpets in our church on Easter—that is going too far!"

What that irritated saint didn't realize was that the young student pastor wasn't being particularly original with the trumpet bit; a preacher by the name of Paul beat him to it by quite a few centuries. In his first letter to the Corinthians he put it this way: "For the trumpet will sound and the dead will be raised…" (I Cor. 15:52.) It was the ringing sound of hope.

For all too many life seems to have too few trumpets and too many struggles. One problem after another, one hurt after another, one dead end after another. Time passes after a joyous wedding celebration and a tearful couple declares their marriage is failing. With fear and hurt in their eyes, bewildered children listen to these dreaded words from a parent: "Mommy and Daddy have decided it would be best if we didn't live together anymore." They have scarred their children for life.

Every day men leave prison on parole, all seeking a new beginning. Within three years, 80 percent will return to prison; they have morally collapsed again. The accountant informs you that if you sell now you might be able to salvage a little bit of your investment. The phone rings in the middle of the night and a stranger's voice informs you there has been an accident. With a somber expression, the physician whispers in a soft tone, "I'm sorry. We did all we could." It is a rare person who has never known failure, pain or grief.

Oh, how we need to hear the trumpet sounds of victory. How we desperately need to hear a word of hope. We have seen too many failures, and stood by too many graves. We observe the weeks, months, years flying by with lightning speed, yet we have accomplished only a tiny bit of our goal. We need more than an emotional shot in the arm or a day or two off. We need much more than that. We need hope.

Some years ago in late March a sudden, unexpected snow storm darkened the great Smoky Mountains in eastern Tennessee and western North Carolina. It was the tempest of its time. Many hunters and hikers were trapped with seemingly no way out. Four medical doctors from Knoxville had chosen that weekend for a hunting excursion in the Smokies. Since they had expected to be gone only one night and had received a favorable weather forecast, they were not prepared to face any adverse circumstances. They had not even bothered to let anyone know their intended location.

Imagine their surprise when the sky opened up, nearly burying them underneath the fury of the snow storm. Much to their dismay, their cell phones were in a dead zone. There was no one in the outside world who knew where they were. They had brought no extra food. They looked at each other with a hopeless, sickening feeling, at a loss as to what to do next. Twenty-four hours turned into thirty-six hours, then forty hours—still no contact with civilization. They found a stale doughnut which they divided four ways. Would anyone find them before they had either frozen or starved?

Suddenly they heard a sound overhead—the unmistakable whir of a helicopter. They screamed and waved their arms. In a near panic, they did everything they could to get the pilot's attention and it worked! He hovered low above them and some could see that the aircraft was already filled with other hunters and hikers. Before long a basket was lowered, containing a canister with a note that read: "Tomorrow." They had received a message of hope. This joyful team of MDs formed a chorus line, kicked their legs as high as the snow would allow and they sang at the top of their lungs, "Tomorrow, tomorrow, I love you tomorrow. You're only a day away." Their fear was gone; help was on its way. They would live to see another day.

George Herbert, Anglican priest and poet, summarized it well when he wrote: "He that lives in hope dances without music." And finally: the Psalmist adds the exclamation point for us with this declaration, "God is our hope and strength: a very present help in trouble" (*Anglican Prayer Book*).

"In compassion a man spares his son..."

Malachi 3:17

He was a preschooler out on the playground and he was singing for joy, "Jesus loves me this I know for my daddy tells me so." A disgusted playmate folded his arms, shook his head and rebuked his friend. "Those aren't the right words." That may be true. That is not exactly the way the songwriter wrote it, nevertheless, happy is the child who is able to sing it with such joy and conviction.

I was blessed to have a father like that who, through word and example, taught me so much about the love and grace of my Heavenly Father. I had just turned sixteen years old and had my driver's license for two weeks. We were a one car family. My father worked the swing shift and participated in a car pool. That meant our Ford would be sitting in the garage on Friday night. I mustered up enough courage to ask him if I could borrow it to go to the movies with some friends. I promised him I would be extra careful and go nowhere but to our local theater which was only about three miles from our home. I was given the keys to the family auto.

Excited, proud, and feeling much like an adult, I picked up some very congenial guys and we were on

our way to the movies. Disappointment awaited us.
The theater featured only one movie and it was not of
interest to three teenage boys. "Let's go to the Glendale
theater. Whatever is showing there is bound to be better
than this," proclaimed my passengers. With this type of
pressure I caved in to their urgings. This was going to
be a ten mile trip and contrary to the promise I made
to my dad. However, they were very persuasive in their
contention that he would never find out and that no
possible harm could come from this.

It was a popular movie and the parking lot was filled
so I paralleled parked out in the street, probably quite
a ways from the curb. I opened the driver's side door
and–WHAM!– a speeding souped-up hot rod hit my
door, ripping it right off. I was stunned and then I began to feel sick. The door was lying in the street. In a
daze I reached down, picked it up, found some old rope
in the trunk, and tied it back on. Much too miserable
now to enjoy a movie, I told my buddies that we were
going home. No one said a word.

When my fourteen-year-old brother saw what had
happened, he gasped, "Boy am I glad I'm not you. Dad
will never again let you drive." Those certainly were not
words of encouragement even though I figured he was
right. Dad worked late hours so he wouldn't be home
until 1:00 a.m. I knew I couldn't sleep so I stayed up
sitting at the kitchen table waiting for the inevitable
hour to arrive.

As soon as he got home a very solemn teenager confessed, "Dad, I need to show you something." I took

him out to the garage and pointed to the damage. Filled with remorse, I explained what happened and where it happened. "Glendale? What were you doing over there?" With shame and regret I reviewed the whole scenario. He put his hand on my shoulder, took a deep breath, "Son, I'm sure thankful you were not hurt." That was it.

The next day the pathetic looking vehicle was taken to the collision center. Eventually the call came that the damage had been repaired. A neighbor kindly gave us a ride into town. The door was as good as new, the bill was paid. Dad handed me the keys, smiled and declared, "Let's go home!"

The grace and love of the Heavenly Father demonstrated in the words and actions of my earthly father. It was a life-changing experience with eternal consequences. God made fathers with the full intention that every child would be able to get a glimpse of the Heavenly Father because he had an earthly father who pointed the way.

"She will give birth to a son...Jesus."

Matthew 1:21

Wally Kurlig was a lonely child whose story brings the Christmas drama to us in a manner that it can't reach us in any other way. Wally happened to be retarded. Already eleven years old and just starting the third grade, he was physically awkward and much larger than his classmates so was seldom invited to play in any ball games. The poor kid would stand by himself on the sidelines and watch. He was gentle and kind and, by virtue of his size, a natural protector of the little kids who had problems. No one would dare cause trouble for the younger children when burly Wally was near.

In the children's Christmas play that year the director chose Wally to play the role of the innkeeper. She figured that because of his size, his refusal would be more dramatic. Everyone was confident that he would act out his part well because when he put his heart into something, he gave it his all.

The annual Christmas program started in the usual fashion and before long, Joseph and Mary had made their way to the inn. Joseph rapped on the door and a gruff voice demanded, "What do you want?"

The expectant mother and her betrothed looked at him with pleading eyes as Joseph implored, "Please, sir, we are in urgent need of lodging."

But Wally bellowed as he had been told, "There is no vacancy. Go away!"

Joseph begged, "My wife is about to give birth. Surely there must be some place for us."

At this point, the exasperated innkeeper was supposed to growl, "I said there is no room in here! Go around back and sleep in the cow shed if you want." However, Wally got caught up with his feelings and forgot that this was only acting. He stood there in genuine sorrow, pondering the situation. For him this was no longer a pretend production–it was really happening.

His Sunday school teacher, assuming he had forgotten his lines, whispered, "Send them on their way."

As Mary and Joseph turned to go, the audience saw Wally's face. It was filled with sadness as tears started to flow. All of a sudden he shouted: "Please come back! I'll sleep in the barn and you stay in my room!"

No one who was present that night will be able to forget how deeply they were touched by that scene. Helen Keller once said: "The only blind person at Christmastime is he who has not Christmas in his heart."

Ezra Brown, a neighbor of mine when I started my ministry in Cleveland, was a simple, diligent, blue-collar worker. He was a husband, father of three children and a follower of Jesus.

It was December 23–one of those harsh Midwestern days when the temperature was near the teens and a frigid wind chilled the bones of anyone unfortunate enough to be outdoors. Every heater in the Brown's household had been turned on. The electrical wiring must have been quite old because a fire suddenly broke out in one of the bedrooms; in a matter of minutes the whole house was in flames. The Brown family, clad only in their night clothes, fled for their lives. They were able to escape the inferno but almost everything they owned was destroyed.

The next day, a news anchor appeared on live TV and proclaimed that while most Clevelanders would soon be sitting down to plum pudding and turkey dinners, admiring a tree filled with beautiful lights and eagerly awaiting the grand gift exchange, this would not be true for the Brown household. He then turned it over to the network's correspondent, Mike Roper, who was interviewing the Browns. It went something like this:

"Mr. Brown, all of Cleveland is saddened with you over the tragic loss you suffered last night. We know that for you and your family it will be impossible to have a merry Christmas. What are your plans now?"

He fully expected to hear, as did we, a weepy Mr. Brown lamenting his ill fortune. Instead, this amazing man of God, wearing clothes donated by a neighbor, exhibited no self-pity at all as he answered: "Of course it isn't easy to lose your house and just about everything you own, but," he added with confidence, "we are still going to have a merry Christmas. We were spared from the fire and we have each other." He smiled as he reassuringly wrapped his arms around his loved ones.

"Christmas is our Lord's birthday and we always sing on his birthday, so we're going to sing now." With sparkling eyes and cheerful expressions, the Brown family broke out singing, "Joy to the world!"

Startled, Mr. Roper nearly dropped his microphone in the snow. Almost in a daze, he murmured to the camera, "We return you now to our newsroom."

It was beautiful and powerful! Ezra Brown had the Christ child in his heart, and consequently, a joy that nobody or nothing could take from him.

"They will call him Immanuel
which means 'God with us'."

Matthew 1:23

I was ordained in June, and accepted the call to be pastor of a small interracial congregation in inner-city Cleveland, Ohio. It was December and I was preparing my first Christmas service. I was also a bachelor at the time and this was going to be my first Christmas Eve away from family. I thought I would be alone this Christmas.

Benevolent families from sister churches and some big-hearted merchants had donated groceries, clothes, and gifts for children for us to distribute. Our youth gathered a week before Christmas for a gift wrapping party. Brightly colored packages were labeled according to age and gender. That week, many homes filled with excited and delighted children were visited and presents distributed with the reminder that Christmas was Jesus' birthday.

December twenty-fourth was a picture-perfect evening. Snow had been falling like fluffy flakes all day. The sanctuary was filled for our seven o'clock candlelight service. We concluded with the singing of "Silent Night" and then worshippers headed for home. Everyone was gone. It was very quiet. I made the rounds to make sure lights were off and doors were closed. On a table in our parish hall, I spotted a box of beautifully wrapped gifts. What were they doing here? I thought all packages had been delivered. Had we missed someone? I reviewed the list of families that were to receive Christmas boxes and all had been checked off. Yet there remained one mysterious box of surprises.

Then, for reasons that made no sense at the time, and because at the moment I had nothing else to do, I put the box of gifts in my little Ford and headed in the direction of a family that had visited several weeks ago. They had not been on our Christmas package list so it seemed like the logical thing to do. I gingerly made my way through the slippery streets and stopped in front of an all but abandoned apartment building. The family had been in Apartment B but it was all dark now. I peeked in the window. There was no evidence that anyone was living there. I sighed and went back to my snow-covered vehicle wondering what to do next.

As I sat there under the street light, I sensed that someone was watching me. Sure enough, staring in my back window was a ragged little waif of about nine or ten. I rolled down the window. "What are you doing out tonight? It's Christmas Eve." He just shrugged his shoulders. "Do you live around here?"

He pointed to a shack tucked away behind a sheet metal shop. He noticed the packages on the seat next to me and in a hopeful tone asked, "Who are those for?"

I answered before thinking when I responded, "I'm not sure. Maybe for your family?" His eyes widened with anticipation.

"Are your parents home?" I inquired.

"Mom is," he said excitedly. "Follow me," and he started running. I trotted on behind. He opened the door to their humble hovel and shouted, "Mom, there's a man here wants to talk to you." A weary woman clad in blue jeans, a soiled blouse and an apron eyed me with suspicion and asked what I wanted.

"I'm the pastor from Peace Church. I have some Christmas gifts I'd like to give your children." She stared at me in disbelief and then sat down on a rumpled couch and started to cry. I had not expected this and just stood there as the snow on my shoes started to melt and left little puddles on her floor. I glanced around the room—no tree, no packages, no special lights, no decorations, no suggestion that anyone here was celebrating Christmas. Nothing but battered furniture, cardboard boxes, and a stack of clothing waiting to be ironed.

The woman, gaining her composure, dried her eyes on her apron and answered my unasked questions: "My husband ran out on us about five months ago, leaving us with nothing. Gary is my oldest, then two girls (five or six years old) and the baby. I was in the kitchen baking a pie when you came. It was to be their Christmas present this year. I had been praying 'O Lord, I feel so alone, so forgotten, please help me.' "

As a child I had read stories, make-believe tales of poor children who had a mysterious visitor drop by on Christmas Eve and leave them delightful surprises. Those fictional accounts had always thrilled me, but tonight was no fairy tale. This was real. Out to the Falcon Gary and I went, and returned with a box load of blessings. As the packages were removed from the box, a sudden chill went up and down my spine. What was in the box was unbelievable: a Christmas miracle! A package labeled "Boy 9-12," two other gifts marked "Girl 5-7," a decorated box tagged "Baby," and at the bottom, a package containing a pretty lady's sweater.

The children danced for joy as the treasures were placed on the table. Mother spoke, "Everyone listen now as pastor tells us the Christmas story." She smiled and nodded toward me.

Never before or since have I told that old, old story in such a sacred setting. The wonderful narrative concluded and Gary piped up and declared with enthusiasm, "Let's sing 'Happy Birthday' to Jesus." Gary's mom took a magnificent baked pie out of the oven, placed a lighted candle in the middle, and we sang, "Happy birthday, dear Jesus, happy birthday to you." The most memorable Christmas Eve of my life finished with group hugs for everyone. I thought I would be alone at Christmas. I should have known better. "Immanuel is God with us," oftentimes making that clear to us in surprising and marvelous ways.

"The Spirit of God descending like a dove..."

Matthew 3:16

We had recently entered the twenty-first century. Life was good. Our congregation was healthy and growing. In so many ways we felt God's hand of blessing. We sensed that the time had come for us to add a third ordained pastor to our staff. A search committee was formed and a job description was placed on our website and in church periodicals.

In no time at all we received dozens of resumes from aspiring applicants. Our search committee selected three candidates to visit our campus and participate in personal interviews, where they were asked to share their life stories, perceived gifts and abilities, passions and special interests, strengths and weaknesses, their favorite Bible passage, and describe their philosophy of ministry in just one word.

Three outstanding pastors had been interviewed. The search team planned to meet again in a week. In the meantime, they were admonished to pray daily for discernment that the person of God's choosing would be the one called to do ministry here. After much prayer and discussion, the associate pastor chosen to be added to our staff was Pastor Charles "Chuck" Daley. For the past decade he had worked for the State of California as a counsellor for those suffering from various addictions, mostly alcohol and drugs. He was convinced that the time had come to return to pastoral ministry in a congregation and thus had responded to our posted job description.

Chuck was middle-aged, father of two grown children, had been widowed, and now was married to Carol, who also had been widowed. During the interview, we learned that his favorite Bible passage was Romans 8. He reminded us that in this scripture, St. Paul lists everything he can think of that might separate him from God's love. His conviction was that nothing exists now or will ever come that has the power to separate us from God's love.

He shared that his conviction was sorely tested when his first wife died suddenly leaving him as a single father with two teenagers. He was depressed and angry and stated that he received no comfort whatsoever from those who piously proclaimed, "She has now gone to a much better place…" Pastor Daley read and reread Romans 8 which brought comforting peace. He said, "I reached the point where I deeply sensed the power of Christ's victory on the cross and it caused my heart to nearly burst with hope."

Our search team provided a list of words and phrases and invited Pastor Chuck to pick out some that he thought described himself. His first choice was "caring." Then he added: "One of the best ways to do that is to listen. The silent cry from so many people is the plea that someone will listen to them."

The search committee was convinced that Pastor Daley was God's choice to join our pastoral team. The congregation agreed with the recommendation and at a celebratory Sunday service, Pastor Charles Daley was installed as our second associate pastor. Several months of exciting ministry followed. Daley commented about the wonderful manner in which the congregation and staff welcomed him and accepted him as a member of the team.

One day he confidentially confessed to me a concern: for unknown reasons he often felt exhausted, as if he'd been in a marathon run. He had scheduled a thorough physical exam to see if there might be a medical solution to his tiredness. An early diagnosis pointed to the possibility that he was a diabetic. Soon treatment was underway, but the results were very disappointing. More exams were scheduled.

A couple of weeks passed. Chuck and Carol were holding hands and wearing very somber expressions as they entered my office. Their countenance told me they were bearers of bad news. "On my most recent test I lit up like a Christmas tree," he stated in a voice barely above a whisper. "I have cancer throughout my body, from my head to my feet. The cause is unknown and there is no cure. My doctor suggested I start hospice care, where every effort will be made to make my final days as pain-free as possible." The shocking news left me stunned. Soon the three of us were embracing and sobbing.

Some time later, following a time of prayer with Chuck, I commented, "You've only been with us a year and soon you will be leaving. Could it be that you came here to teach us how to die?" He paused, took a deep breath, and responded, "Pray that I will be a good teacher."

It was Easter Sunday, a great day of joy for all Christians, and Pastor Chuck fervently desired to be with us. By now he was very weak, barely able to sit up in a borrowed wheelchair. His presence was a very emotional time for all of us, as hundreds of tears were unashamedly flowing. The worship leader declared the greatest news ever proclaimed, "He is risen!" Pastor Chuck raised his head and responded, "He is risen indeed!"

It was early in the morning, before dawn, when my phone rang. It was Julie, director of our Stephen's Ministry program. She had spent the night with Chuck and Carol at their home. "Pastor Chuck has just departed for his heavenly home." I dressed as fast as I could and was at their house in ten minutes. I met Carol in the kitchen where we hugged and wept together. While still holding her, I glanced over her shoulder at the kitchen window just a few feet away. I could hardly believe what I saw. To my utter amazement, I was face to face with a plump-bodied, brown speckled dove. Its feathers were shining like gold in the morning sun. He just stood there gazing at us. "Carol, turn around. What do you see?"

"A big beautiful dove sitting on the window sill."

"Has he ever been here before?"

The startled grieving widow stared in wonder. "No. What could it mean?"

"Carol, the dove appears dozens of times in the Bible. It is often seen as a messenger from God, a bringer of hope, a symbol of God's presence. Carol, God has sent this dove to assure us that Chuck has entered heaven's gates and all is well." The tears continued to come as we clung to each other, comforted by this miraculous and amazing act of God's grace.

"Do not be like the hypocrites..."

Matthew 6:5

Arthur Boyle, an Englishman, decided some time ago to play a practical joke on twelve friends, men who were well-known, well-respected pillars of the community. He sent each a telegram with the same message: "All is discovered. Get out of town now." Within twenty-four hours, three of them had fled the country. Amazing! Virtually all of us have some things in our lives of which we are ashamed, such as an action we would not want others to know about.

In the gospel of Mark, we read Jesus' words, "These people honor me with their lips but their hearts are far from me." So many religious people are sticklers for traditions, rules, and regulations but seemingly blind to love, mercy, and compassion.

For years, Dr. Laura Schlessinger's radio program had millions of loyal listeners. She was a popular talk radio host and family therapist who was appalled by the decline of moral values in our culture. As an example, she received a call from a worried mother whose son was shacking up with his girlfriend. That, however, was not what concerned her. As an Orthodox Jew, she was upset that her son was no longer living within walking distance of a synagogue and to drive would be a violation of Sabbath law. Dr. Laura could not get her to understand the inconsistency between observing one tenet of her faith (honoring the Sabbath) but not caring if another was violated (her son's fornication with his female partner). It is not unusual for people in a high-sounding voice to proclaim some virtue and altogether ignore other moral principles.

A college sophomore was being interviewed on TV about her religious beliefs. She affirmed, "Oh yes. I believe in God but I'm not nuts about Him." According to a Gallup poll taken in June 2011, that is an accurate description of how most Americans feel about God. Over 90 percent of us believe there is a God, but when it comes to translating that belief into action, clearly most are not nuts about him. In an earlier poll, Gallup discovered that 85 percent of Americans felt the Ten Commandments remained very valid and should be obeyed by all of us. When asked to name half of them, most U.S. citizens could not do so. You see the problem? God on our lips but not in our hearts.

Country music star Willie Nelson loves to tell the story of an image of Jesus that appeared in 1987 on the wall of a town in South America. Tabloid magazines reported the story. People from surrounding towns gathered to pray in front of the image; some reported healing from disease. Then came the second miracle. After a heavy rainfall, another face appeared on the wall, that of Willie Nelson. The people had been praying in front of an old poster covered over with whitewash advertising a Willie Nelson concert. A few days later the tabloids ran a new headline: "That's not Jesus; it is just old Willie." People who use religion to whitewash their hearts discover that when the rain of adversity comes, the whitewash fades and people see that it wasn't Jesus at all. It was just old Willie.

Back in the '40s after the creation of the state of Israel, there was a great need to find a top caliber person to be mayor of Jerusalem. This was going to be a very difficult task. Who will face the great dangers of serving in this tinderbox office? Eventually, after the question had been asked many times, one delegate rose to his feet and in an impressive booming voice, proclaimed, "Here I am and I am here to nominate Clarence!" Just about every organization has some people in their midst who are quick to answer, "Here I am. Send Clarence." All too many are willing to stick their toe in the water but will never plunge in all the way. They talk the talk but don't walk the walk.

There is a difference between being a sinner and being a hypocrite. A hypocrite wears a mask pretending to be what he/she is not. However, a Jesus follower admits the truth that he/she is a sinner, one who has fallen short of God's ideal. Jesus loved sinners but had few kind words for hypocrites. A peasant once approached Francis of Assisi and admonished him with the following words: "Brother Francis, I pray that you will be as good as people think you are." Whew! That is pressure, yet by the grace of God we become motivated to be the very best we can be.

I was once asked something that I think is an excellent question for all of us to ponder: "Pastor B., how do you want to be remembered after you're gone?" After pondering that query for quite a while I responded, "By God's grace I would hope that people would be able to state that he made every effort to practice what he preached." Now it is your turn. How do you want to be remembered after you are gone?

Wouldn't it be great if someone followed you around with a secret video camera and they would find something far more newsworthy than a holy hypocrite? Instead they would uncover a forgiven sinner, daily striving to become more and more the person God designed him/her to be. How wonderful life could be if each of us made that our morning prayer.

"Your will be done..."

Matthew 6:10

I was recently ordained and had received a call to pastor a small, struggling, multiracial congregation in inner-city Cleveland, Ohio. I was a bachelor and all my earthly possessions had been placed in my Ford Falcon. The congregation owned a parsonage, located right next to the church building. This would be my home. It was completely unfurnished except for an old stove in the kitchen.

I went over to the church and borrowed a chair and a small folding table. I visited the church cupboard and came home with one cup, one dish, one plate, one knife, one fork, and one spoon. On my next trip I felt quite fortunate to discover a small frying pan which perhaps had not been used for years. A sleeping bag on the floor served as my bed, which was fine with me. Hardly a week had gone by when I arrived at the conclusion that somewhere I needed to find a refrigerator. There was an ad in the weekly newspaper placed by an appliance store highlighting their annual sale which included refrigerators. When the sales clerk discovered how much I could afford to spend, he kindly offered to sell me a trade-in that had been in the storeroom for some time. I considered it a blessing and life was good.

The church building had been well-maintained even as the community around it was disintegrating, with houses and apartments desperately in need of repair. The crime rate was rising, racial tensions were increasing, and broken homes and fatherless children seemed to be the norm. It was not uncommon to hear gunshots during the night. Ministry was a twenty-four hour job and not easy. Two years passed and we were blessed with growth, both spiritual and in numbers of new believers.

I returned home one night to a darkened parsonage. I prepared a pork chop, baked potato, and a salad and sat down to eat. In addition to a table grace I added, "Lord, I am really lonely. You said 'It is not good for a man to be alone. I will make a helper suitable for him.' So here is my idea: I am asking you to bring me a life's partner. I won't go out searching for one. I'll stay where I am using the gifts you have given me to be the best pastor I'm capable of being. Amen."

I prayed that prayer almost daily for the next year. I was left disappointed as the prayer went unanswered. One night, after repeating the same prayer for the umpteenth time, I stopped mid-sentence and said out loud, "This is not a good prayer," and I changed it. "Lord, you are aware of what's in my heart as you have heard me pray it many times. However, if you know that I can be a better servant as an unmarried pastor, then so be it. Amen." Guess what? It is as if the Lord said, "Finally you prayed what I've been waiting to hear. Now prepare to receive the answer to your prayer."

A short time later, a bright, attractive young Christian woman, a graduate student at Case Western University, joined us for Sunday morning services. At the time I did not recognize her as the answer to my prayer since she was there with her boyfriend, but that is another story for another time. Suffice it to say that a year later, the answer to my prayer and I were married. I have become convinced that God only gives three answers to prayer: (1) Yes! (2) Not yet. (3) I have something better in mind.

It seems that a highly skilled American ophthalmologist had undertaken the responsibility of performing delicate eye surgery upon an Eastern monarch. It was a wonderfully successful procedure that saved the king's eyesight. After His Majesty's recovery, the problem of presenting his bill puzzled the good doctor. He had no idea what he should charge. It was common knowledge that in Eastern countries it would be a serious wrong to charge the king more or less than the actual value. He sought the advice of his colleagues but they were as mystified as he was. Then he had an idea: he took a blank bill and wrote across it, "The king can do no wrong" and submitted the bill to his royal patient. His answer was a letter enclosing a sum of money beyond his wildest expectations.

When we are not even quite sure how to pray or what to pray for, then pray as Jesus taught us, "Your will be done..." Just leave it in the hands of the King who does all things well.

"Forgive us...as we have been forgiven..."

Matthew 6:12

Forgiveness is powerful but it is not easy. If we are hurt, slighted, or offended, our inclination is to figure out a way to get even. I'll show them, we think, they can't do that to me.

Human nature being what it is, we are out to get the offender, not forgive him. Ann Landers tells the story of a man who saw an ad in the newspaper for a Porsche in mint condition. The asking price was fifty dollars. He could not believe his eyes. It had to be a typographical error. Even priced one hundred times higher it would be a great buy. So he hurried off to check on this incredible bargain. It was as advertised. It almost took his breath away. The seller assured him the price of fifty dollars was correct. Brimming with excitement, he handed her a fifty dollar bill and in return received the pink slip of ownership and the keys to his fulfilled dream. "How in the world could you sell this for such a ridiculously low price?" With a sadistic grin she responded, "My husband ran off with his secretary and left a note instructing me to sell the Porsche and send him the money."

I am reminded of the account of the deathbed conversation that the Spanish patriot Ramon Maria Narvaez (also known as the first Duke of Valencia) had with his priest. The good father was present to administer the last rites. Narvaez was asked if he had forgiven all his enemies. "I have no enemies," he acknowledged. "I shot them all." I would guess that refusing to forgive them would be as serious a sin as shooting them.

When some of Mahatma Gandhi's followers wanted to use violence to strike back at their opponents, their mentor cautioned, "The person who pursues revenge should dig two graves."

Corrie ten Boom, a most remarkable Christian woman and author of many inspirational books, wrote of forgiving some friends after much prayer. She just made up her mind that she would forgive them and then prayed. At that point she felt a surge of joy. Time went on and she was disappointed that the same problem still bothered her. "I thought all was forgiven. What is the matter with me?" She concluded that it wasn't enough to say "I forgive you." She had to live it out. In a sense she found herself pretending that everything was fine.

One evening some friends came by for a visit and the conversation turned to the people she thought she had forgiven. A guest commented, "They claim you got all upset over such a minor issue." At that Corrie flared, "A minor thing? I saved the letters they wrote. I've got the evidence right here." In a matter of a few minutes she had it all spread out in front of them. Like a bolt of lightning it became clear to her what she had been doing. She had only forgiven with her lips but not with her heart. The repentant woman burned the letters, thus destroying the evidence of their sins. That is the way God forgives. He banishes our sins from his sight forever.

Evangelist Leighton Ford once shared the tale of a man who owned a Rolls-Royce. While he was traveling on vacation hundreds of miles from home, there was a mechanical failure so he called the dealer from which he had purchased the Rolls. They flew in a mechanic from England to repair it. It was soon as good as new. A month went by and the luxury car owner had yet to receive a bill for the work that was done. He contacted the manufacturer in the U.K., requesting a final billing. He received the following message: "We have no record of a Rolls- Royce with a mechanical failure." The evangelist reminds us that this is what our Lord will say someday when we ask about the penalty we must pay for our sins, "We have no record of you ever having done wrong."

"Whoever acknowledges me before men..."

Matthew 10:32

When Margaret Himiniski was seven years old she received a gift from her grandmother. It was a tiny cross on a chain so fine that it weighed hardly anything at all. "Never forget what this cross means," her grandmother admonished as she fastened it with tender loving care around Margaret's neck. Over the years, that cross became as much a part of her as the lone freckle on her left cheek. She could look at herself in the mirror and not even see it.

As a graduate psychology student she took a job tutoring at a school for emotionally disturbed children. Suddenly she was surrounded by children who expressed their displeasure by kicking, biting, and screaming. She found herself scared to death, although determined not to show it. On her first night there the head counselor said that three of the boys asked for permission to escort her to dinner–alone! How would she handle it if the three decided to act out at once? She swallowed hard. She was desperate to have employment so she fought back the panic and walked with her charges to the dining hall.

They passed through the cafeteria line as tantrums and scuffles erupted all around them. She was ever so grateful that none of her escorts exhibited any kind of behavioral problems. They made their way to the table and the boys took their seats. Ms. Himiniski picked up her fork and was about to take the first bite when she noticed that all three boys were staring at her. "What's the matter?" she questioned.

A somewhat bewildered eight-year-old Peter asked, "Aren't you going to say grace?" "This is a state school so I didn't think that I was supposed to ask a blessing."

"Yes," the child responded, "but you are wearing a cross."

Her grandmother's words surged to the surface of her memory: "Never forget what the cross means."

"We thought your cross might mean something special," observed disappointed Charles. "It does," Margaret affirmed, "thank you for reminding me." She bowed her head, no longer afraid, and prayed a table grace. Thank God for Margaret's faithful grandmother. I believe a man named Jose Lozano once said: "I don't pray for God to take my problems away, I pray only for God to give me the strength to go through them."

An American businessman traveled to Europe to witness the famous Oberammergau Passion Play. Following the performance, the tourist had the opportunity to see and speak with Anton Lang, who portrayed Christ in the sacred drama. Seeing the cross that had been used, he decided he would like his photo taken holding the cross. His wife took the camera, ready to snap the picture with the cross on his shoulder. He was shocked to discover that he could barely budge it off the floor. "I don't understand," the surprised American said to Lang, "I thought it would be hollow. Why do you carry such a heavy cross?" Mr. Lang's reply helps explain why this pageant draws people from all over the world to a small Bavarian village: "If I did not feel the weight of this cross, I could not play the part." If being a disciple of Jesus costs us no pain to acquire, no self-denial to preserve, no effort to advance, and no struggle to maintain, then it isn't what Jesus had in mind.

E. Stanley Jones, author, inspirational speaker, and Christian missionary, described the changed life of a Brahman who left Hinduism to become a Christian. As a Brahman, he had been a member of the highest caste and believed that he had earned that rank because of the good works done in a previous existence. Now a new believer, he chose to live in the Ashram community which had been founded by Jones. Everyone there was expected to participate in the daily chores, including the cleaning of the latrines. Upon hearing of that assignment, the former Brahman stopped short, claiming that task was beneath him. His mentor insisted that in Christ there are no unsuitable chores and those converted to the lordship of Jesus should have no trouble cleaning latrines. The Indian responded, "Brother Stanley, I am converted but not that far." That can be our problem, too, can it not? We are converted but not that far.

Teddy Roosevelt was returning from Africa where he had gone to do some big game hunting. As his ship pulled into New York Harbor, a gala celebration was waiting. News reporters, photographers, even several brass bands were on hand to welcome the popular former president back home. The dock was filled with dignitaries and VIPs from across the country, applauding as he made his exit from the ship. In the meantime, an older couple in failing health and walking at a slow pace made their way down the gangplank. They were Christian missionaries who had for forty years been sharing the good news of the gospel with the African people. Their lives had truly been a life of sacrifice in a poverty-stricken part of the world. The husband leaned over to his beloved life partner and said, "Such a marvelous homecoming for Teddy Roosevelt yet there is no one here to meet us." After a pause, his wife responded, "That is because we are not home yet."

"He gave thanks..."

Matthew 14:19

During the winter of 1940, Josephine Kuntz's husband, a house painter, was temporarily without work. It was a very difficult time for the family. They literally had no money. Their eighteen-month-old daughter, Rachel, was recovering from pneumonia and wasn't doing very well. The doctor insisted the child be given a boiled egg every day. Even that was beyond their means.

"Why not pray for an egg?" suggested a young friend. They were a Christian family but the idea of actually praying for their needs was something that they had never seriously considered. Josephine wasted no time. On her knees, she asked that God would provide an egg each morning for her daughter. A few hours later Rachel's mother heard some cackling coming from the hedge fence in front of their home. Among the bare branches sat a fat red hen. She had never seen this robust fowl before and had no idea where it came from. She just watched in amazement as the beautiful chicken laid an egg and then proceeded down the road. In a moment she was gone but the large brown egg sat in the yard.

What do you do under such circumstances but thank God? The next morning Josephine was startled once again to hear cackling near the garden wall. The Rhode Island Red came every morning for a week and repeated this routine. Each day little Rachel had a fresh boiled egg. She got better, the weather improved, and Josephine's husband went back to work. "The next morning I waited and watched," Josephine declared, "but the little red hen never returned."

The Message: The Bible in Contemporary Language in a paraphrase from Psalm 107 declares: "You called out to God in your desperate condition, He got you out in the nick of time."

Beryl Dovid tells about a near tragedy that befell his seventy-four-year-old-father. He was returning from an out-of-town worship service one cold Saturday evening when his old Ford broke down on an isolated stretch of road. As he got out of the jalopy to check under the hood, he slipped and fell, badly twisting his leg. When he tried to get up, the pain was so excruciating that he nearly passed out. He lay in agony on the pavement. The chance that someone would come by before morning was remote. Also, because of his precarious position, a passing motorist might run him over without realizing someone was there. As the frosty asphalt sapped his body of warmth, the old fellow decided that this was a very undignified way to die. He started to pray.

Hours later, a young man driving a white Honda spotted Beryl's father and expertly tended to him. His father was, by then, almost dead from exposure. The good Samaritan took him to a local hospital. After making sure that he would be OK, he disappeared. The only thing the family was able to find out about this remarkable young rescuer was that he may have been a college student. An emergency room nurse said the husky youth was wearing a jacket with "PROVIDENCE" lettered on the back. No one has ever been able to convince Beryl's father that the one who saved his life was to all appearance a student at nearby Providence University. We acknowledge that God's providence does not always come that directly. Still we know He cares for His children.

Prayer is placing our needs in God's care and getting on with our lives, trusting that our Heavenly Father will handle the rest. Sometimes some of us who have lived a few years and have gotten a bit calloused in our prayer life can be revived as we hear the prayers of a child. Dr. Benjamin Lewis told the following story: He will never forget little Jennifer, five years old, who was brought into the hospital for rather serious surgery. As the medical team was preparing her for the operation he explained that soon they would be putting her to sleep. "Oh," she declared, "I always say my prayers before I go to sleep." So everything came to a stop while Jennifer prayed, "God bless Dad, Mom, Grandma and don't let them worry too much. Also bless the doctors and nurses who are going to help make me well. Thank you Jesus for loving every one of us. Amen. OK," she said, now satisfied, "I'm ready to go to sleep now." Dr. Lewis humbly stated, "I suppose I hadn't prayed for ten years but now I do every day."

Then there are those times when God wants to use us to answer someone's prayers. Tony Campolo, popular Christian author and inspirational speaker, was invited to a women's conference where he was to give a major address. These women were being challenged to raise several thousand dollars for a mission project. While Campolo was sitting upon the platform, the chairperson asked him if he would begin with a prayer for God's blessing as they considered how best to reach their financial goal. To the utter amazement of nearly everyone, he smiled, shook his head from side to side and said "no." He got up, approached the microphone, and announced, "You already have all the resources necessary to complete this mission. It is all here, now, within this room. It would be inappropriate to ask for God's blessings when in fact God has already blessed you with the abundance and the means to reach your goal. The necessary gifts are in your hands right now. As soon as the offering is taken we will thank God for freeing us to be generous, responsible stewards that we are called to be as his disciples."

Tony was right on. You can be certain that there are times when we intercede for someone asking God to bless them and then God chooses to bless them through us. More often than we realize, God has given us all that is needed to be the answer to someone's prayer.

"Then Peter got out of the boat..."

Matthew 14:29

When hundreds of senior citizens were asked, "If you could live your life over again, what would you do differently?" A very common answer was, "I would take more risks." I would agree with that. Oh, not foolish chances that serve no good purpose, but risks like the apostle Peter took when Jesus invited him to put all fear aside and walk on water. When Jesus said, "Come," Peter stepped out of the boat and will forever be remembered for his courageous action.

A young man, Jeff McMillan, was once placed in a situation where he could play it safe or take a career-threatening risk. Jeff spent four years acting the character of Ronald McDonald in Arizona and Southern California for the McDonald's Corporation. Once a month he would visit children's hospitals. Two restrictions were placed on him: He must always be accompanied by McDonald's personnel and hospital representatives. He also was never permitted to touch one of these young patients because there was fear he might transfer germs from one child to another. If he ever broke the rules he was told he would lose his job.

After several years in his role as Ronald McDonald, he was heading down the hallway of a hospital on his way home. He heard a little voice calling out, "Ronald McDonald." The voice was coming through a half-open door. He stepped inside the room and saw a small boy, about five, lying in his father's arms. He was hooked up to more medical equipment than Jeff had ever seen. His mother was nearby along with his grandparents and a nurse. It was very obvious that the situation was grave.

He asked the young fellow his name. It was Billy. Jeff did a few magic tricks that brought a smile and look of wonderment to the face of the suffering child. As he stood up to leave, he heard a soft voice pleading, "Ronald, will you please hold me?" Such a simple request. But Jeff knew well the rigid instructions: touch a child and you will be fired. He said, "I'm sorry but perhaps we could color and complete a picture together." Soon a picture of puppies, kittens, and rainbows was ready to be placed on the refrigerator door. When finished, Jeff was once again asked by Billy if he would please hold him.

By now his heart was answering "Yes," but his mind with nearly equal force hollered back, "No. Don't think such things. You'll lose your job." His thoughts were moving at a rapid clip. If I lose my job, he thought, I might lose my car and I might even lose my home but... so what? He politely asked the family and the escorts to leave the room. The nurse tending the medical equipment stayed but he requested that she turn her back. Then he picked up this precious frail little chap and held him in his arms. They laughed, cried, and for the next forty-five minutes talked about things that worried

Billy. He was afraid his little brother would get lost in the playground without Billy being with him. He worried that Sonny, his golden Lab, might not get any more bones because he had hidden them before going back to the hospital and couldn't remember where he put them.

These are the problems of a small child who knows that he may never go home again. On his way out of the room with tears cascading down his cheeks, Jeff gave Billy's parents his real name and phone number (another automatic dismissal for Ronald McDonald). "If I can do anything else, anything, please call me," were his parting remarks to Billy's parents.

Less than forty-eight hours later, he received a phone call from his little friend's mother. She informed him that Billy had passed away and she and her husband simply wanted to thank him for making such a difference in their beloved son's life. Shortly after Jeff had left the room, Billy smiled at his mother and softly whispered, "Mom, it's OK if I'm not here to see Santa Claus because I was held by Ronald McDonald." Jeff McMillan could have settled for playing it safe–most people do–but until his dying day, Jeff will forever be grateful that he listened to the "Yes" in his heart and took a risk.

Sharing the love of Jesus always carries a risk with it. The homeless person might take the five dollars you passed him and purchase a bottle of Thunderbird wine in place of the eggs and pancakes he could have. The foster child you take in might pilfer your heirloom treasures. The shut-in to whom you pay a visit may scold you for not coming more often or, like Jeff McMillan, you may have to risk your job and your reputation to meet someone's needs. Love always carries a risk, but it is often risk worth taking. "Then Peter got out of the boat and walked on water."

Lt. Col. Jeff Patton was flying his F-15 fighter jet over northern Iraq in total darkness when suddenly his plane was locked on by surface-to-air radar. He violently maneuvered his aircraft to break the radar's lock on him. He successfully accomplished that goal but that created a new problem. These radical movements had thrown him off balance, causing him to become disoriented. His mind was telling him his plane was climbing but when he checked his instruments they indicated he was in a sixty-degree dive toward the ground. But he was certain he was in a climb and his mind was screaming to him to lower the nose and halt the climb. His flight instruments instructed him to do the opposite. He was in total darkness so his life depended on making the right choice. Even though it took every ounce of strength within him to overcome what his mind was telling him to do, he made the decision to follow his instruments. So he pulled his F-15 upward. He trusted his instruments, made the right choice, and saved his life.

Later on he realized that if he had delayed just another three seconds he would have crashed in the mountains of Iraq. Even right decisions can be wrong ones if they are made too late. When we give our lives over to Christ's control, we are trusting Him to guide the instruments inside our hearts even when our mind may be telling us to do the opposite. There comes a time when we, like Lt. Col. Patton, must decide whom we're going to trust. It is the beginning of Christian discipleship. Who controls your life?

For nearly a decade I would make regular visits to Donovan Prison, a dark, foreboding place housing over 5,000 convicted felons. There are so many stories about incarcerated inmates. One of the most remarkable is that of a young man who for a while shared a cell with his grandfather. His grandpa spent most of his adult life in prison, his father was serving a life sentence and now, at age nineteen, he was in prison. He told me in a matter-of-fact tone that he knew someday he would be in prison. Just as some kids know they'll go into military service or that they will go to college, he expected to go to prison.

Six months after arriving at Donovan, he was invited by a fellow inmate to come to a chapel service. He was bored and this would provide a change in his daily routine so he accepted the invitation. Almost nothing that happened there made any sense to him but there was some good music so he came back a second time. Several months passed and he found himself in a conversation with the chaplain. He told him his life story, stating that just like his father, he expected to someday be serving a life sentence and would probably die in prison. He said it with an air of resignation and hopelessness. The chaplain reached out, put his hand on his shoulder, and said, "It doesn't have to be that way. You have two fathers and the freedom to choose which one you will follow." The chaplain was right on. We, too, are free to choose who we will follow.

Dave Thomas, the founder of Wendy's, was a big advocate for adoption. He was an adopted child himself and was very grateful for the love and values his family gave him. Dave tells the story of Kandy, a twelve-year-old who was adopted. The young girl had been with her adoptive parents for only about a year when her birth father invited her to lunch. He had been in prison most of Kandy's life and she had never met him. Her parents had a quiet fear that she might choose to go back to him but nevertheless encouraged her to go so she could learn more about her history. She had dozens of questions to ask and he answered them the best he could. Then her anxious parents arrived at the end of lunch and Kandy did something unexpected. Up until now she had never even held the hand of her adoptive dad. She got up from the table, thanked her birth father for lunch, and gathered her doggy bag. She reached out her hand and took the hand of her adoptive father and said, "Papa, I'm ready to go home now." It was only a small gesture but it announced to the world that Kandy was committed to her new family. She had decided who her father would be and who she would follow. That really is the question each of us faces as we begin a new day. Who is our father? Who is in charge? Who do we want to imitate? Who are we willing to follow?

> *"What if he gains the whole*
> *world, yet forfeits his soul?"*

Matthew 16:26

Fred and his young son had stopped at McDonald's for a snack. They were sitting at a table with a bag of french fries in front of the lad. Fred casually reached over to take a fry out of the bag when the little boy cried out, "No, they're mine!" and pulled them closer. Startled, dad looked at his child in surprise and then asked himself what had just happened here. *If it wasn't for me, he wouldn't have any fries,* Fred thought. *I went to the counter, I ordered the fries, I paid for the fries, and I placed them in front of my son. I am his father. I have the power to take them away or to buy $100 worth and bury him in them! He doesn't understand it at all. I don't need his fries. I could obviously have all the french fries I wanted. I really just wanted his willingness to share them with me.*

He continued to reflect, *That is how our God must often feel when he sees how we use what He has given us. When He gave us His Son, He gave us the ultimate and since then He has continued to give to all of us.* The question for each of us is this: How do we react when He reaches over for some of our fries?

A Gallup poll confirms what we thought all along–the more we have, the harder it is to give. Dollars given to charity decreases as income increases. Moderate and low-income Americans donate a much higher percentage of their income than do the wealthy. Tom Stanley, author of *Marketing to the Affluent*, points out how difficult it is to get people with lots of money to see anything else. When wealthy participants were asked if they would like the money for taking part in the survey donated to their favorite charity, the overwhelming response was "no."

I can't tell you the number of people who have told me how generous they would be if they won the lottery. Of course, I don't believe them. Not even for a moment. If one is not generous today what makes him/her think they will be tomorrow? I am convinced that expenses usually rise to meet income. Our giving is a spiritual matter because there are some things in our world that only money can do: feed the hungry, clothe the naked, care for widows and orphans. Dollars can also build a place of worship or a school for needy children.

My grandfather, now rejoicing with the saints in heaven, told the story of a lad carrying a basket of eggs down the street when he tripped and fell, smashing most of the eggs. One person looked on sadly and exclaimed, "What a pity." Someone else reacted by shaking his head as he uttered, "Too bad." A third witness responded, "I feel so sorry for the kid." Then a man stepped forward, reached into his pocket, and announced, "I care a dollar. How much do you care?" An excellent question for all of us.

The Methodist church in downtown Charlotte, North Carolina, had a large number of affluent members. Its social ministry team enabled it to extend its service to the homeless and dregs of society. After a while it was not uncommon to find some poverty-stricken, low-class citizens of the city hanging around the church. One day a sophisticated, well-dressed member of the congregation approached the pastor and expressed her concern about "all those intruders."

Her minister explained that he was trying to save people from hell. The woman grudgingly agreed that the church should do what it could to save these street people from hell. "No, I don't mean them," he replied, "I'm trying to save *us* from hell."

What a powerful statement. Jesus himself warns us of the great danger of gaining the world and, in the process, losing our own soul.

"Lord, how many times shall I forgive.."

Matthew 18:21

"To err is human, to forgive is not our policy." So read the sign tacked on the wall in the thrift store. For all too many, to forgive is not our policy. Our policy, dictated by our sinful human nature, is to hold a grudge, plot revenge, or break off relations with the offender. It is probably not our intention to forgive because it is such a difficult thing to do.

The well-known team of Gilbert and Sullivan of light opera fame had a fight, or so it is claimed, over the cost of carpeting in a theater they had purchased. As a result, they never spoke to each other as long as they lived. Sullivan would write the music and mail it to Gilbert, who would write the words and mail it back. When they were to receive an award jointly, they refused to appear on the same stage together so they came in separate entrances. The honor was divided so they wouldn't have to look at each other.

Louis XII, King of France, fought in many battles before he ascended the throne and made many enemies. When it became common knowledge that he had a list of the names of those who had opposed him and beside each foe he had placed a black cross, all those whose identities appeared on that list were certain that he planned to execute them. Imagine how stunned they were when they were brought into his presence and given pardons by His Majesty. The cross next to their name, he told them, was to remind him of Jesus Christ who forgave his enemies and expected all who followed him to do likewise.

I met Louie Zamperini at a Kiwanis Club luncheon in Compton, California in 1970. He had been a lieutenant in the Air Force during World War II and his plane crashed somewhere in the Pacific Ocean. He bounced around in a life raft for forty-seven days surviving on raw fish and rescued rainwater. Eventually he was captured by the Japanese, severely tortured and beaten, a prisoner until the end of the war. What helped him keep alive, the former POW testified, was his hatred of his enemy and his vow that someday he would get even. After the war ended, he was free and home again, determined to fulfill his vow and gain revenge. He acquired as much information as he could about his guards. He had planned to search them out one by one. But a strange thing happened to him on the angry road to retribution.

Zamperini was trying to pray the Lord's Prayer but could not do so. When he got to the petition, "Forgive us as we forgive others," he knew it was a lie because he hadn't forgiven others. The love of God just seemed to overcome him and the ex-captive determined, by God's grace, to be a forgiver as he had been forgiven. He returned to Japan, sought out his prison guards, and faced them. Two of his guards were so profoundly moved by his act of forgiveness that they asked how they could become Christians. There is enormous power in forgiveness. It can revitalize spiritual lives, it can make the weak strong, it can rebuild friendships, renew marriages, and open the highway of heaven for God's people.

Jim was thirty, his wife Mary twenty-eight, and they had been parents of little Elizabeth for a year and a half. As far as Mary was concerned, it was a good life. She loved her husband and child and thought it was a two-way street until one weekend, Jim took off with his secretary, deserting his wife and daughter. Mary was heartbroken but constantly prayed a rather remarkable prayer. Her petition was not one of revenge or even that Jim would come back. Instead she daily requested on her knees that Jim would open his heart to Jesus and become His follower. The day came when Jim sat in a pastor's office pouring out his prayers of confession. He asked the minister to help him write a letter to his wife imploring her forgiveness. This the preacher did. Forgiveness was sought and it was given.

At this point something else needs to be written. Louie Zamperini was able to forgive his Japanese prison guards and Mary was able to forgive the unfaithfulness of her husband, but I'm certain that neither will ever forget what happened. We make a serious mistake when we link forgiveness with forgetting. Jesus has forgiven us and those that nailed him to the cross but I'm sure he'll not forget, because the nail prints are still in his hands. In like manner, the pain or hurt may have been so great and so deep that it can never be forgotten, but that doesn't mean it can't be forgiven. If it is easy to kiss and make up then maybe the offense wasn't so great. We cannot equate forgiving with forgetting. However, true forgiveness means reconciliation has taken place and the issue will never be brought up again. Thus we pray, "Forgive us our sins as we forgive those who sin against us."

"Give to Caesar what is Caesar's ..."

Matthew 22:21

A young man, fresh out of college, was looking for work. He was in conversation with his minister. He told the pastor, "As soon as I get a job I'll give ten percent of my check to the Lord's work and I promise that as long as I am employed I'll continue to tithe." His mentor prayed with him that the right doors of opportunity would open for him and thanked God for his commitment to be a tither.

Before long the recent graduate landed a job. His yearly salary was $40,000 and he immediately donated 10 percent just as he promised he would. The next year he received a salary increase and, true to his pledge, he kept his vow and gave 10 percent to his church. His excellent work ethic led to a major income increase and in less than two years his yearly paycheck of $40,000 had jumped to $140,000. The youthful executive was back in the pastor's office and asked to be relieved of his commitment. "When I promised to tithe I had no idea my wages would increase so fast. There is no way I can afford to contribute ten percent any longer." "Shall we pray about this?" the preacher suggested. Then he addressed the Lord by praying, "Will you greatly reduce this brother's earnings so that once again he can, with joy, keep his promise?"

"Ah!" he pleaded. "Please don't pray that way."

Sad to say, but it is a simple fact, the more people earn, the less they give proportionally to charitable causes. Why is this so? It is a part of sinful human nature; the more we get, the more we want. It really is a question of our hearts, isn't it? Render to God the things that are God's. Number one on that list is our heart.

There is a silly story going around that makes a powerful point about where many of us are now. According to this rumor, the pope needed a heart transplant. Thousands of people gathered outside the Vatican screaming and waving their hands, "Take my heart, Papa, take my heart." The pope had no idea what to do until a thought popped into his head. He declared that he would toss down a feather and whoever the feather landed on would be the chosen donor and his heart would be removed and transplanted into the chest of the Holy Father. And so the feather was released and floated down toward the people. All were still crying out, "Take my heart, Papa," while blowing the air above their heads. I suspect that is where all too many are. We say "All I have belongs to you, Lord, take my heart," while we blow the feather away.

I am reminded of a wonderful account of hearts truly given away. The tale is from the days of the Depression. Newlyweds, deeply in love but as poor as church mice, desperately wanted to give each other a special gift on their first Christmas together but they had no money. The wife was aware that her beloved could not wear his prized watch because of a broken watchband. She wanted with all her heart to present him with a new watchband but she didn't have a dime in her pocket. She saw an ad in the paper from a company that manufactured wigs offering to purchase hair. Well, one of her most striking features was her long, beautiful hair. She made a decision: she would cut off her locks in order to get cash to buy her husband's gift. So she did, covering her head with a scarf.

With much love, she handed her husband the sacrificial gift she had purchased for him. They opened their presents and fell sobbing into each other's arms. She sold her wondrous hair in order to buy for him a watchband. He had sold his watch in order to give her a hairbrush for her crown of beauty. Each, out of love, gave the best they had.

So many Christians are missing the blessings that could be theirs because they don't truly believe His promise, "Give and it shall be given to you." God doesn't need our money. After all, in Psalm 50 we hear the Lord reminding us that "the cattle on a thousand hills belongs to me." It is we who need to give for we have been blessed to be a blessing.

The ancient tale has been told of a very wealthy merchant who was determined to take his treasure with him after he died. He prayed and prayed until he convinced God to let him bring his earthly treasures inside the pearly gates. There was only one condition: he must condense it all in a single suitcase. That is what he did.

He filled his luxury luggage piece with gold bullion.

The day came when he was met at heaven's door by Saint Peter who told him that he couldn't bring anything with him. The newcomer objected, informing the gatekeeper that he had made a personal deal with the Almighty Himself. A baffled St. Peter asked, "Are you certain? This is highly unusual." He was assured that an exception had been made for this sinner. "OK. Please let me see what you have brought." The baggage was opened to reveal several pounds of bright gold bullion. The Lord's sentry shook his head in confusion and disbelief, "Why are you bringing more pavement to heaven?"

There is nothing that God needs. Our gold is as asphalt to pave the streets of heaven. What our Heavenly Father wants from us is our hearts, that is, everything we are and everything we hope to be.

"Therefore go and make disciples..."

Matthew 28:19

John Ortberg, Presbyterian pastor and author, wrote a marvelous book called *When the Game Is Over It All Goes Back in the Box.* He writes about an experience he had when he was ten years old, playing Monopoly with his beloved grandmother. Grandma was very competitive and always played to win. Her strategy was to buy as much property as she could, as fast as she could. And guess what? She would always win. But this day was different. John adopted her approach and, for the first time in his life, he won. He later reflected that, at the time, he sensed it was the greatest moment of his life. Nevertheless Grandma had one more lesson to teach her grandson. Yes, he had won. Key properties, railroads, utilities and thousands of dollars were on his side of the table, but now it was time to put it away. But the young winner wanted to savor his victory. To bronze it would be a great idea. He wanted to leave it out on the table so that the whole world could see and admire his success. But the game was over and it would be put back in the box. Ortberg concludes: "It's not bad to play the game. It is not bad to play to win. But the danger is that we forget to ask what really matters. We race around the board with shallow relationships, frenzied schedules, grasping for rewards, lulled into thinking the game will never end. But it will and everything will go back in the box."

There is a synagogue in Budapest that has an empty coffin built into the wall as a constant reminder that life's end is always near.. The Jewish Talmud teaches that every person should repent one day before his/her death. Treat every day as if it were the day before the last. Arrange your life around that which matters most, starting today. The box is waiting.

Pastor Bill Hybels once preached a sermon about a meeting he attended where the speaker stood in front of the room with a roll of stickers in his hand. Behind him were tables filled with props that represented the stuff in our lives: a toy car, a doll house, a bank book, a little desk, etc. He walked around and placed a sticker on each item. Each sticker carried the same word: "TEM-PORARY." He went on to explain that everything on the tables may give us a momentary thrill, but the excitement will be short-lived. He also posted "TEMPO-RARY" stickers on resumes, SAT scores, on MBA's and PHD's. All of these material things are fleeting and will someday be forgotten.

He then took another set of stickers and wrote "ETERNAL" on them. "Put one on your family, put one on your friends, put one on your boss, put one on the guy next door and put one on your own forehead. When all is said and done, only love never ends. Love for God, love for each other; only love has ultimate value." We need to ask ourselves what we are doing–or not doing–now with our lives that could lead to regret. In the game of life, we can't go back once a move is made. Oftentimes we regret something that we did, but it is usually tempered by time. But when our regret is for that which we did not do, we may very well take it to the grave.

Southern Baptist pastor Adrian Rogers once said: "If the devil can't make you bad, he'll make you busy." God never gives us too much to do; He will give us the time to finish what he wants us to accomplish. If we're not getting done what God wants us to do, then we know our priorities must be out of whack. Jesus said, "Seek first the Kingdom of God and his righteousness and all these other things will be taken care of" (Matthew 6:33).

The author of the Book of Hebrews writes: We are surrounded by so great a crowd of witnesses so let us run with perseverance the race set before us" (Hebrews 12:1). Imagine walking through the scriptural Hall of Fame. You read the names. You see on each plaque two dates: the date the race began and when it ended. There is a little dash in between. Then you come to your plaque. You had nothing to say about the date on the left side–the date of your birth. Soon the blank spot on the right will have a number, but you probably don't have much to say about that either. Which brings us to the great question: What are you going to do with your dash–your life? What will you do with the opportunities you get to play the game? Ready or not, it's now your turn.

*"Jesus reached out his hand
and touched the leper..."*

Mark 1:41

Our annual mission trip to India always included setting up a portable medical clinic in a remote Dalit village. A native Christian evangelist had been sharing the good news of the gospel with these untouchables for a year or more and many had joyfully responded to God's love and were becoming followers of Jesus.

Their lifestyle was that of a poverty-stricken people, the poorest of the poor, unable to read or write, with little access to pure water, and existing on one meal a day, probably some type of rice. Few if any in the village had ever received professional medical treatment or had any type of health exam.

Traveling in a couple of four-wheel drive vans over dirt roads, our team arrived at the village where the Dalits, informed that we were coming, had been waiting for many hours. We then set up four tables under some shade trees while a half dozen monkeys were swinging in the branches just a few feet over our heads, noisily scolding us for interrupting their daily routines.

Next we unboxed our donated medical supplies: aspirin, vitamins, some first aid kits, and various prescription drugs. Also, such staples as soap, body lotions, toothpaste, and Band-Aids were distributed. Indian translators were on hand to assist us as we got underway.

A bilingual native's task was to record each person's name, age, and health concern. A team volunteer would take their blood pressure. Someone else took a blood sample, then the doctor would use that information along with a brief physical exam, to determine what sort of medication and/or treatment should be given. After a dozen or so patients had reached this point, they would then gather with a hygienist who would teach them through demonstration how to use soap, toothpaste, body lotions, and other cleansing items. Oftentimes these sessions would conclude with visual aids describing how germs are spread. Then they were told that if they so desired there would be someone available to pray with them. Almost all requested prayers.

Our Indian evangelist was asked if he had witnessed any miracle healing. "Yes," was his firm reply, "we have seen amazing healings with no medical explanation. One of the great blessings is the quiet joy and value the Dalits sense when you touch them. Remember they are untouchables. Most of them have never been touched by anyone other than another untouchable. When you, a Christian from America, touch them they feel valued. That is always positive."

On one of our trips I had been praying for several hours, one-on-one, with over a hundred untouchables.

My translator was Daniel, a fourteen-year-old follower of Jesus who had an amazing command of the English language. This delightful young Christian would tell me what the prayer request was, I would pray a few sentences, he would translate, and we would continue. The day was drawing to a close and both of us had been on a spiritual high but were also exhausted. I thanked my prayer partner and told him that I had a small gift in the van and so I headed off to retrieve it. When I returned he was nowhere to be found. Then I saw, off in the distance, Daniel coming my way and beside him was someone walking in a precarious manner, leaning on a huge walking stick. This person was wrapped in an old black cloth from head to feet.

My young friend called out, "Pastor, will you pray one more time?" I hustled in their direction where Daniel introduced this person to me. "This is Mujica. She is a brand-new Christian."

With joy I responded, "Praise God! That is wonderful. She is my sister. What is her need?"

"Pastor," he softly replied, "Mujica is a leper."

I froze. A leper. I'd never met a leper. Leprosy is almost non-existent in the Western world. However, I had read that there were still pockets of leprosy in India. My mind started racing. What do I remember about this dreaded disease? There are basically three kinds. One is a severe skin ailment, where boil-like sores pop up over the whole body. While painful, treatment can result in complete healing. A second form, far more serious, attacks the nervous system, killing nerves so the body no longer feels pain. This can be fatal since wounds may appear, bones be broken, animal or insect bites go unnoticed, or infection come from numerous causes and lead to death. The third type begins with an attack in the extremities causing toes and fingers to rot, like so many spoiled tomatoes, and eventually fall off. The disease will do similar damage to ears and nose. This form of leprosy can be contagious, traveling through such body fluids as a sneeze, cough, perspiration, or something as innocent as tears.

My heart was pounding as I stared at this pathetic woman. She had no toes, only small nibs where toes had once been. No fingers, just tiny stubs on her hands. Her nose was missing and her ears, only partially visible, were bent and folded over. In a voice that was shaking, I asked Daniel how she would like me to pray for her. He asked her and she responded in a deep, guttural sound. "What did she say?" I asked while catching my breath. He replied, "She said you are a man of God and know how to pray."

I hung my head, closed my eyes, and felt like I was about to cry. No, no, I thought, I'm not the righteous man of God she believes that I am. I don't know how to pray. Now my heart and my head started to battle with each other. My heart encouraged me to pray for her just like I did for the others but my head said don't be so foolish. You dare not place your hands on her. My heart spoke again: you just told her she was your sister. Treat her with the same love and tenderness as you would treat your sister. My head answered that is, of course, theologically correct but–come on–be practical , it would be an unnecessary crazy risk. One more time my heart's turn. I'm reminded that Jesus touched a leper. My head responds with a smirk, so you think you're Jesus?

My heart was the ultimate winner. I wrapped my arms around her while she placed her head on my shoulder. I thanked God for my sister Mujica. I praised God that He promised to make all things new. The time would come when Mujica would run and jump, shout and sing, her life wonderful, exciting, filled with peace and joy, soaring with the angels and dancing with Jesus. She was loved by Jesus and would be so beautiful.

Tears were running down my cheeks as I finished the prayer and announced, "Amen." She looked at me through dark, piercing eyes buried in the back of her head and exclaimed, "Alleluia!" I stared into the hollow that held her eyes, spellbound. I was awestruck. It was as if I was looking into the eyes of Jesus.

"The smallest seed...grows..."

Mark 4:31

There comes a time in nearly everyone's life when they are just about at wit's end.

Teachers have certainly experienced this. Sister Helen Mrosla remembers teaching her ninth grade class "new math" a number of years ago. Her students were working hard but it was obvious that they just did not understand the subject. They were getting more and more frustrated and discouraged with each passing day. Then one Friday afternoon Helen decided to depart from her lesson plan. She instructed each student to list every person's name in the classroom on a sheet of paper and write something nice about each one. The unusual assignment took the entire class period to complete.

The next day, Saturday, Sister Mrosla took those papers and compiled a list for each person on what others in the class liked about them. On Monday, all pupils received a paper with what their classmates had written. The atmosphere in the class changed instantly; happy smiles were popping up everywhere. She heard one excited young lady whisper, "It makes me feel so much better about myself." It was a marvelous, uplifting experience for her students. Soon they were back tackling their math lessons and nothing more was said about the papers.

Years passed. Time went on as the members of the class grew older, graduated and went their separate ways. Some years later at a class reunion, Helen's former students, now young adults, gathered around her. One of them had something to show her. Opening his wallet, he carefully removed two worn pages of notebook paper that had obviously been taped and refolded many times. The smiling teacher knew without asking that this prized document was one on which she had listed all the good qualities of each classmate. She was amazed as a young mother who had been a member of that ninth grade class shared that she, too, still had that special paper and kept it in her top drawer of her desk at home. Another student who was now a naval officer had placed his list in his wedding album. Yet another ex-pupil of hers expressed her heartfelt gratitude for that highly valued list that she carried in her purse just about everywhere she went. Helen Mrosla was simply overwhelmed.

Who would have thought that what a junior high school teacher did out of desperation on a warm Friday afternoon would have such lasting effect on so many lives? You never know for certain how something you might do may affect the life of another. The irony is that you might not think that what you did was that important, but it could be life-changing to someone else. Jesus told us that the kingdom of God is like that. The tiniest of seeds can produce an enormous harvest.

Some years ago a movie producer caught the gist of this in his film *Oh God!*. It was actually a good story performed by excellent actors. God is played by the incomparable George Burns, and Jerry, the assistant supermarket manager to whom God is revealed is portrayed by John Denver. In one of the final scenes, they were discussing the success of their mission in the world. Very few seemed to be listening to the message that God told Jerry to deliver. The young man thought that he had failed. In a defeated tone, he sighed, "We blew it." However, God didn't see it that way. "Oh I don't think so," he mused. "A seed here, a seed there, something will catch hold and grow."

Patience and trust is what is needed. For those of us caught up in the midst of roaring autos, clanging phones and whirling electronics–people seemingly so busy, always on the go, forever in a hurry–this is a hard lesson to learn. Growth can be painstakingly slow. A tiny seed may seem worthless and yet when it takes hold, it has the power to burst stone.

Sometimes we are so near something or someone that we are unaware of the growth that has taken place. Many years ago, our family was getting ready to travel by plane to Chicago to visit our children's grandparents. I asked our youngest son what he thought Grandma would say when she saw him. "She will cry out, 'Oh, Benji, how you have grown!'" And, of course, when we deplaned in Chicago, Grandma exclaimed, "Oh, Benji, how you have grown!" He looked at us and rolled his eyes as if to say, "What did I tell you?"

Small seeds, acts of kindness, goodness, and charity can all reap huge dividends tomorrow. On occasion we may need to back up or get another perspective and we will be amazed at the amount of growth that has taken place. I remember hearing an inspirational address where the presenter began by asking, "Who was Jim Thorpe's coach? Who was Albert Einstein's third grade math teacher? Who was ten year old Paderewski's piano instructor? Who was Billy Graham's youth group advisor?" From tiny seeds, faithfully sown, God promises a bountiful harvest.

It had been one of those evenings. The local foot-ball team had lost another close game. The coach in the privacy of his own home was lamenting the fact that poor blocking was the cause of yet another defeat. "What I need is a good blocking back," he growled. "If I just had one tough blocking back we'd have a winning team."

His six-year-old son, ready for bed, looked up at his dad and promised, "When I grow up and go to high school I will be a blocking back."

His father smiled with approval at that comment.

Then, with a puzzled expression on his face, the little fellow asked, "What is a blocking back?"

"He is the one who does the hard work, clears the way for others, and lets somebody score the touchdowns and get all the glory."

"Oh," his young son responded, "I didn't know that. I don't want to be a blocking back."

The six-year-old was sharing the feelings of millions of others. Tough job. Lots of hard work and no glory?

I don't want to be a blocking back. Our culture, our society, human nature itself do not condition us to be a blocking back. Rather, we are taught that our goal is to be praised as number one. Our desire is to be the one who scores the touchdown and gets the cheers.

Note: there is nothing wrong with wanting to be the best, to be successful. God has given us personal ambition and we are encouraged to strive to be excellent in all that we do. If I have a medical problem I want a doctor who is dedicated to being the best he can be. When I go to a restaurant I would like to think that the cook or chef is determined to be the very best that she can be. When I have my Hyundai cared for I would like to believe that my mechanic is the best in town. It is commendable to strive for excellence. It can be healthy as long as we keep everything in proper perspective.

An anonymous writer put it like this: "Imagine life as a game in which you are juggling five balls in the air. You name them Work, Health, Family, Faith and Friends and you are trying to keep all of them in the air. You will soon understand that work is a rubber ball. Drop it and it will bounce back. But the other four balls are made of glass. If you drop one of these they will be scuffed, marked, nicked, damaged or even broken beyond repair. They will never be the same." That struck me as powerful imagery. Work is a rubber ball, but the other important things in life are made of glass. If you neglect these concerns in your quest for excellence, in your goal to be number one, you will most certainly come to regret it.

Marion Mill was born into a very wealthy family in Hungary. She was sent to school in Vienna where she became an actress. There she fell in love with a young medical student named Otto. They married and moved to Beverly Hills. He also started to dabble in movies and became so interested that he gave up his medical practice and went on to become an award-winning movie director, Otto Preminger. Marion's wealth, beauty, wit, and charm brought everything she desired. In Europe, New York, and Hollywood she became a famous international hostess.

But the fast life took its toll. She slipped into alcohol, drugs, and numerous affairs. She divorced Otto and moved back to Vienna. There she met another doctor, Albert Schweitzer. She knew her life was a total mess and had no purpose at all—a complete contrast to that of Schweitzer's. When it came time for him to return to work in a primitive hospital in the heart of Africa, she went with him. She spent the rest of her life as a hard-working, humble servant. When she wrote her autobiography, she chose as the title: *All I Want Is Everything*. She penned, "Dr. Schweitzer claims there are only two kinds of people. There are helpers and non-helpers. I thank God that He allowed me to be a helper for in helping I found everything."

Do you see what she is saying? The most content people in the world are those who understand that life is about serving. They have the great satisfaction of knowing that as a "blocking back," they have paved the way for others. The least contented people are those who think meaning is found in being served. Motion picture producer and actor Ben Stein mused, "I came to realize that life lived to help others is the only thing that matters."

There was a feature article in *People* magazine about a self-serving man who regained his life's focus thanks to his little daughter. Randy Leamer had a weight problem and, like untold millions, he had tried scores of weight reduction programs, diets, and exercises but none had any lasting results. Then he was informed that his eighteen-month-old daughter Meagan, had severe kidney disease. Various types of treatment were administered but nothing worked; she just got worse. At age five, she was in desperate need of a kidney transplant. Her mother's side of the family had a history of kidney problems so a transplant from her would be extremely high risk. That left Meagan's father, Randy. However, he weighed over three hundred pounds and might not survive the removal of a kidney.

Now what? Randy had already failed numerous attempts to lose weight, but he had never been motivated like this. Friends, family, coworkers cheered him on as he vowed to shed one hundred pounds. Within eight months he had lost 106 pounds. His support group purchased new clothes for him as the old togs no longer fit. A kidney transplant took place and both father and daughter recovered fully. Because of his love for his little girl, Randy Leamer took a needed action that will probably, in the long run, give him a longer life. It is amazing how love and service can help us refocus our life.

> *"Whoever welcomes one of*
> *these little children..."*
>
> Mark 9:37

Nancy Dahlberg and her husband were enjoying their new Honda SUV and were traveling from San Francisco to Los Angeles. They had stopped in King City for lunch. The restaurant was nearly empty and Erik, their fifteen-month-old son, was the only child there. Soon he started squealing with delight, "Hi there. Hi there." His eyes were smiling and his face alive with excitement. He wiggled and giggled and his parents turned to see the source of his joy. There was a man wearing a tattered coat and dirty, greasy trousers. His toes were poking out of one of his shoes. Lots of ring-around his collar and a face about as ugly as you could imagine.

He was waving at Erik and was blaring, "Hi there little buddy. I see you buster." Nancy's husband looked at her as if to say, "So, how do we handle this?" Their meal arrived but the noise continued. Now the battered-looking bum had elevated his voice, "Hey little fella. You know how to play peek-a-boo? Sure you do." The young innocent continued to laugh and pound his tray and holler, "Hi there!"

The lad's parents didn't think this was cute or fun, not by a long shot. The tramp was either drunk or had a mental problem. Erik's father got up to pay the check and suggested that Nancy meet him in the parking lot. She nodded and then whispered a prayer, "Just let me get out the door in peace." She took a deep breath and headed for the exit.

However, it was obvious that the Lord and a little boy had other plans. As Nancy drew closer to her antagonist, she made an effort to sidestep him. At that moment her precious baby reached way out with both hands in a toddler's pick-me-up position. His mother made eye contact with the poor fellow whose expression seemed to implore, "Would you please let me hold the boy?" Before she could resolve what she was going to do, Erik propelled himself from her arms into his. Suddenly a very old man and a very young child clutched each other in a loving embrace. The grizzled guy's eyes were closed and tears were running down his cheeks. His gnarled hands so gently, so very tenderly, cradled the little boy's bottom and stroked his cheek.

Erik's mother was awe-stricken as she watched him holding the contented little tot in his arms. The old gent opened his eyes and commanded in a firm voice, "You take good care of this baby. You hear me?" In a soft and meek tone, his mother promised that she would. He pried Erik from his chest and handed him back to his mother. Then the gentleman declared, "God bless you, Madam. You have given me a wonderful gift." The humble mother managed to mutter, "Thanks." With

Erik back in her arms, she hurried toward their SUV. Her startled husband wanted to know why she was crying and why she was pleading, "My God, my God. Please forgive me."

Jesus said, "Unless you become as a little child you will never enter the kingdom of heaven." In the city of Chicago there is a small playground that was donated to the city by a young couple in memory of their two-year-old daughter who succumbed to leukemia. It is called "Tiny Tot Playground." In order to get in, one must be able to walk upright through an entrance shaped like a key. It is a very, very low gate and has above it a sign which states: "For Children Only." Size, too, determines whether or not a person enters the kingdom of heaven.

One of my favorite characters from church history is Francis of Assisi. He is sometimes pictured as the patron saint of children and innocent animals. This spiritual and intellectual giant was an amazing man of God. It was once said that he left the following instructions for his staff: They were admonished not to disturb him under any circumstances as he had very important work to complete. If anyone would come to see him they must be told that an appointment was necessary, then he paused and added, "Unless, of course, a child should come."

Isn't this what Jesus is saying, too? Philosophers and theologians, presidents and kings may come with boldness, rapping at his door and there is no answer. But if a child or someone with a childlike faith should come the door will immediately spring open. Dwight L.

Moody, the great evangelist of years ago, returned from a revival service and was asked by a friend if the message resulted in any converts. The preacher replied that there now were two and a half new believers. His companion questioned, "You mean two adults and one child?"

"No," responded Moody. "Two children and one adult. The adult's life has been half lived already, the children have their lives ahead of them."

This final thought: Benjamin, a young man of eighteen years, was about to leave home for the first time. From the age of six he had lived with his grandparents, hard-working farmers. They loved him, cared for him, and provided a wonderful example of godly living. As he prepared to board his plane, he wrapped his arms around them and asked, "How can I ever repay you for all you've done for me?" With a soft and tender voice Grandma replied, "Benjamin, a parent's love isn't to be paid back. It can only be passed on."

"A cup of water in My name..."

Mark 9:41

I t was Christmas Eve in 2010 and we at Peñasquitos
Lutheran Church in San Diego were preparing to
celebrate Jesus' birthday. We had heard much about the
giving and receiving of gifts during the festive season.
Then the question was raised, "What will our birthday
gift to Jesus be this year? How can we actually give Him
anything?" Jesus answered that query long before we
even asked it when He said, "Whatever you did for one
of the least of these brothers and sisters of mine, you
did for me."

Earlier in the year I had joined a mission team and
visited a Dalit village in India. Dalits are on the bottom of Hinduism's notorious caste system and are also
known as "untouchables." Most are illiterate, malnour-
ished, anemic, have never seen a health professional,
and have a life expectancy of less than fifty years. The
majority of the villagers were ill and some had even
died because they had no access to clean water–only a
dirty polluted pond. To drink that contaminated water
would make them sick, but not to drink any water at
all would result in certain death. That was the dilemma
these poverty-stricken children of God faced. From this

experience came our congregation's response: "Let's give Jesus the life-giving gift of fresh water for the Dalits."

Moved by the Spirit, our people opened their purses and wallets and a generous Christmas offering was received and designated for a fresh water well for Jesus. We hired a respected Indian geologist who started his search for clean water in this village of "untouchables." The government had attempted to dig wells in nearby communities but had not succeeded. The wells they dug were either dry or the water found was unfit for human consumption.

Local Christians gathered with our chosen geologist and fervently prayed that God would bless his efforts to find clean water. The location selected for the drilling was near a primitive road so that passersby from neighboring villages would be able to share in the hoped-for blessings. He drilled a borehole to the depth of 650 feet and struck water: fresh, clean, sweet, life-giving water!

Dozens of thankful families joined together to build a church near the well site that would soon be flowing with a river of life. The building was constructed through the loving hands of unskilled laborers. The result was a simple chapel consisting of four walls, a roof, a door, two ventilation glassless windows, dirt floor, and a handmade rustic cross placed up front.

The happy day soon arrived when our well drillers informed us that the prayed-for fountain was ready to be dedicated and put to use. I was given the sacred and joyful opportunity to lead the worship for that gala celebration. Nearly one hundred smiling Dalits entered the chapel where all would sit on the floor; the men sat in the back and the women and children up front. Our worship leader, equipped with only a tambourine and lots of enthusiasm, led the singing for the next twenty minutes. Then our Indian evangelist, Pastor Kondiah Paul, introduced me and served as my translator as I shared the story of the woman at the well and the Lord's promise that she would receive "living water welling up to eternal life." Prayers of thanksgiving followed and then with songs of joy we left the sanctuary and marched to the well site.

The pump handle had been securely wrapped but now the moment had arrived for it to be unveiled. I was granted the privilege of inaugurating this life-giving tool. I pumped the handle and joined in a chorus of joyful voices as fresh, pure water gushed forth. Men and women, the young and the old, started dancing, clapping their hands, and praising Jesus. A little girl ran to the glistening flow, cupped her hands under the refreshing water and with a squeal of delight splashed her face. The tears started to come as I thought of Jesus' words: "Of such belongs the kingdom of God." This precious child had received the gift of love, hope, and life. It was a very emotional experience that will be remembered for a lifetime.

The well continues to be a godsend to the Dalits. John Peter Kirubbagaran, Director of the United Evangelical Mission, reports, "I have just spoken to the young congregation's pastor, Satish Kumor. The water continues to gush with force. In the area of Chandramaulapalle there are one thousand families belonging to various Dalit tribes. All these families now fetch water from our borewell. When the well was dug there were thirty baptized members of the church. That number soon doubled and now more than one hundred believers gather together on Sunday morning to worship Jesus. The fresh water well is a great blessing."

A cup of cold water given in Jesus' name opens the door to the fulfillment of His promise: "The water I give will be an artesian spring within, gushing fountains of endless life" (*The Message,* John 4:14).

"And the two will become one flesh."

Mark 10:8

Some time ago our local newspaper carried a story from India. Two brides and two grooms discovered that a rather serious mistake had been made on their wedding day. The ladies

had been wearing long veils; they were hardly able to see anything around them. To make matters worse, the simple ceremonies had been rushed. Hence both weddings were over before it was discovered that the brides had been paired with the wrong grooms. A ruling by the village elders confirmed that the marriages were binding as performed and nothing could be done to change the situation. Imagine that. Married to the wrong person and nothing you could do about it. According to divorce statistics, a whole lot of people feel they married the wrong person. A pastor once told me after officiating at a wedding that he feared he had mispronounced them husband and wife.

What did Jesus have to say about marriage and divorce? "God made them male and female. For this reason a man will leave his father and mother and be united with his wife and the two will become one flesh... what God has joined together let no one separate." This simple statement has some powerful implications. One is that it does away with all such notions as same sex marriages. It is not possible for the two to become one flesh. Jesus said it takes a man and a woman to have a marriage.

Jesus always reminds us that marriage is the highest relationship possible in life. It takes priority over all other human relationships. "The two shall become one." "Become" is a key word here. It does not mean immediately or automatically; marriage is a process of the two becoming one. Then our Lord gave this warning: "What God has joined together let no one separate."

Here is where it gets personal and sticky. Jesus states plainly that divorce is contrary to God's plan. It is a violation of God's intention for marriage. Divorce always involves some form of sin. But thank God this sin, like every other sin, can be forgiven. Jesus paid the penalty on the cross for the sin of divorce.

So what does God think about sex? He thinks it is important. After all, he created it and it is so special that he put boundaries around it and intended it only for married couples. God doesn't change. This was His intent yesterday, it is today, and will be tomorrow. However, even Christians are being seduced by the culture and watering down God's clear revelation. For example, the record number of couples who are living together but are not married. What about that?

First of all, we know from divorce statistics that those who cohabit before marriage are more than twice as likely to get divorced as those who do not live together before marriage. Some question that thinking. "Wouldn't it be better to try it out first to see if we're really right for each other?" The question misses the point. If we're going to be right for each other, we first need to be right before God. His Word is very clear–sexual intimacy is to be reserved for marriage.

"It is not a very courageous thing," stated theologian Joe Sittler, "to say 'I will shack up with this one, and this one with me, as long as the delectability continues.' There is nothing commendable about that. To be sure it is understandable and may even temporarily be delightful but it has nothing to do with marriage. In no way can we suggest that it has God's approval."

We cannot expect non-Christians to listen to what Jesus has to say, but we have a right to assume that followers of Jesus will listen and strive to obey His Word. Where does this leave us? The Scriptures declare, "If we confess our sins he is faithful and just and will forgive our sins and cleanse us from all unrighteousness." This day can be the day of new hope and new beginnings. How beautiful to be cleansed.

This final thought: A little boy sat through a Sunday school class and learned about a time when Jesus was invited to a wedding and there performed a miracle of turning water into wine. "And what do we learn from this story?" asked the teacher. The little fellow pondered for a moment and then answered, "We learned that if you are going to get married, be sure you invite Jesus to the wedding." Good advice. The husband and his wife will become one...for life.

"What God has joined together,
let no one separate."

Mark 10:9

Pastor Neal Parker says that he insists on only two things before performing weddings: that he has premarital counseling with the couple and he does not do weddings in unusual places like hot air balloons or underwater. But he broke both rules once. He agreed to do a wedding on a day's notice when the minister who was to officiate was unavailable because of a family emergency. All he knew was the names of the bride and groom, that the wedding would take place outdoors on a farm, and the congregation would include 140 bikers who had come up for the weekend.

He had considerable misgivings as he turned off the road and caught his first glimpse of the site. Motorcycles were everywhere and loud music came from a tented refreshment area. It looked like Woodstock all over again. He was startled to discover that except for bride, groom, and their parents, most of the guests seemed unaware that a wedding was to take place. He met the bride wearing blue jeans, a tee-shirt and a few flowers in her hair. The groom was introduced as "Bear." He had a thick, bushy beard, heavily tattooed arms, and outweighed the officiant by at least a hundred pounds. The good reverend checked to see that the marriage license was in order and everything was ready. He headed for the tent, requested that the music be turned off, asked for a microphone, introduced himself, and announced that the wedding was about to begin.

Several of the bikers immediately headed to the parking lot. Then, with almost military precision, the bikes streamed out of the parking lot and toward the pastor. Only a few feet from him, they turned off to form a double row facing each other–an honor guard to create an aisle for the bride. With engines in full throttle, the roar was echoing throughout the valley. As the bride walked slowly and gracefully down the aisle, each bike she passed shut off its engine. As she passed the last pair and all engines were stilled, a beautiful silence filled the air. The bride walked shyly up to Bear. His eyes were overflowing with tears. The melodious tones of song birds could be heard. Surrounding the bride and groom were their friends, members and families of the Sober Riders, each one a recovering alcoholic, each one a biker, each one quiet and reverent in this holy moment.

The bride had given the minister only one instruction for the service: "Please be sure you talk about the ingredients of a Christian marriage. Our friends need to hear a word from God." The gratified minister stood in the middle of the field in a congregation of tee-shirts, blue jeans, and tattoos, in front of a bride and groom who knew exactly what they were doing and why, in a cathedral of fence posts and Harleys. In response to the bride's request, what could be said about Christian marriage in that setting?

I would start off with the conviction that the key to lifelong God-pleasing marriage is to be found in preparation for marriage. Sadly, many couples devote more time, energy, and effort in their plans to buy a new house or new car than they do in selecting a life partner. The Bible makes it clear that no major decision in life should be made by Christians until we've first sought the Lord's guidance through prayer.

Rarely have I counseled with couples who sincerely sought the Lord's will before they were married who later wound up in a divorce court. It is so easy to get caught up in the romantic notion that "some enchanted evening you will see a stranger across a crowded room... and somehow you will know." It is far better to call upon the one who made marriage in the first place and ask Him to guide you to the partner of His choosing. That is a prayer that should be prayed by all followers of Jesus and by all godly parents for their children. This is the best guarantee that I know of for a good marriage that lasts a lifetime–the conviction that God brought the two together and that His blessing is on their union.

Jesus said, "The two shall become one flesh and what God has joined together let no man put asunder." Jesus does not like divorce. He hates it. To be sure, He knows about human weakness and frailty and no one is more compassionate than He is. The end of marriage can be devastating, even more tragic in many cases than death. The effects on children are well documented. Every situation is different and we need to respect that, but still we are part of a culture where it is far easier to get a marriage license than it is to get a driver's license. Our contemporary society does not take marriage very seriously, but God does. I would want Bear, his bride, and all their guests to hear that.

Then I might remind them that there are no super-excellent marriages because there are no sinless people. But there are some very good marriages because both partners have learned to be big forgivers, slow to speak, slow to anger, and quick to say "I love you." There are no perfect marriages but if Jesus has been invited into the home, He will provide grace enough each day to overcome the bumps in the road.

Finally, I would remind the soon-to-be newlyweds that love is a decision. Begin each day with a conscious decision to love your partner and look for ways to demonstrate that love. In the words of Martin Luther, "Apologize for each other, speak well of each other and put the most loving construction on each other's actions and each other's words." Great, lasting marriages take place when two people commit themselves to God and to each other—to become one flesh, "for better for worse, for richer for poorer, in sickness and in health, to love and to cherish, till death us do part..." It may not always be easy but with God's blessing it happens.

*"He went away sad, because
he had great wealth."*

Mark 10:22

Oh, to be young, healthy, and rich! Can anything be more grand? Not only to have youth and energy to enjoy life but also to have money and the means to truly relish it. Wow! It sounds like the perfect destination.

There are a few for whom riches and youth are not just a fantasy. For example, take Rosemary Russell of Newport Beach, California. At age twenty-five, she was already highly successful in her chosen career. Ms. Russell was pulling down $150,000 a year in a financial firm, and wise investments resulted in the acquiring of a staggering string of properties, including her mortgage-free home with a silver Mercedes convertible parked out front. What more could she possibly want? It seemed all her dreams had come true. But something was missing. One day Rosemary drove her Mercedes to a Laguna Beach motel, checked in, and then checked out of life with an overdose of pills. She left behind a note that said she was ending her life because "I am so tired of clapping with one hand."

In the gospel of Mark, chapter 10, we encounter a young man also blessed with youth, health, and wealth. He, too, sensed that he was clapping with one hand. Joy, purpose, and meaning were also missing from his life. Jesus told him all that could change if he would go home and have a gigantic garage sale. "Sell what you have and give the proceeds to the poor. Then come and follow me." The rich young man could not commit to such a drastic remedy. He had become accustomed to living in a world where a bank account was highly prized. He had asked, "What must I do?" but he could not accept the answer to his question. He went away sadly to live out his life trying to clap with one hand.

Dennis Levine, made famous by Wall Street insider trading scandals, was once asked by his wife why he really needed more money. He thought it was a foolish question and didn't even bother to answer it. However, the more he thought about it, the more he realized that he didn't really have an answer. Levine remembered that when his income reached $100,000 a year, he yearned for $200,000. Then he made his first million and felt a strong desire to have three million. He wrote, "I don't know why I ever thought that if I was unhappy at one million that I would be happy at three million. I guess it is human nature to think that if I just had a little bit more I would be happy. I'm convinced that is a bald-faced lie sent to us by Satan himself."

In Greek mythology, the god Dionysus offered to give King Midas whatever his heart craved. Midas' immediate response was, "I desire that everything I touch be turned to gold." His wish was granted and he was overjoyed. He stuck out his hand and touched a stone; it turned to gold! He plucked a leaf; it turned to gold! Wow! He roared with laughter, "I will be the richest and happiest man this world has ever known." He clapped his hands with joy, leaped in the air, shouted with glee, and danced all the way home.

King Midas ordered that a banquet be held to celebrate his good fortune. But as the bread touched his hand, it turned to gold. The wine touched his lips and it, too, turned to gold. The hungrier he became, the greater his dismay. As he reached out to his young daughter for comfort, she, too, became a chunk of gold, and Midas cursed himself for being such a fool.

Dr. Glendon Harris, former member of the faculty at Michigan State University, wrote that there is nothing in biological necessity to account for the drive to get rich nor is there any equivalent for it in the animal kingdom. Indeed, by definition, to "get rich" is to get more than one needs. And yet this seemingly purposeless drive is one of the most powerful known to the human race. Money in itself is neutral. It is a measure of value, a medium of exchange. But the other side of the coin is that it can become intoxicating, maddening, and inflaming.

In his best-selling book *Margin,* Dr. Richard Swenson reminds us that way too many people are suffering physically, emotionally, and spiritually because they have not been able to separate needs from wants. All we really need, he states, is God, love, food, relationships, meaningful work, clothing, and shelter. Anything beyond that is merely a want; it may be OK yet it is not necessary. He adds that a major problem we face is that we are part of a culture where a daily bombardment of advertisements create a sense of need within us. Almost no ad we ever see or hear is for something we truly need. Advertisers spend millions in an effort to create a sense of need in us. They are having phenomenal success.

"Give a man everything he wants," wrote Immanuel Kant, "and at that moment, everything will not be everything." Oh, to be young, healthy, successful, and rich. Surely that would be the essence of happiness. It was all an illusion. It left her clapping with one hand—a life not worth living.

*"Watch and pray so that you will
not fall into temptation."*

Mark 14:38

I'm quite certain that many of you have read Homer's epic poem *The Odyssey*. You may remember the Sirens: mythical evil creatures who were a combination of bird and woman. They lived on an island surrounded by submerged, jagged rocks. As ships approached the reef, the Sirens would sing the beautiful, seductive songs, luring the sailors to their deaths.

The hero of this classic narrative was Odysseus, captain of the ship. When the vessel approached the isle the skipper ordered the crew to fill their ears with wax in order to escape the charm of the Sirens' songs. Once this was done, he commanded them to bind him to the mast as the schooner passed by so that he could not change his instructions. Smart. Very smart. All of us are weak at different places but one thing we never want to do is test the Tempter's power.

It all started in the Garden of Eden, where a talking snake seduced Eve with the alluring words concerning the forbidden fruit: "God knows when you eat it your eyes will be opened, you will be like God knowing good and evil." Fascinated by the serpent and his smooth tongue, she turned covetous eyes back to the Tree of Knowledge of Good and Evil. The fruit looked so good, so pleasing, so desirable and, not only that, the Tempter promised her equality with God. His words were so enticing that she could no longer resist; she took one bite and then shared it with her husband.

Wham! The first temptation. The first sin. Why the Tree of Knowledge of Good and Evil? Because now they could decide what was good and what was evil. They would be their own gods. We certainly have a multitude of people in modern society eating from that same tree today, don't we? Ignoring God's words and His will with each person deciding in his/her own mind what is right and what is wrong. Each is his/her own little deity. Jesus taught us to pray, "Lead us not into temptation..." He could take on the Tempter and win, but as much as we would want to be like Jesus, we are not Jesus. For most of us, the best course of action is to avoid temptation whenever possible.

An old Native American legend sums it up well. A young Indian brave, in order to prove his manhood, had scaled a high mountain. He stood on the rim of the obstacle that he had conquered, rejoicing in his hard-earned accomplishment. Then he heard a rustle at his feet. Alarmed, he discovered the strange noise had been caused by a poisonous snake. Before he could utter a sound the serpent beseeched him, "Oh conqueror of this mighty mountain, have mercy on me. It is very cold up here and there is no food. Put me under your shirt and take me down into the valley."

"No, never. I can't do that. I know your kind. You are a rattlesnake. If I pick you up you will bite me and I will die."

"That will not happen," pleaded the reptile. "I will treat you with tenderness. I would never hurt such a compassionate soul."

The youth resisted for awhile but finally gave in to the very persuasive deceiver. He picked it up, and tucked it under his shirt, and gently carried it down into the valley. The soft-hearted young man removed the sidewinder and placed it on the ground. Without warning, it coiled, rattled, and bit him.

"No, no," the victim cried out in agony, "you promised!"

"You knew what I was when you picked me up," replied the deadly creature as he slithered away.

That is a powerful little parable. The snake for you could be drugs, alcohol, infidelity, greed—anything contrary to God's will. Satan knows full well that all of us, no matter how strong we may think we are, have our weaknesses and he will never give up trying to break us. What tempted us yesterday may not tempt us today, but we'll soon be facing a whole set of new temptations. Oftentimes the best protection we have is avoidance. Get away from whatever it is.

I was in my twenties, single, recently ordained, and adjusting to wearing a clerical collar. The church I had been called to pastor was a struggling little multiracial congregation on Cleveland's east side. The people had been without a pastor for six months. I had been going door to door for several weeks informing city dwellers that the church was back in business and inviting all who were willing to come and see. It was twilight, not yet dark, so I decided I still had time to knock on a few more doors before it got too late. One of my mentors had suggested I always wear the clergy-identifying clerical collar. This way suspicious residents would know that I was not someone's probation officer or an insurance salesman.

I entered an apartment building, went upstairs, and rapped on a door. A feminine voice seductively bid me to "come on in." I thought that she must have been expecting a friend; why else would she invite a total stranger into her apartment? I knocked again. The same charming voice purred, "The door is not locked. Come on in." I opened the door and was met by an attractive woman with a surprised smile on her face. She reached out, took my hand, and led me into a room where I encountered a number of young ladies in various stages of undress. The stunned expression on my face caused my hostess to burst out laughing. She was having fun. Still holding my hand, she giggled, "We offer clergy discounts." It took me a few moments to get my bearings and realize that I had walked into a brothel.

A braver preacher than I might have thought, "What an opportunity for a sermon," opened his Bible, and expounded on the Scripture. Ah, but not me. I'm not that courageous. I fled the scene on feet that had wings. And so we pray, "Lead us not into temptation."

"He is risen!"

Mark 16:6

You probably don't remember the name Nikolai Ivanovich Bukharin and there is really no reason why you should. But there was a time when he was one of the most powerful men on earth as a Russian Communist leader in the 1920s, he was editor of the state-controlled newspaper *Pravda*, and was a member of the Politburo. His works on economics and political science are still read in colleges today.

In 1933, he took a journey from Moscow to Kiev to address a huge assembly on the subject of atheism. Speaking to the crowd in his usual pompous manner, he aimed his big guns at Christianity, hurling insults, arguments, and so-called proof against it. An hour later when his harangue was at last finished, he looked out at what seemed to be the smoldering ashes of the people's faith. "Any comments or questions?" he bellowed. Total silence filled the massive auditorium. Then one older citizen began his slow but steady march to the lectern.

Standing beside the powerful Communist leader, the elderly gentleman surveyed the crowd first to the left and then to the right. Finally, he mustered all the strength he had inside him and shouted the ancient greeting known well in the Russian Orthodox Church: "Christ is risen!" In mass, the crowd stood to their feet and the response came crashing like the sound of thunder, "He is risen indeed!"

When all is said and done it is all about the resurrection, is it not? St. Paul wrote: "If there is no resurrection than all our preaching is useless; if there is no resurrection our faith has no value; if there is no resurrection we become false witnesses; if there is no resurrection we are still living in our sins, if there is no resurrection, then of all people we are most to be pitied." But he is quick to proclaim, "But Christ has indeed been raised from the dead." It is the resurrection that gives our life meaning and hope.

For all too many life seems to be a constant struggle: one problem after another, one hurt after another, one dead end after another. Each year we see eager young people starting off for their first year of college; a few months later they come circling back, sadder but not too much wiser. They have failed. Many times I have been part of a joyous wedding celebration where couples stood before the altar of God and pledged their undying love and faithfulness to each other. Time goes on and one or both are found in the counselor's office with tear-stained cheeks, telling of a failed marriage. Every day men leave prison on parole looking for a new life, and a short time later three-fourths of them are incarcerated again. Every hour a physician somewhere is battling to save the life of a critically ill person, and every hour the hearse is backing up to the door of the hospital to receive the failures. Our televisions preview new shows, highly touted and then quickly cancelled as failures. The financial pages of our newspapers tell of foreclosures and business failures.

I read of a small town hospital that received a bomb threat. The police took no chances and evacuated the hospital. Most patients were taken to a nearby armory but, due to lack of space, some were taken to a local mortuary. One woman, in surgery when the bomb scare was received, gradually came to and realized that she was staring at the surroundings of a funeral parlor. Imagine for a moment her fears and concerns. Although she misunderstood her situation, she was only premature, not wrong, in her conclusion. Each of us are certain to face the time when life on this earth is over. Surely this is a reminder to make the most of each day. We are all labeled terminal cases the moment we make our appearance in this world. We just don't know how long we will be here or where it ends. But we do know for certain that the grave is waiting for all of us; that is why it is all about the resurrection. It is only here that meaning and hope is found.

The following information comes from the Alaska Department of Fish and Game: Both male and female reindeer grow antlers in the summer each year; male reindeer drop their antlers at the beginning of winter. Female reindeer retain their antlers till they give birth in the spring. Therefore, every single one of Santa's reindeer had to be a girl. We should have known. Only women, while pregnant, would be able to drag a fat man in a red velvet suit all around the world in one night and not get lost.

In the gospel of Luke, chapter one, we read, "Do not be afraid, Mary, you have found favor with God. You will be with child and give birth to a son, and you are to give him the name Jesus. He will be great and will be called the Son of the Most High."

Names are important; they hold meaning and bring back memories, both good and bad. In a recent survey the most popular names for American newborns were : Emily, Emma, Madison, and Kaitlyn for girls and Ryan, Michael, Jacob, and Matthew for boys. Did you notice that Judas and Jezebel did not make that list? As a matter of fact they have never cracked the top 1,000. What girl's name do you think has been in the top fifty for over a hundred years? Of course, it is Mary. The name rings with gladness. God chose a teenage virgin named Mary to be the mother of His one and only son. What an honor, what a blessing. Her reputation lives on today as the epitome of what it means for a mother to trust in God.

If you and I had been giving advice to God 2,000 years ago, we would surely have suggested that the last thing the world needs is another baby. Give us instead a spectacular display in the heavens. How about providing us with advanced satellite television so we could broadcast God's love to the whole world? Perhaps pass along a few billion dollars so we could feed the world's hungry. But another baby? That makes little sense.

Ruth Harden spins an interesting tale in "Let Nothing You Dismay." Her story features an absent-minded old woman who realizes with horror that she had switched two Christmas gifts and sent them to the wrong people. The thick woolen socks which she had made for her poor friend, Hilda, were sent to her granddaughter instead. The lovely lace and satin nightgown that she bought for her granddaughter had been sent to Hilda! The elderly gift giver was mortified. Her friend, Hilda, is plain, poor, simple, and unadorned. Such a beautiful nightgown would almost seem a mockery of Hilda's plainness.

However, a few days after Christmas the chagrined grandmother received two thank you notes. The first was from her granddaughter expressing her delight for the fashionable ski socks. The second was from an ec-statically grateful Hilda. No one had ever thought to give her something so beautiful. Hilda wrote that she put on the nightgown and danced across her rough, wooden floor. For the first time in her life she felt pretty. It was the perfect gift.

God's perfect gift to us was given through Mary. Mark Lowry in his album "*Happy Christmas,*" repeatedly asks the question "Mary, did you know...?"

"Mary did you know that your baby boy would someday walk on water? Mary did you know that your baby boy would save our sons and daughters?

Did you know that your baby boy has come to make you new? This child that you delivered will soon deliver you?

Did you know that your baby boy has walked where angels trod? When you kiss your little boy you have kissed the face of God?

Mary did you know that your baby boy is Lord of all creation? Mary did you know that your baby boy will one day rule the nations?

Did you know that your baby boy is heaven's perfect lamb? The sleeping child you're holding is the great I AM? Mary did you know?"

Of course she couldn't know. Nevertheless she responded, "So be it. I am the Lord's servant." Or a more literal translation, "I am the Lord's little slave girl."

*"You will be with child and
give birth to a son..."*

Luke 1:31

Alan and Patricia Trent are the authors of *Barren Couples, Broken Hearts: A Compassionate Look at Infertility.* It is about married couples who desperately want to have children but for one reason or another, are unable. It is one of life's ironies, isn't it? Some couples have unexpected and even unwanted pregnancies. Other couples who are totally unfit to be parents have no trouble breeding. Then, too, there are those young marrieds with so much to give but who are denied the opportunity.

Wouldn't it be wonderful if all children would be greeted with joy and enthusiasm? Unfortunately we know that is not the case. Almost every year the abortion rate and the number of child abuse cases go up. One American child dies every four hours from abuse. The cost to society is staggering. Two out of every three prisoners in our penitentiaries who are convicted of violent crimes report childhoods of physical cruelty. 80 percent of prostitutes have histories of sexual perversion as a child. If you are a product of a loving home, give

God thanks every day of your life. You may already have received the richest blessings life can bestow. And if you have children of your own, make these years count!

Sam Levenson tells a wonderful story about the birth of his first child. The initial night home the baby would not stop crying. His wife frantically flipped through the pages of *Dr. Spock's Baby and Child Care* to find out why babies bawl and what to do about it. Since Dr. Spock's book is rather long, the baby continued to exercise her lungs for a long time. Grandma was in the house but she knew better than to offer advice that had not been asked for. The baby's cries were not about to end. Finally, Grandma could be silent no longer. "Put down that book," she ordered her daughter, "and pick up the baby."

Good advice. That was exactly what the infant wanted and needed. Every parent would do well to listen to those words from Grandma: "Put down the book and pick up the baby." In the eyes of children, LOVE is spelled T-I-M-E. In a survey done of 15,000 schoolchildren, the question was asked, "What do you think makes a happy family?" Of course a myriad of responses were offered but the most frequently given answer was "doing things together." We don't want to ever lose sight of that.

To have a baby implies a big risk. It is the risk of loss. Some of you have lost children. Death struck in infancy. For others, it was after the child reached adulthood. Regardless of when it happens, it brings indescribable pain. All one can do is to trust in the mercy of God whose love is eternal.

Marie Pemberton lost her beloved four-year-old to leukemia. Jeremy died in June, and as Christmas approached, the pain of the loss was still crushing her heart. She stood at her kitchen window numbly staring out at the new fallen snow. She saw Chris Martin, Jeremy's little friend, struggling to build a snowman. Poor child, Marie thought, he always seemed so alone since Jeremy died. Marie had not been much comfort to the little fellow. Her grief had been so intense that she could barely look at him. For when she did, thoughts of Jeremy leaped to mind. When Chris came to the fence between their backyards trying to get her attention, she totally ignored him. One day, when speaking to him could be avoided no longer, and he asked her where Jeremy was, she mumbled, "Go ask your mother." After that, the young boy no longer wanted to talk to Marie. Instead he went out of his way to avoid her.

Marie was thankful that her husband, Joe, had decided to go light on Christmas this year. No Christmas tree, no decorations, no holiday visitors. They would eat out on December 25. She also decided to keep the kitchen curtains drawn so there would be no Chris Martin to remind her of Jeremy.

Later in the afternoon, looking out the living room window, she was surprised to see Chris's father in his driveway taking a magnificent tree off the top of his car. She quickly closed the drapes. At dinner, Marie told Joe that the Martins already had their Christmas tree.

"I thought you weren't interested in Christmas this year," he said.

"I'm not," she snapped as she went to answer the door. It was Ellie Martin.

"Come over and look at our tree, Marie. There is something there that you just have to see."

Marie was not the least bit interested but Joe nudged her; it would be the polite thing to do.

It was newly decorated and beautiful. "Look," Ellie said as she took Marie by the hand and led her over to the nativity scene where two little babies were tucked into a blanket in the manger. "Chris says they are baby Jesus and Jeremy." Her eyes got misty as she continued, "Last summer when you sent him back home to ask about Jeremy all I told him was that he had gone to heaven to be with baby Jesus. When I placed the Christ child under the tree this afternoon, he ran and got a doll and placed it in alongside. When I asked him why, he reminded me of what I told him last summer."

Jeremy with Jesus, Marie thought to herself. It sounded so right. "And a little child will lead them" were the words racing through Marie's mind as she went looking for Chris, to hug him. Christmas had arrived. It is a time of healing. "For unto us a child is born, unto us a son is given."

"There was no room for them in the inn..."

Luke 2:7

Many people spoke of Ralph as a spoiled and obnoxious kid. He did all that he could to live up to his reputation. When it came time to select characters for the Sunday school Christmas play, Ralph insisted that he be given the part of Joseph since that was one of the major roles. Someone else, however, was chosen to be Joseph, and Ralph, much to his displeasure, was cast as the innkeeper. He deeply resented that and determined on the day of the pageant he was going to get even–he would show them.

Pageant day came and the children were all doing their parts very well until finally they reached the place where Joseph approaches the innkeeper and asks for lodging. He expected to hear, of course, that there was no room in the inn, but that was not what happened. Ralph responded by declaring, "Come on in. We have lots of room." The audience gasped and the director just about fainted. A startled Joseph took Mary by the hand and entered the inn. The young fellow playing Joseph, however, was up to the occasion. He looked around and then said to Mary, "Phew. This place is really a dump. Let's go. Even a stable would be better than this."

The Christmas story is an old, familiar classic. It is because most of us have heard it so often that we are in danger of letting the heart of the message slip right through our fingers. It is so easy to get caught up in the maddening quest to focus on material things. After all, that is what most of society is doing.

Did you hear about the hoodlums that broke into a department store shortly before Christmas? Surprisingly they didn't steal anything or damage any items. Instead they were mischief makers who had a grand time rearranging price tags. Customers the next morning were startled to see fur coats on sale for $5, televisions for $1.95, and diamond rings 2 for $3. On the other hand, panty hose were priced at $395, umbrellas at $299, and a plastic banana for $1,077.

Has something or someone come into our lives and switched around the price tags? Have material gifts become of more value than spiritual gifts? Under most Christmas trees this year are many special prizes and surprises, presents which will bring momentary joys. Soon almost all of them will wear out, break, be used up, or discarded. The treasures that last will not be gift wrapped at some department store and found under the tree.

Pastor Harry Griffith told me about one of the first pastoral calls he made soon after his ordination. A member of his congregation was hospitalized for no apparent physical reason. She was heartbroken and desperately alone. He figured that he had to muster some words of encouragement for her so he piously stated, "Never forget that God loves you." She blurted out, "I don't care if God loves me or not. I want my husband to love me," and she burst into tears.

The fresh minted preacher said he learned a lesson that day. It doesn't do much good to just tell someone that God loves them unless we, as followers of Jesus, family, neighbors, friends are willing to wrap that love in our own flesh and express it in practical and helpful ways—not words about love, but demonstrations of love.

Several years ago a college professor was arguing for the value of exchange student scholarships. He was not thinking of Christmas when he said, "The best way to send an idea is to wrap it up in a person." That, of course, is what God did on Christmas Day.

Marc Connelly in his marvelous play, *The Green Pastures,* has the angel Gabriel walk on the stage with his horn under his arm and approach the Lord who is in deep thought. God is very disturbed by what is happening on earth. People are refusing to listen to his prophets and messengers. Sin seems to be abounding more and more. Gabriel offers to blow his horn—the final trumpet—which would end it all. But God takes the horn from Gabriel. The surprised archangel asks what God plans to do. God answers, "I'm not going to send anybody this time, I am going myself."

"I bring you good news of great joy..."

Luke 2:10

Akbar Abdul-Haqq, Indian associate of Billy Graham, told the following story: Once there was a wealthy merchant who was moved with pity over the plight of a destitute neighbor. At an opportune time, he sent him large gifts and a sealed envelope. The recipient was surprised by joy. However, in his excitement and preoccupation with the many things he had received, he neglected to open the letter from his friend. The following day his wife found the envelope in a pile of wrapping paper. She set it aside in order to show it to her husband at a more convenient time.

A year later, the merchant passed away suddenly. The poverty-stricken mourner was shocked to hear the sad news. As he shared his grief with his wife, she remembered the long-forgotten letter. After a lengthy search, she discovered the elusive letter and presented it to her husband. To his utter amazement, he found a blank check duly signed by the rich businessman. He could put down any amount that he might want. He was ecstatic.

The excited beneficiary filled in the blanks to the tune of many thousands of dollars. Overflowing with joy, he raced to the bank with his incredible gift. To his utter dismay, he learned that his deceased patron's accounts had all been closed and his enormous wealth passed on to his heirs. The check was worthless. So there he was, a poor man who remained a pauper because he had failed to avail himself at the right time of the great gift he had received.

Christmas is a time of giving and receiving gifts. But in the abundance of material items it is all too easy to neglect the greatest treasure of all and thereby miss the very heart of Christmas. The apostle John writes, "The Word became flesh and made His dwelling among us." The Almighty Himself had broken into human history. Amazing grace, a God with a face.

Our son, a Navy physician, received orders that would take him away from his family for a while. His young daughter, Emma, was very upset by the news. Her mother attempted to comfort her with the message that through Skype she would be able to have video chats quite often with her father. This appeased her for awhile. Arrangements were made a few days later to visit via Skype. The little girl was excited and filled with anticipation. However, barely had the Skype contact been made when she burst into tears. Flooded with disappointment, she stammered that she wanted a daddy she could hug. Of course. That is the kind of father we all want.

A chaplain in a rehabilitation home for emotionally disturbed children was struggling to prepare his Christmas sermon. He wanted something fresh and exciting to share. It was December 24 and three quarters of the children had gone home at least overnight and the ones who remained were very uncomfortable with empty beds and a changed routine. Hence, the harried minister had been faced with many interruptions. The house mother, once again, broke his train of thought by announcing that Tommy had crawled under his bed and refused to come out.

The shepherd of the flock headed for the young fellows's room. He couldn't see a hair or toe under the bed so he addressed himself to the cowboys and bucking broncos on the bedspread. He described the brightly lighted tree downstairs, the exciting packages underneath it, and all the other good things that were brightening up the night.

No answer.

Concerned about the amount of time he was wasting, he dropped to his hands and knees and lifted up the bedspread. Two enormous blue eyes met his. Tommy was eight but looked no more than five. It would have been no effort to just yank him out. But that was not what the little guy needed. So, crouched there on all fours, the loving father figure launched into a menu of the special Christmas Eve supper to be offered soon. He even reminded Tommy of the Yule stocking with his name on it. All this was met with total silence. There was no indication that Christmas had any meaning for the troubled lad.

At last, since he could think of no other way to make contact, the chaplain got down on his stomach and wiggled in beside the child. In the process he snagged his suit jacket on the bed springs. For a long time he simply lay there with his cheek pressed against the floor. For the next few minutes he described the big wreath above the altar and the candles in the windows. He reminded Tommy of the carol he and the other children were going to sing at the festive Christmas Eve service. He ran out of things to talk about and so simply waited there beside him.

After a while a small, chilled hand crept onto his. "You know what, Tommy? It's not very comfortable here. What do you say that we go out where we can stand up?" So they did, however not in a hurry. But, as the chaplain later reported, "It suddenly dawned on me that I had my Christmas sermon. Flattened there on the floor, I had been given a new glimpse of the mystery of Christmas. Hadn't God called us too, as He had called Tommy? But we wouldn't listen. Finally, God stooped to earth itself and joined us in our loneliness and alienation. It was then that we, like Tommy, dared to stretch out our hands and take hold of His love."

"And when he saw him, he took pity on him."

Luke 10:33

David Hunter, a reporter for the Knoxville News Sentinel, wrote an article about a woman known as the Good Samaritan. She was a senior citizen who spent each day on a street corner in downtown Knoxville collecting money from those passing by. The dear lady impressed many people with her neat uniform, pleasant smile and her simple appeal, "Would you like to help the Good Samaritan?" Who could say no? Hunter, himself, on occasion had given her a few dollars. Only after her death did Hunter learn that there was no Good Samaritan charity. The sweet little old charmer was keeping all the money for herself.

This story exemplifies the fear that many people have that if they try to be a Good Samaritan and help someone else, they will be taken advantage of. I must confess that I have been bitten many times by cons and scams when I thought the story was real and someone had a legitimate need. Even so, I have adopted a personal philosophy which is: when in doubt, it is better to help someone who really didn't need the aid than to turn someone away who had a real need. There is much joy that is found in assisting someone who truly can use a helping hand, but it is amazing the excuses that most of us can conjure up on why we are just too busy to get involved.

Tony Campolo told of a young woman who made a commitment to Christ and joined a local church. Nevertheless, she continued to feel frustrated and depressed. She went to a therapist for help but seemed to be making little progress. Then one happy Thursday she came into her counselor's office with her face radiant with excitement. "I've had such a wonderful morning," she exclaimed. "The day began on a bad note; I could not get my car started. I knew that my pastor would be driving by on his way to church so I called him and asked if I could hitch a ride. He kindly consented to pick me up adding, however, that he planned to stop by the hospital to visit with a patient. I went in with him and dropped in on some elderly people in one of the wards. I read the Twenty-third Psalm and prayed for them. It was such a great feeling. I haven't felt this good in years."

The therapist smiled and responded, "Now it is clear what makes you happy. Today we learned how to lick your depression and to pump meaning into your life." Much to his surprise, the young woman answered, "You don't expect me to do this sort of thing every week, do you?" She realized what the solution to her problem was. She knew what gave her joy and what filled her life with meaning but she still resisted. Sometimes I fear her story is all too common.

Just about everyone would recognize America's cat, Garfield. In one of his cartoons, Garfield is seated in a comfortable chair and as he looks out the window he sees his friend Odie outside the window peering in eagerly. Garfield says to himself, "Poor Odie locked outside in the cold. I can't bear to see him like this. I gotta do something." At this point America's most famous feline gets up from his chair and closes the curtains.

I read of an experiment that a professor of psychology and some of his students carried out in New York. An unsuspecting person walked by a dark alley when a woman cried out claiming that she had been raped and beaten. Nearby were two students who were part of the study. As instructed, they ignored the pathetic cries and hurried by. The unsuspecting passerby hesitated, not knowing what to do, but when he saw the others rush on by then he did likewise.

The test was repeated many times with generally the same result. This led the psychologist to conclude that our response to another person's plight is often determined by how other people respond. So the most important person in any situation that calls for courage and compassion is the first person to act. After one person acts then others are prone to follow suit as well. But someone has to take a risk to step out of the crowd and go first. God has placed us in the world to set an example of compassion and courage. After people see our willingness to get involved then they most likely will react in a positive way. This is what following Jesus is all about.

*"You are worried and upset
about many things..."*

Luke 10:41

I recently came across a cartoon in my files that had been clipped from a magazine several years ago. Approaching a bridge plainly marked "Load Limit–8 Tons," was a truck with a notice printed on its back door: "8 Tons." When the eight-ton truck was about in the middle of the bridge with the eight-ton limit, a bluebird landed on the top girder. At that point, the bridge gave way and crashed with the truck in the river below, to the obvious surprise of the bluebird.

The bridge was built as indicated for eight tons; the truck weighed exactly that. The bridge could hold up under its load limit but not under eight tons plus one bluebird. Of course this story is wonderfully ridiculous. Most bridges could stand up under their load limit and several bluebirds extra (perhaps several thousands), but obviously it isn't the bluebird that causes the breakdown–it is the fact that eight tons are already present.

We all have bluebird troubles, don't we? We're all burdened by the facts of our lives which load us to the limit. We let little things get the best of us, little bluebirds of nothingness, tiny bluebirds of no importance, but just the thing to bring us down. Every one of us has a limit and we would do well to watch for the warning signs of one bluebird too many.

While attending graduate school some years back, I recall the instructor, a psychologist, pointing out to us that we are fast producing an anxiety-ridden society. He stated that most of his clients are people riddled with guilt, apprehension, and worry. He even went so far as to claim that a friend of his, a veterinarian, has concluded that in metropolitan Los Angeles there are 200,000 neurotic dogs. It sounds a bit silly, but he is convinced there is evidence to confirm this. If their owners are nervous and anxious, then the pet is apt to pick up that personality trait. Consternation and worry not only hurts us, our spouses, and our children, but it even has a detrimental effect on the family pet.

One of the chief causes of our fearfulness is that we reach out and start to collect bits and pieces of nonsense, little worries, irritations, troubles, and allow them to remain as we approach our load limit. We find ourselves dwelling on the negative things and all of life starts to turn sour.

A pretty young wife came to a marriage and family therapist all weepy and terribly distressed. She felt that her marriage may have been a mistake. Her husband, she wailed, was often moody and was making her life miserable. The counselor waited for her to say more, but she ended there. "Well that is distressing but I'm sure that's not the whole story. What about the other woman?"

"Why, there is no other woman!" she cried out indignantly.

"Well that is certainly a relief," her therapist sighed. "We'll cross that off our list of issues that need to be dealt with. Does he have a drinking problem?"

The young woman raised her voice as she exclaimed, "Of course not! He's never been drunk a day in his life."

"That is another blessing. Perhaps his big problem is the way he handles money? Buying foolish gadgets or maybe gambling?"

Again she flew to her husband's defense. "He is a wonderful provider and is careful what we do with our paycheck."

"That's marvelous. Let's thank God that all we have to deal with are his moods." He suggested that she attack this problem with a good dose of love, prayer, and patience. The enlightened bride saw in reality that her blessings far outnumbered her problems and that her marriage difficulties were really not so desperate after all. With God's help, this too, would be taken care of. Happiness or unhappiness is not conditioned so much by what happens to us as it is by our attitude towards what happens to us.

Matthew Henry, a Christian gentleman with an amazing capacity to deal with life situations that would have caused anxiety, bitterness, or deep resentment for most people, was taking a walk through a city park one evening when a stranger approached him, pulled out a revolver from his pocket, pointed it at Matthew Henry and demanded, "Hand over your wallet or I will pull the trigger." He handed over his wallet to the gunman who fled into the darkness.

Under similar conditions, many people, perhaps most, would have either cussed out the police for not being where they were needed or lambasted their own bad luck and worried themselves sick over the incident or blamed God for allowing this to happen. But that is not what Matthew Henry did. He instead returned to his room, got out his diary, and wrote: "Tonight I am thankful for three things. I'm thankful that although my life was threatened, I was not harmed. I am thankful that although my wallet was taken, it was not all that I had. I am thankful that I was the one who was robbed and not the one who did the robbing."

"Lord, teach us to pray..."

Luke 11:1

Dave Peterson, a Lutheran minister now retired, was walking down a city street some years ago when he heard a public telephone ring. His first reaction was to answer the call. Then he thought that would be ridiculous. What would he do with someone else's call? He shrugged his shoulders and answered the phone anyway. On the other end of the line was a woman whose tone of voice indicated that she was in deep distress. She pleaded, "Please sir, I need help." The befuddled preacher asked, "Who are you calling?"

"I don't know," was her troubled response. "I've got a terrible problem and I have no idea what to do next. I was on my knees praying and the number I just dialed came up before my eyes. So on impulse I called the number. Maybe you are the answer to my prayers?" She then blurted out her pain, her problems, and her heartache. Peterson listened, got out his pocket Testament, and read some of the promises of God and prayed with her. From a grateful and relieved heart came the words, "Thank you, thank you, God bless you. He has used you to answer my prayers." Coincidence? Maybe, but as someone once put it, "The more I pray the more coincidences occur."

All around us are men and women, young and old, who have learned the power of prayer.

Ray Phibbs was a graduate student at Yale University when Reinhold Niebuhr served on the faculty. Dr. Niebuhr was an intellectual giant, a much respected theologian with a world-wide reputation for his insightful biblical commentaries. There was one thing, however, that puzzled and even irritated some of his students. It was the childlike manner in which their esteemed professor prayed. The God to whom he prayed was like a loving parent who was powerful, personal, and present.

His naive praying just didn't seem to square with his sophisticated theology. So, Ray was commissioned by his colleagues to approach the distinguished professor on this disparity. Ray reported, "I caught up with him one day while he was walking across the campus toward his office. Skillfully and tactfully, I popped the question: 'Dr. Niebuhr, some of us have been discussing the theology of prayer and we are wondering what is your theology of prayer?' He didn't even look at me as he replied, 'I don't have a theology of prayer.' There was a long, embarrassing period of silence as I tried to think of something to say. 'Prayer is not something you talk about. It is something you do.' "

There was a time when Mother Teresa appeared on Robert Schuller's television program, *Hour of Power*. Schuller reminded her that the show was being carried all over America and in twenty-two foreign countries. He asked her if there was one message that she would like to convey to all those viewers. The diminutive sister declared, "Yes. Tell them to pray, and tell them to teach their children to pray." Prayer is the beginning of anything really worthwhile. We connect with Christ before we connect with our neighbor.

If you really want to help someone, pray for them. God often answers prayers in ways that we cannot even imagine. A grateful parishioner stopped by the church office and invited her pastor to offer a prayer of thanks that she had been spared—not even a scratch—in an accident that totaled her Volkswagen. After hearing her story, the minister prayed, "Lord, I thank you for protecting my friend from all harm in the accident in which her car was demolished. But I also thank you for saving her life, and mine, many times when our vehicles were spared from accidents which so easily could have happened. Lord, you have rescued us on numerous occasions even when we were unaware that we were in danger." How true! God often answers our daily prayers in ways we never realize.

"Be on your guard against all kinds of greed."

Luke 12:15

According to African legends, there once was a certain remote tribe that elected a new king every seven years. For seven years the tribal leader enjoyed all the perks of a king with absolute authority. Every wish of his became a command for his subjects. But when his seven years were completed, he was killed and a replacement chosen. Every member of the tribe was aware of this custom but there were always plenty of applicants for the post. For seven years of luxury and power, men were willing to sacrifice their life.

In like manner, untold multitudes of sophisticated and intelligent people are making the same choice between things now and total bankruptcy later. Countless numbers are willing to be paupers in God's eyes if only they may have stacks of dollars now.

A science teacher took a frog and placed it in some cool water. The little creature was perfectly content to stay there. The classroom instructor placed the water over a Bunsen burner and applied heat. The jumper could easily have popped out at anytime. The water was gradually getting warmer and warmer but the pathetic croaker was oblivious to what was happening.

Before long the water was boiling and he roasted to death.

There must be a warning there for all of us. No one sets out with the intent of self-destruction but it happens when our priorities get all bent out of shape. God is then placed somewhere on the back shelf. This is usually a gradual process, so much so in fact that we might not even be aware of it. It is its subtle nature that makes it so deadly.

Russian author Leo Tolstoy, philosopher and a master of realistic fiction, shared with us this classic: A young man had received a small farm as an inheritance from his father who had recently died. He was approached by a well-dressed stranger who made a remarkable offer to him. In exchange for his farm the stranger offered him as much land as he could walk around in a single day. The youth's heart was beating with excitement as he looked out on acres and acres of plush, beautiful land. He agreed to the offer.

The next morning at his father's grave site he once again met the mysterious stranger. He was reminded that all the property he could walk around in one day would be his, but he must be back to the starting point by sundown. He immediately set out–no time to pack a lunch or fill a jug of water and no time to say farewell to anyone. He was on his way with the goal in mind to cover six square acres, but after getting off to a fast start he increased his goal to twelve square acres. It was getting late. He knew he had to be back by sundown. He was utterly exhausted and aware that he was running out of time. His heart felt like it was about to explode as he frantically plunged at his father's grave just as the sun went down. He collapsed and died. The sinister character asserted, "Through all his mighty effort he now has a plot of ground next to is father's that is six feet long and two feet wide." With a sly smile on his face, the well-dressed stranger went on his way. Tolstoy informed his readers that the stranger's name was death.

"You fool," Jesus proclaimed to the man who was building his future on material wealth, "For tonight your soul is required of you and what good will all your stuff do you now?"

Two young men asked an old Indian sage to help them settle a dispute over ownership of a piece of land. They had been quarreling over boundary lines and agreed that they needed a third party to help them resolve the issue. The aged Indian listened to their respective arguments and then said he would have to ask the soil who owned it. So after putting his ear to the ground, he arose and in a solemn tone stated, "The land said that it belongs to neither one of you but you both belong to it."

"Watch out!" Jesus said. "Be on your guard against all kinds of greed; a man's life does not consist in the abundance of his possessions."

A hen and a pig were discussing what they could do to help the poor. It wasn't long before the hen came up with a positive suggestion: why not provide them a tasty meal of bacon and eggs? The pig thought about it for a moment and then replied, "For you it requires only a contribution but for me it demands total commitment."

Everything of any value comes at a cost. Some athletes training for the next Olympics are preparing to pay a heavy price. They adopt rigorous measures for four or five years in hopes that they will qualify to participate in the games, enduring years of self-denial just for the opportunity to compete. Jesus asks any who would be his disciples if they have counted the cost.

Some of you may remember comedian Yakov Smirnoff. He recalled that when he first came to the United States from Ukraine he wasn't prepared for the incredible variety of instant products available in American grocery stores. With a note of amazement in his voice, he reflected on his first shopping trip where he saw powdered milk–just add some water and you have milk. Then he saw powdered orange juice. And then he saw baby powder, and he thought, "Wow. What a country!" If only life was that easy.

Jesus said that following him would come at a high price, so before making such a commitment we need to count the cost. The example he gave us is that of a farmer who needed a place to store his tools and his crops. A brand-new, state-of-the-art tower would do several things for him: The level of respect from his neighbors would be elevated. The value of his property would increase. Everything of worth would be safely stored. In the event of an attack it would be a fortress, a place to take a stand. But he better count the cost before he starts because if he runs out of funds and is not yet finished he will become a laughing stock. The point is it doesn't make much difference how you start if you don't finish well.

Some time back there was a TV commercial about a fellow and his girlfriend in a tattoo parlor. He had instructed the artist to inscribe the words, "I love Donna." Somewhere in the midst of the procedure he asked what it was going to cost.

"Fifty dollars," was the answer.

"I've only got forty."

"Then we are done," declared the artist as he put down his pen.

The commercial ends with the message "I love Don" scrawled on his arm and a young woman staring at him in contempt and disbelief. He failed to count the cost.

When we focus on what it means to be a disciple and review the cost it will nearly always require stepping out of our comfort zone. Milton Cunningham, a Christian missionary home on furlough, had just settled in for his flight from Atlanta to Dallas. Next to him was a young girl with Down syndrome. She turned to Milton and in all her innocence asked, "Mister, did you brush your teeth this morning?"

A little awkwardly he answered, "Yes."

"Good," she smiled, "that is what you are supposed to do."

Her next question, "Mister, do you smoke?"

That was easy to answer as he told her, "No, I don't smoke."

"Good," was her satisfied reply, "because smoking can make you die."

The third question was even easier to answer when she asked if he loved Jesus.

She was happy with his reply: "Because we are supposed to love Jesus."

Just then another passenger sat down in the seat next to Milton. Immediately the girl asked Milton to find out if the new fellow had brushed his teeth. He didn't want to disturb the stranger but the girl was persistent. Sheepishly he commented, "My little friend wants me to ask you if you brushed your teeth today?" He looked at the child and knew it was an innocent question and nodded his head.

With a sinking feeling Milton realized where this was going. He asked the second predictable question and got ready for the third one. He thought it was too personal but the girl insisted. The missionary squirmed and asked embarrassed, "She wants to know if you love Jesus?"

His face darkened. He started talking about his search for meaning and purpose and his conviction that maybe he was looking for God. The rest of the flight was a conversation about Jesus and his love, and it all started with a question asked by a naive child.

President Harry Truman once made a trip to the Old West town of Tombstone, Arizona. Ghosts of the famous and notorious alike were said to crowd the streets, people such as Wyatt Earp and Doc Holliday. When Truman returned, he shared that the most powerful impression made on him were the words engraved on the headstone of a simple man buried on Boot Hill: "Here lies Jack Williams. He done all the good he could." When we have counted the cost, stepped out of our comfort zone, and life in this world comes to an end, may that be said of us as well.

"Rejoice with me; I have found my lost sheep."

Luke 15:6

In the early '30s George Burns and Gracie Allen were enjoying moderate success with their new radio show but they were not drawing the audience they wanted to have. They needed somehow to get people talking about their comedy. The solution came, quite by accident, through one of Gracie's scatterbrained comic routines. Gracie started making up crazy stories about her brother, George Allen, who was actually somewhat of a reserved gentleman, an accountant for an oil firm. Burns hit upon an idea of starting a search for George, as if he were missing. It became a running gag on their show and carried over to other popular programs. Gracie would pop up on various network shows and announce that she was looking for her brother. People all over the country liked the joke and thus the George Burns/Gracie Allen production became a nationwide hit.

There was, however, a problem with this. Gracie's brother, George, was a very private person who suddenly was yanked out of his comfort zone and thrust into the national spotlight. He was so uncomfortable with what his sister had done that one time he actually disappeared for a while. This caused an embarrassed Gracie to put a stop to it. But even after he came out of hiding he remained the butt of many jokes. One of the problems today in looking for that which is lost is that it might not want to be found.

The world is full of lost people, living right on the street where we are and just about everywhere else in the world. People who have lost their focus in life, their enthusiasm, their joy, their hope, their purpose for living. It is easy to get lost. In the killing pace of progress, in the race for power and prestige, in the frantic pursuit of more dollars, in the out-of-control dash for entertainment and pleasure and finally, in the frenzied fear that we are marooned in a state of confusion and no longer have control of our lives. In the midst of all this, God's word tells us that His love doesn't depend on us and our actions; it depends on God's character.

John Ortberg, Christian pastor and author of several inspirational bestsellers, one time told us the story of Pandy. Pandy was the favorite doll of Barbara, John's sister. Wherever his sibling went, there was Pandy too. After years of devoted love from the little girl, Pandy was a mess. But Barbara never noticed her ugliness and Pandy remained her constant companion. One year the family vacationed in Canada. On their way back home the Ortbergs realized that the beloved dolly was missing. The family had already driven over 100 miles. Her father turned the car around and the whole household headed back across the border to retrieve the ugly little rag doll. Barbara's daddy knew that she would not rest until she had Pandy in her arms again. The child's parents made that long tiring trip back because they knew of the love their daughter had for her precious doll.

Barbara's love didn't depend on Pandy's beauty. Pandy was nothing more than a grubby toy. It certainly didn't depend on anything Pandy could do for her. Pandy was and always would be a lifeless doll. Anyone else in the world would have tossed her on the trash pile and forgotten about her. But Barbara and the whole Ortberg family went to great lengths to bring her home again. Our God isn't willing to give up on anyone, from the worst of us to the best of us. That is the attitude he wants us to have, too.

Roy Angel tells the following story. It seems that a widow had lost her only son, a young man in his 20s. In the midst of her grief she had a strange dream. An angel of the Lord stood before her and told her that she could have her son back for ten minutes. The angel asked if she wanted him back as a baby, as a young child romping with his dog, a teenager graduating from high school, or an adult leaving for military service. She thought about it and then in her dream said, "None of the above. Let me have him back when, as a small boy in a fit of anger, he doubled up his fist, scowled, and shouted, 'I hate you!' and stormed out of the door. A short time later a weeping little fellow came back with tears all over his dirty face, put his arms around me and said, 'Mama, I'm so sorry. I don't hate you. I love you with all my heart.' Let me have him back at that moment," she sobbed. "I never loved him more than when he changed his attitude and came back to me." Jesus said that is how he feels about us. Heaven rejoices when the lost are found.

"He ran to his son…"

Luke 15:20

In his short story "Capital of the World," Ernest Hemingway wrote about a father in Spain who had a son named Paco. Because of his rebellious attitude, Paco and his father had become estranged. The father was so angry that he kicked the boy out of his house. A year went by before the father came to his senses. He recognized that he loved his son and that he had made a big mistake and needed to be reconciled with him. He could not, however, locate the young man so in desperation he placed an ad in the Madrid newspaper. The advertisement read: "Paco, meet me at the Hotel Montana. Noon Tuesday. All is forgiven. Papa." Then the father prayed that his son would see the ad (Paco is a rather common name in Spain). Hemingway wrote that when the father arrived at the hotel on Tuesday he could not believe his eyes. Eight hundred boys–all named Paco–were waiting and hoping to receive forgiveness from their father.

In one of the best known stories in the Bible, Jesus told a parable about a forgiving father whose youngest son complained that he couldn't just sit around waiting for his father to die to inherit his share of the estate. He wanted it now. So the father granted his wish. In no time at all, the youth had packed his bags and headed for a distant land where he wasted his money on wild living and before long, it was all gone. He was destitute and, if that wasn't bad enough, a severe famine was gripping the land. The only way to stave off starvation was to accept a job with a local farmer feeding his pigs. He was so hungry he would have eaten the pigs' slop but that was forbidden. He could sink no deeper and at last came to his senses. Now barefoot, dirty, in rags, and smelling like a hog, he headed for home.

While he was yet a long way off his father saw him coming. Filled with compassion and love, he ran to meet his son. The repentant youth confessed that he had sinned against God and against his father. But even before the words were out of his mouth, his father embraced him and kissed him. The forgiving father soon gave orders to his servants to bring some clean clothes, sandals, and a family ring for the prodigal's finger. Then they were told to kill the grain-fed calf and roast it and prepare to feast and party. "For this son of mine was given up for dead and now alive! Given up for lost and now found!" This is the only time in the Bible when we see God in a hurry. He is rushing to embrace and welcome home a repentant sinner.

Years ago there was a homeless bag lady in New York City who attended a preaching service at a Manhattan Rescue Mission. Afterwards, while standing in the soup line, she mentioned to the preacher she was now ready to give her life to Jesus. She said, "I never knew until today that my name was in the Bible."

The chaplain smiled and asked her what her name was.

She replied, "My name is Edith and it's in the Bible."

He told her in the kindest way possible that she was mistaken. He was sorry but Edith was never mentioned in the Bible.

"Oh, yes, it is," she insisted, "I heard you read it."

He retrieved his Bible (King James Version) and reread the passage in Luke 15, "Jesus receiveth sinners and edith with them."

Indeed the good news is that Jesus does receive sinners and Edith, Jerry, Marcia, Rod, Ben, and anyone else who comes to him.

We have seen a wonderful picture of what God is like. He is heartbroken when we head off to the far country but filled with great joy and forgiveness when we return. Before I close this chapter, I know that some readers may identify more with the brokenhearted father than the wayward son. You may be a parent or grandparent of a son or daughter who is far from home because of rebellion or a sinful lifestyle. Perhaps they just walked out of your life. Whatever the reason—you are in pain. God knows exactly how you feel and He cares. He is the suffering father in this story. Please note: He did not jump into the pigpen to bail out his child. He knew that would have been a mistake. The son had to come to the conclusion that he was at fault, sinning against God and his father. So don't go to the pigsty and attempt a rescue, but let them know the door at home is unlocked and that you'll leave the light on for them.

Like the Prodigal Son, they may need to reach absolute bottom before coming to their senses. When they at last turn toward home, run with outstretched arms to welcome them. In the meantime, keep praying, keep hoping, never give up.

"At his gate was a beggar named Lazarus."

Luke 16:20

A young, successful entrepreneur was traveling down a neighborhood street, going a bit too fast in his shiny new Mercedes-Benz. He was watching for kids darting out from between parked cars and slowed down when he thought he saw something. As he cautiously continued, no children appeared; instead, a brick smashed into the side of his prized possession. He slammed on his brakes and, with his tires burning rubber, backed up to the spot where the brick had been thrown. Furious, he leaped out of the car, grabbed the nearest kid, and pushed him up against a parked SUV demanding: "What the devil was that all about?! That's a brand-new car and that missile you tossed is going to cost your parents a bundle. Why would you do such a thing?!"

The trembling boy was apologetic as he explained, "Please, mister, please. I had to do something and I didn't know what else to do. I threw the brick because no one would stop." Tears were running down his cheeks and off his chin as he pointed to a spot just beyond where they were standing. "It's my brother," he sobbed, "he rolled off the curb and fell out of his wheelchair and I'm not strong enough to lift him up."

His tears continued to flow as he pleaded with the stunned driver: "Will you please help me pick him up and put him back in his wheelchair? He's hurt himself and is crying." The shocked young executive found himself fighting back tears of his own. With painstaking care he lifted the handicapped child back into the wheelchair, then took out a clean handkerchief and with compassion cared for the fresh scrapes and cuts.

At last satisfied that the situation was under control and everything would be OK, the boy smiled and placed a reassuring hand on his brother's shoulder. "Thank you, mister. God bless you," the grateful youth solemnly addressed his benefactor. Shaken by the entire experience, the chastened good Samaritan watched in silence as the brothers headed down the sidewalk toward home, then in a pensive mood walked back to his beloved chariot. The dent was quite noticeable but the man never bothered to repair the damaged door. He kept the nasty scar there to remind him of a message, "Don't go through life so fast that somebody has to throw a brick at you to get your attention!" God whispers to our spirit and speaks to our hearts. Sometimes when we don't have time to listen, he has to throw a "brick" at us.

In the story that Jesus told about the beggar Lazarus we see how God was trying to get the attention of the rich man. He threw a "brick" named Lazarus at him everyday, yet the rich man ignored the message delivered to his front gate. The parable doesn't say that the recipient of the tossed "brick" was a bad man; by today's standards he would be considered a good guy.

We assume he was faithful to his wife. He never robbed a bank, he wasn't nasty or cruel to anyone, and as far as we know he got his money honestly. He never kicked Lazarus in the ribs or ordered him to go beg elsewhere.

Now let me ask you a question: do you think the rich man saw Lazarus lying there at the gate? Of course he did, at first. But then he soon got used to him. Lazarus began to blend in like shrubbery. His presence and his needs made less and less of an impression on the rich man as time went on. After awhile it was as if he wasn't even there. Is this possible? Of course it is. It could even happen to you and me. We need to recognize that we have far more in common with the nameless man than we do with Lazarus. There are millions of people in other countries who would think they have died and gone to heaven if they visited the average supermarket in our land.

There are needy people all around us, but their needs are not necessarily financial concerns. People need someone to look up to—a role model or a mentor, a friend, and, on occasion, someone who will cry with them. And everyone needs to know of God's love. People have all sorts of needs that go unnoticed if we don't open our eyes and look in their direction. They could be next-door neighbors, coworkers, or classmates. It could be a child or even a member of the family. Will a "brick" have to be tossed at us before we notice the Lazarus at our door?

"Be always on the watch..."

Luke 21:36

Some time ago the San Diego Chargers football team came from behind to defeat their arch rivals, the Oakland Raiders. For most of the game the Chargers' star player, LaDainian Tomlinson, had been running the ball as expected. After all, he was the best running back in the NFL. In the fourth quarter he started to run and as the Oakland defenders closed in on him, he suddenly stopped and passed the ball to a wide open receiver for a touchdown, tying the game.

After the contest was over, the Raiders said they had been told in advance that Tomlinson might do that so be prepared but they had gotten so used to trying to stop the run that they had forgotten about the pass. In an instant the game changed because the defense let down their guard.

We know better, but it is still easy to get lax in our preparations for the coming of Christ.

Ignore the signs of high blood pressure long enough and you could have a stroke. Ignore a traffic light and you can be arrested or have an accident or both. Ignore the indicator on the fuel gauge and you'll run out of gas. Ignore the skull and crossbones on the bottle and you can be poisoned. Ignore the signs of the times the Bible presents to you and you can be caught off guard and face disaster. "Be always on the watch," the Scriptures declare, otherwise the day could close unexpectedly like a trap.

Ole was a hermit who made his home in northern Minnesota. He lived way back in the woods where he hunted and fished whenever he wanted to. The recluse paid no attention to the hunting seasons or fishing regulations and knew the woods better than the game warden. The keeper of the forest with his badge on his chest had been trying to catch the elusive offender for a long time. Today was the day. He knew that Ole would be up early to go fishing. So the confident sleuth sneaked down in the middle of the night and hid on top of the hermit's hut. This way he would have the jump on his crafty quarry. He would let him head out and then he'd follow him. His plan was to hide in the woods until his victim caught a large illegal fish and then nab him.

As the light of dawn began to peek through the tree-tops, the hidden pursuer could hear Ole get up, start a fire, and begin to brew the coffee. The nearly frozen agent felt his stomach start growling as the aroma of coffee and fresh-baked biscuits reached him. He could hardly contain himself. Suddenly the cabin door opened and out stepped Ole who hollered, "You're welcome to come on in for fresh biscuits and coffee while they're hot. I know you're out there." With that parting comment, the door was closed.

The stunned game warden could not believe it. He slid down from the roof and unto the porch and rapped on the door. "How did you know I was out there?" Ole responded, "I didn't. I walk out and say that every morning just in case you are there." Ole may not have been a genius but he knew enough to always be on watch, to be prepared.

A few years ago, a bright young high school freshman stopped by the pastor's office for her pre-confirmation interview. I asked this articulate young lady about her future plans. Unlike most of her classmates, she had actually written down a series of personal goals. She would be taking very specific courses in high school and expected to graduate with a 4.0 GPA. She then named a very prestigious university that she planned to attend after winning a competitive scholarship. Following college graduation she would enroll in California Western and pass the bar exam. She would be hired by a well-known law firm and eventually be a full partner. In the meantime, she was confident that she would find a wonderful soul mate and get married.

I was amazed. She was fourteen years old and had her whole life all planned out. She was intelligent and determined and I was convinced that she had reachable goals. Then I asked, "How does the Lord fit into all your plans?" I received a blank stare.

We make our plans. We sock away something in IRAs. We set short and long range goals. For some, the retirement date is circled on the calendar years in advance. But where does the Lord fit into all of this? The question is met with silence and a blank stare.

Eugene Peterson in his paraphrase of Proverbs 16:9 writes, "We plan the way we want to live, but only God makes us able to live it."

*"Jesus, remember me when you
come into your kingdom."*

Luke 23:42

Minnie Perkins was a middle-aged woman with an incredible capacity for hard work and a heart as big and pure as any the Almighty has ever produced. She had four bright, healthy children but a heavy cloud hovered over her life. Her husband, Abraham, was a hopeless alcoholic.

As a result of his drinking problem, he'd lost a fine job as a school principal and ruined his health. Minnie was forced to obtain employment as a housekeeper for a wealthy family in the suburbs of Cleveland. Some days she would put in twelve hours and return home to care for her children and alcoholic husband. Her family and friends had tried to convince her to leave him. "Get a divorce. Get him out of your life," was their ongoing advice. "Oh, no, no," she would respond, "he has a good heart. I pray every day that he will return to his old ways. He really is a sweet and kind person when he is sober."

One evening I stopped at their home for a visit and found Abraham in his usual drunken stupor. He started to get up and then he flopped back down on the couch.

"So what are you doing here?" he slurred as he weaved from side to side. "I suppose you've come to talk about the Lord. Well, I don't see any Lord. Where is he? Is he hiding in the closet or maybe he's under the couch?" Mocking me, he grinned and peered to his left and then to his right. His distraught wife pleaded, "Abraham, please don't talk that way."

I closed my eyes and started to pray when I was interrupted, "Hey, preacher," he called out while trying to focus his eyes on me, "did you fall asleep?" The younger children started to giggle as their mother shooed them out of the room. "Abraham," I asked, "look at that precious wife of yours. Can't you see the Lord living in her?" His head was bobbing up and down as he tried to focus on his beloved Minnie, standing before him with big tear drops sliding down her cheeks. His glassy eyes momentarily connected with hers and then he collapsed. It was not much longer after that when the doctor informed Minnie that her husband was dying. He had literally drunk himself to death.

From time to time Abraham was alert enough to recognize that his condition was fatal. Those moments were very frightening for him. His wife was a constant presence by his bedside praying for him, comforting and encouraging him. I made a point to visit often and, at Minnie's request, read from the Psalms which I was told once had been his favorite book of the Bible. Recently he seemed glad to see me but still we couldn't seem to calm his fears.

He was admitted to the hospital on a Friday night in critical condition. It was obvious that the end of his life was only days away. His faithful life partner, eyes filled with tears, was sitting at his bedside where her hand was gently coddling his hand, the one wearing the wedding ring. He was covered in a white sheet from his feet to his neck with only his arms exposed. I approached his bed and called out, "Abraham, can you hear me?"

He nodded his head.

"Good. I'm going to read you a story from the Bible that Jesus told, a wonderful parable of the Prodigal Son." When I finished reading, I asked, "Abraham, who is this prodigal son that Jesus is talking about?"

There was total silence then he whispered, "Abraham."

The eyes of his wife opened wide and suddenly lit up with hope. "Yes, yes, and who met him at the end of his journey with outstretched arms and joy that his son had at last returned?" With conviction he spoke the words, "His father."

"And do you see how his father loved him and forgave him?"

"Yes," was his simple reply.

"Abraham, not long ago you asked me where the Lord was. You said you couldn't find him anywhere. Do you know where he is now?"

Inch by inch he moved his hand along the sheet, stopping when he reached his heart. "Here," he quietly affirmed.

Minnie, his "till death do us part" partner, wrapped her arms around him and cried out in joy, "Oh, Abraham, Abraham. You've come home!"

Early the next morning Minnie called with the news that Abraham left for his heavenly home shortly after my visit. There was calmness and peace in her voice.

> *"They found the stone rolled
> away from the tomb..."*
>
> Luke 24:2

In his book *There I Go Again,* Steven Mosley writes about Anna Pavlova, a Russian ballet superstar in the early 1900s. This tiny, graceful woman has been acclaimed as the greatest ballerina of all time. Her most memorable performance took place after her death. This legend was to play the role she made famous, the dying swan, at the Apollo Theatre in London. Tragically, she died of pneumonia two days before the event.

Still, on the appointed night, a crowd of her fans packed the Apollo. The orchestra started playing, the curtain rose, a spotlight flashed through the dark, wandering around the stage accompanied by the orchestral theme. As the light danced and the musicians performed, they remembered Anna. In their hearts they could see her on stage, dressed in white with her dark and flashing eyes. When the music at last stopped they gave the vanished dancer a thunderous ovation that echoed on and on into the night.

It was an empty stage with only a spotlight but in their hearts she still lived. For some, this is the experience of Easter morning. The Lord was crucified, he died as all of us will one day, and he was placed in a tomb, but in the hearts of his disciples he lives on forever. An empty stage but not an empty tomb.

This is not the testimony of the New Testament. He was crucified, dead, and buried but on Sunday morning when his loved ones came to visit the grave, they discovered the stone in front of the burial site had been rolled away. The risen Lord later met with them, ate with them, laughed and talked with them, and loved them. He wasn't just a pleasant memory dancing in the spotlight. He was alive! This is the heart and soul of the Christian faith. Not an empty stage but an empty tomb.

Is this important? You better believe it is. Ultimately you and I have a choice to make. It is by far and away the most important decision we will ever make. Do we accept an empty stage or an empty tomb? Does Christ merely live on in the minds and hearts of his disciples or has he truly conquered death and lives today?

Death is often an ugly experience. It means loss, separation, and heartache beyond description. Even so, we often do our best to try to pretend that it is not so. Have you ever heard of Mrs. Martin van Butchell? Probably not. She died over 200 years ago, leaving behind a will which specified that her husband had control of her fortune only as long as her dead body remained above ground. Mausoleums were little known at the time so her husband hired a chemist, William Hunter, to embalm his deceased wife. This he did and then dressed her in fashionable attire and put her on display in the family parlor. Daily visiting hours were held for those who wished to view the corpse in the glass-laden coffin.

As news spread of how lifelike Mrs. van Butchell appeared to be, more and more people expressed interest in this new art. Before long undertaking became a thriving business. Families were encouraged to soften the loss of loved ones through embalming the departed one to look as lifelike as possible. Some embalmers, to drum up new business, took their prize corpses on tour, exhibiting embalmed bodies in the windows of barbershops, public buildings, and special booths at county fairs. Everywhere they went they received amazed and positive responses. The public was duly impressed.

We attempt to disguise death in many ways. For example, through our language: "He passed away," "Mother is no longer with us," "She left us last night," or in medical terminology, "The patient expired." We dress the recently died in his finest suit (or maybe even buy expensive burial clothes) while she is placed in her prettiest dress with a necklace around her neck. The mortician smiles with satisfaction when he is told, "She looks so peaceful."

I've heard mourners declare their conviction that eternal life means that we live on in the memories of our family and friends and that is what the future is really all about—living on through others who will keep our memory alive. However, all it takes is for a generation or two to pass and so does memory.

Have you lost a loved one? A parent, spouse, child, friend? Is it enough for you that their memory lives on?

You know it's not! Death is repulsive, a horror, if the Easter story is only a spotlight on an empty stage. But if the focus is on the empty tomb, then death is an entirely different matter and is seen in a whole new light. No empty stage but an empty tomb. Death is swallowed up in victory.

The day after the Japanese bombed Pearl Harbor bringing on World War II, the Imperial Army invaded the island of Guam and soon gained complete control of the entire country. Among the occupying forces was Sgt. Shoichi Yokoi, a tailor who had been drafted in the army. Three and a half years later, on July 21, 1944, U.S. troops landed on Guam and three weeks later the island was captured. The enemy forces had been destroyed.

Sgt. Yokoi survived the attack and for the next thirty years lived a wretched existence hiding in the jungle. He built and dwelt in a tunnel-like underground cave in a bamboo grove. He made his clothing out of the fibers of wild hibiscus plants and managed to stay alive on a diet of coconuts, papayas, snails, and rats. It was three decades of a frightening, miserable experience as he fought off capture and starvation. The fearful fugitive hid during the daylight hours and scavenged what he could during the night. Every day was a struggle until finally he was discovered by some hunters while he was getting water at the Talofofo River. The pathetic straggler never knew that the war was over.

How many people continue to live frightened, defeated, hopeless lives, dreading what tomorrow may bring because they have not heard or cannot believe that the war is over? Death has been conquered. Christ has won the victory for us.

Anna Pavlova danced on in the hearts of those who loved and admired her. The resurrection of Jesus was so much more. Death was put to death. It is more than an empty stage–his is an empty tomb. The battle has been won.

"Why do you look for the living among the dead?"

Luke 24:5

Tony Campolo, college professor, author, and re-nowned public speaker lives in Philadelphia. He is Caucasian, but for most of his life has been a member of an almost all black church. Campolo once told us about a funeral he attended there when he was in his early twenties. His friend and classmate, Clarence, had been killed in a subway accident. At the beginning of the service, the pastor read the familiar Bible passages about hope and the resurrection. Then he came down from the chancel area and went over to the right side of the sanctuary where the family of Tony's deceased friend was seated in the first three rows. There he shared special words of comfort and peace with them.

Then the preacher did something which seemed very strange. He went over to the open casket and spoke as though to the corpse. "Clarence," he confessed, "there were a lot of things we should have said to you while you were alive but we never wound up doing it. I want to make up for that right now." What followed was a wonderful litany of deeds done by Clarence for so many people present and for the church. The list recalled how lovingly this servant of Jesus had served others without the need for recognition or thought of reward. When he had finished, the minister looked at Clarence's body and stated, "Well, Clarence, that's it. I have nothing more to say except this: good night. Good night, Clarence." Having said that, he slammed down the lid on the casket as a stunned silence fell over the crowd.

Then a smile appeared on the pastor's face as he shouted, "And I know that God is going to give Clarence a good morning!" With that as the cue, the choir leaped to their feet and started singing, "On that great gettin' up morning, we shall rise, we shall rise!" Soon everyone in the congregation was on their feet singing along with the choir. "On that great gettin' up morning, we shall rise, we shall rise!" There was clapping, cheering, and tears of joy flowing. Celebration had broken out in the face of death. A preview of the heavenly party that is to come was underway. Death was swallowed up in victory.

Hall of Fame quarterback, Joe Namath, said that he never played a game without pain due to his gimpy legs. Then he went on to add, "When you win, nothing hurts." There is a sense in which that is true for all followers of Jesus. As Max Lucado has written, "I think the command which puts an end to the pains of earth will be two words. NO MORE!" The King of Kings will raise his pierced hands and declare, " NO MORE." Every child of God will turn toward the heavens and hear God announce, "NO MORE!" No more loneliness, no more sadness, no more tears, no more pain, no more sin, no more death. We have read the last chapter. We know how the story ends. The tomb is empty. Death is conquered. Jesus' resurrection seals the victory.

Some of you may recognize the name Clarence Jordan. He was a wonderful man of God best known for his homespun translation of the Scriptures, *The Cotton Patch Version of Paul's Epistles.* When he died, a host of friends gathered to talk about his strength and his gentleness, his simple life and his eloquent words and his love for people, both the great and the small.

Jordan was buried on a hillside near his farm in his native Georgia. Family and friends were shedding tears as dirt was shoveled on top of the cedar casket. But just then a little girl, no more than two or three years old, spontaneously stepped up to the grave and sang her favorite song. She had sensed that this was a special day for Clarence. So in her girlish voice she chirped joyfully: "Happy birthday to you. Happy birthday to you. Happy birthday, dear Clarence. Happy birthday to you."

How beautiful! How wonderful! Yes! Yes! By his death and resurrection Jesus has made it possible for Clarence and for you and me to experience the jubilant victory of a new life.

"The Word became flesh..."

John 1:14

O n December 17, 1903, Orville and Wilbur Wright
  kept their handmade airplane in the air for fifty-
nine seconds. They sent a telegram to their sister in
Dayton, Ohio: "First sustained flight today 59 seconds.
Hope to be home for Christmas." Their sibling was so
excited that she took the telegram to the local newspaper editor. The next morning, much to her surprise, she
read the headline in bold print: "Popular Local Bicycle
Merchants to be Home for the Holidays." The biggest
news of the time passed by Dayton all because the editor
misunderstood what the cable was saying. It is easy to
see how he could have gotten the wrong meaning; after
all, no one had ever flown an airplane before.

Miscommunication can result in some serious problems or some truly bizarre situations.

Such is the case in the hilarious story authored by
Bindeshwar Pathak. It is a tale about a British woman
intending to travel to India, and her correspondence
with her probable Indian host, which vividly reveals the
strange places to which miscommunication can take us.

In preparation for her upcoming trip to India, the
woman had made reservations to stay in a small cot-

tage owned and managed by the local schoolmaster. At that time, public places like bus stations, religious sites, railroad depots or tourist attractions did not have access to restrooms, often discouraging foreigners from visiting. She was concerned about whether the guest house contained what she called a water closet or WC, so she wrote to the landlord to inquire. The homeowner, not fluent in English, had no idea what she meant. He consulted his local priest and asked if he knew the meaning of WC. His friend was as mystified as he was. Together they pondered possible meanings of the letters and concluded that the lady wanted to know if there was a nearby Wayside Chapel. It never entered their minds that she was referencing a toilet. So the schoolmaster responded to her question in what he thought was a positive and helpful manner. What he wrote went something like this:

> Dear Madam, I take great pleasure in informing you that the WC is located nine miles from the house. It can be found in the middle of a grove of pine trees, surrounded by lovely grounds. It is capable of seating 229 people. The doors open every day at noon and it is open all day on Sunday. It is quite busy during the summer months (tourist season) so I suggest that you arrive early. There is usually plenty of standing room. This is an unfortunate situation especially if you are in the habit of going regularly. It may be of interest to you that my daughter met the man who would

become her husband at the WC. As "dame for-tune" would have it, the usher seated them side by side. It was love at first sight. They also chose the WC for their wedding celebration. The WC was filled and it was wonderful to see the expressions of happiness on everyone's faces.

This further note: My wife loves to visit the WC. It is a place where she feels she can commune with God. I'm sad to say that my beloved has been unable to go recently. In fact, she hasn't gone in several months and brings her much pain. You will be pleased to know that many people bring their lunch and make a day of it. Others prefer to wait until the last minute and arrive in the nick of time.

I would humbly recommend that you plan to visit regularly on Thursday. Come at noon for at that hour, to everyone's delight, there will be an organ accompaniment. You will discover that the acoustics are excellent and even the most delicate sounds can be heard in every corner of the WC. The newest addition is a bell which rings every time a patron enters. A marvelous colored brochure describing the vision that led to the building of this most unique and beautiful structure will be given to you as a keepsake on your first visit.

Thank you for your interest. I look forward to escorting you there myself and seating you in a place where you can be seen by all.

It is certainly possible for a written message to be misunderstood. It is also not uncommon to confuse a spoken word. But when I see the message lived out I am most apt to understand. Our Heavenly Father, therefore, caused the "Word to become flesh and made His dwelling among us."

"His disciples recalled what He had said."

John 2:22

M ark was three years old when his pet lizard died. Since it was her grandson's first brush with death, Grandmother Marie suggested that he and an older boy in the family hold a funeral for the lizard. Granny explained that a funeral was a ceremony where you said a prayer, sang a song, and buried your loved one. She provided a box and a burial place in the backyard. The boys thought it was a splendid idea and so they proceeded to the grave site. The older brother said a prayer and then asked Mark if he would like to sing a song. With tears in his eyes, he clasped his hands, bowed his head, and belted out the opening line of Ray Charles' famous song, "Hit the road, Jack!"

One of the most difficult tasks for most of us to do at the time of death is to know what is or is not appropriate. We usually don't have to worry about what to sing, but we are concerned about what to say and what to do. When someone we love is dying what can we say that will comfort them? Words are so inadequate. And what about when we are dying? What can we say to encourage those who are left behind?

There was a time when people recorded the last words of their loved one. The custom has almost vanished and

I suppose the reason is because so many people die in the hospital or a rest home—alone. This is sad, as so often comfort is found in those final words.

Daniel Poling's son had been to see his very ill father. As he got up to leave the room his father murmured, "Son, if I'm not here when you get back you will know where to find me." Those were the final words he ever heard his father speak. The last recorded words of Ludwig van Beethoven, who was stone deaf, were, "Soon I shall hear heaven's beautiful music." Peter Marshall, former Chaplain of the U.S. Senate, was being carried from his house on a stretcher and whispered to his wife, "I'll see you in the morning." The last words of the nameless criminal who was crucified on the cross next to Jesus were, "Jesus, remember me when you come into your kingdom."

Winston Churchill died in 1965 and his funeral was held at St. Paul's Cathedral in London. It was a typical state funeral with high church liturgical orders and traditional hymns and after the benediction, a lone trumpet from the back of the church slowly and solemnly played "Taps." However, before his death, Churchill had planned a dramatic twist. The postlude had been played, "Taps" had been sounded, thousands of people got up and were silently making their way toward the exits when all of a sudden a loud blast from the balcony erupted. A trumpet was playing the reveille, "It's time to get up! It's time to get up! It's time to get up in the morning!"

Yes, yes, yes. God has taken the cross of His son and used it as a battering ram to knock the ends out of the grave and let in the light of a glorious new day. St. Paul, prompted by the Holy Spirit, declared, "The trumpet shall sound and the dead shall be raised."

There is a humorous story of a man whose wife had a cat that he despised. The feline was always under his feet, constantly leaving scratch marks on the furniture, forever shedding cat hairs on the gentleman's slacks. One weekend while his wife was away visiting her mother, the long-suffering husband took the Cheshire out and drowned it. His wife was in hysterics when she returned to discover her beloved pet was gone. To comfort her, the husband made the grand gesture of taking out an ad in the local newspaper and offering a $1,000 reward for the tabby's return. A friend, reading the man's offer, shook his head and pronounced, "Man, you are crazy. That is a huge amount of money to risk." He responded with a sly smile, "When you know what I know, you can afford to do what I did."

Pastor Bohdan Vadis, a friend of mine from Minnesota, commented that he was out walking one afternoon when he stopped to gaze at a painting in the window of an art store. An original painting of the crucifixion of our Lord was on display. He stood there in silence pondering again the enormity of the sacrifice on the cross made on our behalf. He was so engrossed in thought that he was barely conscious of another person standing nearby. It was a small boy of ten or eleven. Bohdan smiled as he made eye contact with the little guy and asked, "Do you know who that is on the cross?"

"Yes, sir," he responded, "that's Jesus." Then thinking that perhaps this stranger didn't know the rest of the story, he went on, "See, there are the soldiers who nailed him to the cross, and there are the religious leaders who mocked him. There is his mother. She is crying…" He paused and then concluded, "That's Jesus alright. I learned all about Him in Sunday school."

Bohdan thanked the young fellow and walked away. Several minutes later he heard the sound of small feet racing after him.

"Mister, Mister! I forgot to tell you the best part. He rose from the dead! He really did. That's the most important part."

"I am the Living Bread..."

John 6:51

An Armenian Christian claims that westerners do not understand what Jesus meant when he proclaimed, "I am the Bread of Life." In the Middle East, bread is not just something extra thrown in at lunch time; it is the heart of every meal. People would never take forks and put them in their mouths. Put it in, pull it out, stick it back in; it would be disgusting. Instead, you break a piece of the bread, pick up your food with it, and eat it. Indeed, the only way you get to the main dish is with the bread. Jesus was explaining that the only way you come to life is through Him. Our Lord uses many metaphors to define his ministry. Let's consider one, bread, and discover the unique message it has to convey.

First of all, the Bread of Christ is universal. No one is excluded: "If anyone eats of this bread he will live forever." It makes no difference who you are or what you have done, where you are from or how you got here. Celebration of Holy Communion has been called the holy of holies in the Christian church. For over twenty centuries, followers of Jesus have gathered in homes and in catacombs, in chapels and in cathedrals, on battlefields and in hospitals, in public and in private, in sick-room and on deathbed. We eat the holy bread and drink the sacred wine and derive from it forgiveness, strength, and hope for our lives. The Bread of Christ is universal yet personal; it is personal yet communal, and there is another paradox. The Bread of Christ is to be kept and it is to be given away.

Jamie Buckingham for twenty-five years was senior pastor of a large Florida congregation. When Holy Communion was celebrated, designated servers would approach the altar where they would be handed the trays of bread and wine, and then station themselves at various locations throughout the sanctuary. Worshippers would then simply move to the nearest server and receive the elements.

One Sunday service the pastor requested that "those prepared to serve come forward at this time." As he handed the trays to the appointed assistants, he looked up and was very surprised to see someone that he had never met. Standing there was a big, bearded fellow with numerous tattoos on his arms. The presiding minister assumed that he must be subbing for someone and so he handed the stranger the two trays: one with the bread and the other with the wine. The newcomer stood there staring at what had been placed in his hands, then he walked off to join the other officiants. A minute or two later, he returned and questioned, "Which of these do I consume first?"

Buckingham whispered, "Bread first then drink from the cup."

"Should I do that right now?" was his earnest inquiry.

"Sure. Why not?" the pastor responded with a big grin.

The young man took a deep breath, then ate the bread and drank the wine. The minister placed his hand on his new friend's shoulder and declared, "The true Body and Blood of our Lord which you have now received will strengthen and preserve you unto eternal life. Go in peace and serve the Lord."

The blessed man tried to cover his watery eyes. Somewhat embarrassed, he returned to his seat. The hour of worship concluded with a hymn of praise. Pastor Jamie saw the new communicant making a beeline toward him. Before he knew it, the big fellow wrapped his arms around him and started sobbing. The preacher just stood there hugging him.

A few minutes later an emotional young lady came and stood with them. "I am his wife," she explained with moist eyes. "He has been hopelessly hooked on drugs for years. This week he opened up his heart to Jesus." Now her eyes were swimming. "This morning he said that he wanted to go to church with me. I told him that there might be a time when he could go forward and publicly announce that he had invited Jesus to take over his life. When you asked the servers to come forward he thought that you were asking for all who wished to serve Jesus to come forward. Then you handed him the communion trays and he didn't know what to do next."

Pastor Buckingham stepped back and looked into the radiant face of this new child of God. "God loves you so much," he answered him, "that when He saw you coming forward, He got so happy that He placed in your hands the Bread of Heaven. Then He directed you to share the gift you had just received with others."

"But I didn't know what I was doing," he responded in a quivering voice.

"None of us know fully what we are doing; we just obey and God honors our obedience by blessing us. There is no wrong time to reach out to Jesus and invite Him in."

And so it is. The Bread of Heaven is to be kept yet given away.

"The truth will set you free."

John 8:32

During the Civil War one of the primary Union objectives, almost from the beginning of the conflict, was to capture the Confederate capital, Richmond. Numerous attempts were launched but all proved futile until the very last week of the war when General Robert E. Lee decided that the only way to save his army was to abandon the city. So on the morning of April 3, 1865, Union forces entered and occupied Richmond.

President Abraham Lincoln knew that with the fall of Richmond the nation's horrible nightmare would come to an end. So the following morning, a Union ship put the president ashore. Without troops, without escort, without Secret Service guards, President Lincoln began to walk from the James River to the ex-Confederate capitol building, a mile and a half away.

As he walked, black slaves started to cluster around him, first just a few, then dozens, then hundreds, and finally thousands who had spent a lifetime in bondage were swarming around the president, patting his back, touching his garments, hoping just to be close to him, shouting for joy in the presence of the man who had set them free. Most believed he had been sent by God as the answer to their fervent prayers. They realized that they were no longer slaves. This just man, the Great Emancipator, was walking unescorted down the main street of Richmond. Norman Lucas, a news reporter, described the scene this way: "It was like rolling thunder, echoing and re-echoing, ever increasing in intensity, piercing, penetrating, deafening, unprecedented and unforgettable: Glory! Glory! Glory! Hallelujah! Hallelujah! Hallelujah! They were free."

Freedom has been the passionate desire of almost every person who has walked the face of this earth. Nearly all from every country of every time has shared a deep longing for those great freedoms named by President Franklin Roosevelt in his message to Congress in 1941: "Freedom of speech, freedom of worship, freedom from want, and freedom from fear." Sadly, those who truly find it are few. Those who keep it without sacrifice are none. It is so precious because freedom has always been so costly.

Jesus would have preferred some other way than the way of the cross, but ultimately He knew that was the only way. He was free to do what He knew He ought to do. This is also where the Christian finds purpose and meaning to life. George Washington was free to enjoy the good life as a gentleman-farmer on his plantation in Virginia. He was also free to command a ragtag army at Valley Forge. Abraham Lincoln was free to practice law in rural Illinois. He was also free to suffer the heartache of a nation torn asunder. Albert Schweitzer was free to live as a distinguished scholar in an ivory tower. He was also free to go into the heart of Africa and bind up the wounds of hurting people. They all chose the greater freedom.

There is always a certain bondage in being free. We sing, "Make me a captive Lord, and then I shall be free." The musician is never free to make music unless tedious hours of practice and struggle have paved the way. A kite will not stay up in the sky very long after the string is cut. It is free to truly fly only when it is securely tied. A ship is not free to reach its destination without a rudder. If it has no rudder it'll be free only to drift aimlessly. The strings of a violin will not make beautiful sounds unless it is taut on the instrument.

In a Classroom Classic song, Paul Colwell reminded us that "freedom isn't free. You've got to pay the price, you've got to sacrifice for your liberty." Derek Ibbotson, track star of a few generations ago, was invited by some friends to take part in a wild orgy the night before an important race. His reply to the offer: "No. If I accepted your invitation I would not be free to run…" Jesus said, "I am the way, the truth and the life." Not a way, or a truth, or a life but *the* way, *the* truth, *the* life.

A young Chinese youth wanted to learn all there was to know about jade. He sought out an expert, a wise and famous old teacher. The elderly gentleman put a piece of jade in the boy's hand and told him to hold it tight. Then he spoke to the young man about philosophy, psychology, science, and the sun and just about everything under it. After that, he took back the jade and sent his student home. The procedure was repeated for several weeks. The teen was getting frustrated. When would he learn about jade? One day the teacher put an ordinary stone into his student's hand. He cried out immediately, "This is not jade!" Ah, yes. Now he knew the feel of jade and would never be fooled by something artificial.

There are so many ideas in the religious marketplace today, so many claiming that they have the right answer. When all is said and done there is only one truth by which all spiritual practice should be judged. That reality is: What would Jesus do? What would He say? He told us that if we continue in His word we will know the truth and to know the truth is to be set free.

"Jesus wept."

John 11:35

A mother was upset because her young daughter was late coming home from school. "I was getting worried about you. What took you so long?"

"Well," she exclaimed, "Emma fell off her bicycle and it was broken."

"So?" her mother said. "You don't know anything about fixing a bicycle."

"I know," the little girl responded, "I just stopped to help her cry."

Sometimes that is just about the best we can do. Take our time to mingle our tears with someone else's tears. Jesus understands the language of tears. He knows the great power that glows through tears of the faithful.

W. P. Mackay was a medical doctor who was raised in a Christian home, but while a college student, he rejected the Christian faith and turned his back on his family's values. Nevertheless a day never went by when his mother did not pray for him. Oftentimes with tears.

One evening this Scottish physician was treating a poor day laborer who suffered critical injuries when the tunnel he was digging collapsed on him. He seemed to find comfort and peace reading an old Bible. After his death his physician was gathering up some of the deceased's belongings and happened to open the Holy Bible. His mouth dropped and his heart started to pound as he saw the name written inside the cover. It was the Bible his mother had given to him. He had donated it to charity along with some other books nearly a decade ago. The doctor was convinced this could not just be some coincidence. He started to read some of the passages that had been underlined by a previous reader. His heart was broken as he remembered his mother's prayers and her tears; right then and there he dedicated his life to Jesus. Next he placed a call to his mother, whose tears now were tears of joy. Her wayward son had come home.

There is a postscript to our story. This prodigal son, Dr. William Paton Mackay, wrote the words to a beautiful hymn that has become a favorite in some Christian communities, "Revive Us Again" with its memorable refrain, "Hallelujah! Thine the glory. Hallelujah! Amen. Hallelujah! Thine the glory. Revive us again."

A three-year-old girl had been given a helium-filled balloon at Sunday school. It was bright blue and almost seemed alive, dancing on the end of her string as she ran through the halls of the church, pulling it along behind her. The balloon bumped into something with a sharp edge and popped. With a single loud "bang!" it burst and dropped to her feet. She looked down and saw what had been her beautiful plaything, now no more than a blob of wet, blue rubber. The tears started to come but then her composure changed as she bent down and picked up the remains, marched cheerfully to where her father was standing, and handed the mess to him. "Here, Daddy," she said with confidence. "Fix it."

Sometimes our lives resemble that wad of wet, broken balloon lying there on the floor. "Here, Daddy," we say to God. "Fix it." It is true we have a God who can do the impossible, but sometimes we have some crazy expectations of our Father. Sooner or later, by some means, everything in this world comes to an end.

Dr. Diane Komp, a pediatric oncologist, described herself as an agnostic when she first entered the medical field. But working with dying boys and girls has given her an unshakable faith in God. With misty eyes, she related an experience that she had soon after starting her work with children at Yale. Seven-year-old Anna had fought leukemia for most of her young life. She reached the point where all her strength was gone and death was fast approaching. Just moments before she died, the little girl suddenly sat up in bed and with a glorious look of wonder on her face, she announced that she saw angels. With her cheeks aglow, she described their beauty and their wonderful singing. Then, this little child, radiant with joy, placed her head back on her pillow and died. The stunned medical team stood spellbound by her bedside, all with tears running down their cheeks. Later Dr. Komp wrote, "Surely a dying child has no agenda, no reason to deceive me. She only reported what she saw. A reliable witness."

In the gospel of John we see Jesus shedding tears. Mary, the sister of Lazarus, is speaking to Jesus. Through her tears she stammers, "If you had been here my brother would not have died." Now a word of caution is in order. There are times when we have some foolish assumptions of God. It is understandable why we do because it is always so difficult to let go of someone we love. That day is coming for all of us and we need to accept the inevitable.

Even so this is an exciting story. We see a compassionate Jesus weeping alongside of Mary and Martha, grieving over the death of Lazarus. This picture gives each of us the go-ahead sign to shed tears, unembarrassed when we are hurting. "Jesus wept." This is the shortest verse in the Bible but is packed with meaning. It is a powerful and unforgettable glimpse of our Lord. This passage allows us to look into the eyes of Jesus. There is love and comfort for the breaking heart. The Father hurts, too, when His children are in pain.

Tears often speak when words cannot. Our Lord understands the language of tears. Sometimes He sheds tears with us but He has promised that the day is coming when He Himself will wipe away all our tears and pain and death shall be no more.

"Greater love has no one than this..."

John 15:13

The Rev. Ian Biss, former pastor of Grace Brethren Church in Johnstown, Pennsylvania, relates the following story: One Sunday morning he invited an elderly gentleman to come up to the pulpit and share with the congregation a very personal memory. This was not the traditional way for a sermon to be delivered in this church and no one recognized the old man. People were filled with curiosity.

He began, "One day my son and his best friend and I set out on a fishing trip we had been planning on the Outer Banks. We were having a wonderful time. Our new boat was truly a marvelous sea craft to be in. It was exciting and joyful and it seemed as if the fish were jumping right out of the water to latch on our hooks. As you can imagine we were having so much fun that we lost track of time. It was getting dark and we had drifted further out into the ocean than we realized. It suddenly dawned on us that a storm was approaching–fast! Before long we found ourselves in ten foot swells. Our boat was being tossed up and down and then it happened..." The speaker, overcome with emotion, stopped, choking back tears.

The misty-eyed host pastor stepped forth to comfort his guest. He regained his composure and continued his story. "A wave smashed over us sending both my son and his friend into the raging water. By the time I finally got a rope to throw to them they had separated and drifted out of reach. I was desperate. Another wave came crashing over the boat, stalling the engine." He paused again, his voice quivering. "There I stood with only a few seconds left to save one boy, my son or his friend. I made the decision and tossed the rope." At this point in his gut-wrenching tale he could no longer control his emotions and started to sob. The minister wrapped his arms around him and continued the powerful narration.

"You see," explained the church's pastor, "the boys had drifted so far apart that he had to make an instant choice: which boy's life would be saved and which one lost. This man of God knew that his own son was a follower of Jesus, a deeply committed Christian. He also was quite certain that was not a description of his son's best buddy. If his son were to die that day he was confident they would meet again in heaven, but he feared that would not be true for the other boy. The father chose to rescue his son's friend." Now the pastor could no longer control his own tears and wept openly. Finally, after taking a couple of deep breaths, he was able to continue. "He sacrificed his own son to save his son's best friend–ME." John 3:16 is the heart of the gospel, "For God so loved the world that He gave His only son..."

When Norwegian Fridtjof Nansen, Nobel Peace Prize winner and renowned oceanographer, tried to measure the depth of the ocean in the far north he used a long measuring line, and when he discovered that he had not yet touched bottom, he wrote in his log book, "Deeper than that." Several times he tried until finally he fastened all his lines together and let them down, but his last record was still like the first: "deeper than that." He finally had to give up. He left without knowing the depth of the ocean at that point except that it was deeper than any he'd ever known.

We may know of a love of a husband for his wife or a wife for her husband. We may know the love of a parent for a child, or a friend for a friend, or a Christian for the Lord. But in each case the measuring line will be too short. We may even add all these measurements together and still we cannot fully measure the love of Christ. We must conclude it's "deeper than that," deeper than anything we've ever known.

"This is my command: Love each other."

John 15:17

In one of the *Peanuts* cartoons, a little girl calls Charlie Brown. "Marcie and I are about to leave for camp, Chuck," she informs him. "We're going to be swimming instructors."

Marcie takes the phone and adds, "We just called to say goodbye, Charles. We are going to miss you. We love you."

The perennial loser, Charlie Brown, stands by the phone with a grin on his face.

A curious friend asks, "Who was that?"

He answers, "I think it was a right number."

Jesus was speaking to us when He said, "This command I give you that you love one another." Love was the mark of Christianity for the first two centuries. It is said that outsiders marveled and declared, "Behold how they love each other."

Philip Yancey in his book, *What's So Amazing About Grace?*, tells the following story: A prostitute came to a man who worked with the down and out in Chicago. She was in wretched straits, homeless, sick, unable to buy food for herself and her two-year-old daughter. Through sobs and tears, she told the counsellor that she had been renting out her daughter–two years old!– to men interested in kinky sex. She made more money leasing her little girl's body than she could make on her own. She confessed it was done in order to support her enormously expensive drug habit. The shocked advisor could hardly bear to hear her sordid account. He had no idea what advice to give her or how he could assist her. At last he asked if she'd ever thought of going to a church for help. The would-be mentor said he will never forget the look of pure, naive stress that crossed her face. "Church!" she cried. "Why would I ever go there? I already feel utterly rotten about myself. They'd just make me feel worse."

So how are followers of Jesus supposed to befriend and love one's neighbor? Jesus gave the answer: "As I have loved you." He didn't just tell us how to love. He showed us what unconditional love is all about.

In Sweden, a nurse working in a government convalescent home was assigned to an elderly female patient. This pathetic resident had not spoken a word in over three years. The whole staff disliked her and avoided her as much as possible. The newly hired caregiver decided to try unlimited love. The old lady sat in a rocking chair and rocked in silence all day long. One day the new staff nurse pulled up a rocking chair beside the silent one and just rocked along with her and spoke softly to her even though she received no reply. On the third day the long-term patient opened her eyes and uttered the first words that she had spoken in years, "You are very kind." Less than a month later she was well enough to leave the hospital. It doesn't always work that way, of course, but it is amazing how many times love does heal.

Shortly after my eighty-nine-year-old widowed mother came to live with us, she was placed in hospice care. Her physician determined that her condition had been deteriorating at a rapid pace and nothing more could be done to restore her health. We were advised to simply do all we could to make her comfortable during her final days. Within six months she had "graduated" from hospice care and was enjoying good health. Mom remained in our home until the Lord took her to her heavenly home at age ninety-eight.

What happened? Her doctor suggested that love works miracles. There was no logical medical explanation for her renewed health. His conclusion: a caring, loving family environment was health giving and also provided an incentive to go on living.

Garbage truck operator Craig Randall sometimes brought his work home with him. For example, the old-fashioned sewing machine he plucked out of the dump. There were some books from the bestseller list. Against all odds, a Wendy's soft drink cup that just happened to be worth $200,000. The stunned twenty-three-year-old driver reported that he lifted the cup off a pile of trash while he was hard at work earning his daily bread. On an earlier trip he had peeled another sticker from a cup and won a chicken sandwich. "I figured maybe I could get some fries or a Coke to go with it." This time, much to his amazement, written on the ticket were the words, "Congratulations! You have won $200,000 toward the purchase of a new home." Neither the shocked scavenger nor his bride-to-be believed it until Randall drove his waste management truck to Wendy's restaurant and picked up his check. A treasure lifted from a garbage dump.

The cross of Christ lifted above the garbage dump of humanity is where the best ever gift, the greatest treasure of all, is to be found. "If I am lifted up I will draw all unto me," declared Jesus. This is what has happened. People have been drawn to Christ not because of His teachings or His miracles or His personality, but by the sight of Him hanging between two thieves. The cross is a revolting spectacle. We survey its horror and it turns our stomachs. Yet we are strangely attracted to the cross. It grips us and we cannot take our eyes off it. These two beams of wood teach us what no prophet or philosopher could ever impress upon our minds. We know that when we accept what Jesus has done we will never be the same again.

The church I pastored in Cleveland was on a busy thoroughfare with many passersby. A budding young artist in our congregation painted a very moving work of art depicting Christ on the cross. We placed it inside a glass message board for all to see with this bold caption under it: "Is it nothing to you, all you who pass by?"

A man from our congregation was dying of cancer, daily growing weaker and weaker. All hope of recovery was gone. His voice had been reduced to an undecipherable whisper. I stopped by for a visit early one morning and his wife told me her dying husband had been struggling to say something to her for the past hour. In total frustration she stammered, "I just can't figure out what he wants." Her life partner fastened his eyes on me and pursed his lips in a futile effort to communicate. Try as I might, I could not fathom what his wishes were. Then, literally climbing in his bed, I placed my ear over his lips while praying, "Lord, please help me understand." Suddenly it was clear to me what he wanted: "the cross." Stunned, I turned to his beloved and related what I had clearly heard, "He wants his cross." The grateful lady, eyes brimming with tears, gave me a hug while crying out, "Thank you, Jesus, thank you."

In a flash she reached a cabinet, opened a desk drawer, and produced a rustic cross that she had given him eons ago. With love and tenderness it was wrapped around his neck. Using great effort, he moved his hand ever so slowly up the side of his bed and over to the cross where his fingers closed around it. Peace and contentment showed on his face as he closed his eyes.

His wife enfolded him in her loving arms, tears running down her cheeks, as she sang:

> On a hill far away stood an old rugged cross,
> The emblem of suffering and shame;
> And I love that old cross where
> the dearest and best
> For a world of lost sinners was slain.
> So I'll cherish the old rugged cross
> Till my trophies at last I lay down;
> I will cling to the old rugged cross,
> And exchange it some day for a crown.

Over 100 years ago, John Bowring wrote, "Bane and blessing, pain and pleasure, by the cross are sanctified; peace is there that knows no measure, joys that through all time abide."

Chester Szuber was in need of hope and received the gift of life, though the cost was so dear he could barely accept it. He had undergone three open heart surgeries and was a candidate for a heart transplant when the youngest of his children, an exuberant twenty-two-year-old nursing student named Patti, was killed in a car accident. Patti's death came on a mountain road in Tennessee while she was on a trip with a friend before her return to nursing school. The little blue Chevy coupe had been struck by a drunk driver. She was airlifted to a hospital in extremely critical condition. Her family rushed from Michigan to Tennessee.

Patti had previously indicated that she wanted to donate her organs, and it soon became clear that her father could be the recipient of her heart. The family had precious little time to consider a transplant. Five hours and fifty-one minutes after his daughter's heart had stopped, it was beating in Chester Szuber's chest. Bob, Patti's brother, shared with a news reporter his conviction that his sister's heart now giving new life to their father was an immense help to the family getting through the tragedy.

I trust that anyone reading these lines will make the connection between this true story and what happened on a cross near Jerusalem two thousand years ago where the heart of God's Son was broken in order to give us hope and a new life.

"Here is your mother."

John 19:27

Dr. James Dobson, psychologist and founder of Focus on the Family, learned a great deal about effective and creative discipline from his mother. His father traveled a good bit when Jimmy was growing up so his mother was the primary disciplinarian. He was a rambunctious boy who often got in trouble in school and his mother was running out of ideas on how to keep him in line.

One day after yet another visit to the principal's office, Mrs. Dobson sat down with her son for a heart-to-heart talk. She announced that she no longer would punish him for getting in trouble at school. Instead, the next time she got a call from the principal she would become his shadow. She would go to school with him, attend all his classes, hold his hand as they walked through the hallways, and participate in all his conversations with his friends. No parent could have thought of a worse punishment. It was a brilliant idea and resulted in an immediate change in James' behavior. He became a model student.

Most of us can identify with young Dobson's situation. At a certain age, the idea of our mother following us around is sheer humiliation. But as we grow older, most of us soon realize that our mothers will always follow us wherever we go. We cannot escape their influence. Many things change over the years–our appearance, our address, our hobbies, and our priorities. But there is one thing that remains constant from the day of our birth to the day of our death: the sound of mother's voice influencing us. For many of us, our mother's voice was the first voice to communicate with us, comfort us, rebuke us, or call us by name. It was the tone of her voice that shaped our identity, our values, our view of the world. No wonder we still carry that voice with us even if our mothers have passed on.

Newly elected President Abraham Lincoln, reflecting on the influences in his life, stated: "All that I am and all that I hope to be I owe to my angel mother." These heartwarming words were in reference to Sally Johnston, his stepmother.

A junior high science teacher lectured on the properties of magnets. A day or two later he gave his students a quiz. The question read like this: "My name begins with an 'M', has six letters, and I pick things up. What am I?" Over half the kids in class answered, "Mother."

A young father was trying to explain the concept of marriage to his four-year-old daughter. He got out their wedding album, thinking visual images would help. He patiently reviewed the entire wedding service for her. When he finished, he smiled and waited for her reaction. She pointed to a picture of the wedding party and asked, "Daddy, is that when Mommy came to work for us?"

Eight-year-old Finn borrowed some money from his father to purchase a birthday gift for his mother. He decided he would use the money to buy her a pretty dress. When the sales clerk asked what size dress he wanted, the boy responded that he didn't know the exact size but his mother was the perfect size. The clerk wrapped up a size eight and sent it home with him. Two days later the mother was in the store exchanging it for a size sixteen.

A very heart-touching scene in the movie *The Passion of the Christ*, takes place when Jesus' mother is watching her son, beaten and bleeding on the way to the cross. Then there is a flashback–we see Mary, a young mother, running to the boy Jesus, who has been playing outside and has fallen and injured himself. She is rushing to pick him up, hug him, kiss away the pain. It was a powerful and sober moment showing the heart of a godly mother and how she suffers when her children suffer.

To those of us who have been blessed with a self-sacrificing, God-fearing mother, stepmother, grandmother, or godmother, how do we best honor her? There really is only one way to say thanks to a godly mother or the memory of such a mother, and that is striving to live a God-pleasing life.

"Jesus said, 'Take care of my sheep.' "

John 21:16

Baseball fans will remember the name Larry Doby. He was the first African American to play for an American League team. The year was 1947. Doby was a promising rookie for the Cleveland Indians. He didn't look promising, however, his first time at bat—tense and nervous, swung at three pitches and missed each by a country mile. It was his first time at bat and he never came near hitting the ball. Humiliated, he walked back to the dugout with his head down. He picked out a seat at the end of the bench and placed his head in his hands.

A marvelous player by the name of Joe Gordon was on the same Cleveland team. He was an All-Star second baseman and batted in the lineup right behind Doby. Gordon had never had any trouble hitting against the pitcher who was on the mound that day. But something extraordinary happened. This outstanding hitter struck out on three pitches, missing each one by a foot or more. He tossed his bat aside and walked deliberately to the end of the bench and sat down next to his dejected teammate. Then Joe closed his eyes and put his head in his hands. Did he strike out on purpose that day? We'll never know for sure. However, it is interesting that

Larry Doby, who would one day be a member of the All-Star team, did something quite unusual. As he went out to field his position, he first picked up Joe Gordon's glove and tossed it to him. This grateful center fielder did that every game for the entire season.

That's brotherhood. That's family. That's caring. What a better world it would be with more Joe Gordons in our neighborhood. He set a Christ-like example for all of us. We do have a responsibility for each other. It really used to bug me when Hall of Fame basketball player Charles Barkley used to smirk, "I'm no role model..." We are all role models of some kind to somebody, whether we like it or not.

One time a businesswoman was flying on a plane across the country. She was somewhat self-centered, surly, and annoyed by petty things. She was particularly upset by the sniffling little child sitting next to her. At last she scolded the man on the other side of the little fellow for not paying more attention to him. "What are you talking about?" he questioned. "The boy is not with me. I thought he was with you." The sad youngster murmured, "I'm with nobody. When my Aunt Maggie gets tired of me in New York she sends me to my Aunt Patty in California and when she doesn't want me anymore she ships me back to New York. I don't belong to anyone."

So now what did our selfish middle-aged passenger do? She forgot about herself, her fears, her loneliness, her annoyance, and all her sour feelings. She put her arm around her little seatmate and before long he was peacefully sleeping with his new friend's shoulder providing a comfortable cushion. That's family. That's caring.

A group of war refugees was planning to escape over a rough and dangerous route. The leaders hesitated about taking a young mother and her very small daughter because they feared the little girl would not be strong enough to make the journey. They decided that the men in the group would take turns carrying the little one.

The refugees had hiked for three days and the terrain had become more difficult. One old man became very weary and decided he was not strong enough to keep up with the others. The aged traveler begged them to go on without him. If he perished it would be no big loss. He had lived a full life and was ready for it to conclude. Persuasion didn't work so the others grudgingly decided to leave him behind and started out again. But the mother ran back and placed her daughter in the exhausted elder's arms. "You can't quit. It's your turn to carry the child!"

She left to join the others but glancing over her shoulder she saw the revived fugitive back on his feet with renewed strength and fresh determination walking after them with the precious bundle in his arms. That's family. That's caring. In the memorable words of William Penn, "I expect to pass through life but once. If, therefore, there be any kindness I can show, or any good thing I can do to any fellow being, let me do it now, for I shall not pass this way again."

"The promise is for you and your children..."

Acts 2:39

The following scene is from the movie *It Could Happen to You*. A New York cop named Charlie is having coffee in a little diner. Finished, he reaches into his pocket to pay and to leave his usual tip. To his dismay, he discovers that he just has enough money to pay for his coffee, not even a quarter for the waitress. Embarrassed, he offers her a choice. He promises to return the next day with double the tip or, taking a lottery ticket out of his pocket and holding it up, he promises to split the winnings, if any.

Poor Yvonne didn't need to hear that. She had had a bad enough day without losing her tip. In fact, she felt her life was in the pits. She really didn't like her job but desperately needed a paycheck. Her runaway husband had run up her Visa card balance so high that just that afternoon she had been in court to declare personal bankruptcy. Could things get any worse? Still, she is good-natured about it. She smiles helplessly at her bad luck and takes Charlie up on his offer to halve the lottery ticket's potential winnings.

Well, as Gomer Pyle used to say, "Surprise, surprise, surprise." The ticket beats incredible odds and wins four million dollars. Charlie comes to the diner the next morning to give Yvonne the astonishing news. Her tip for serving a good cup of coffee with a smile is not two bits but two million dollars. Of course you can imagine the beleaguered waitress' reaction to the startling report. Utter disbelief covers her face. "It can't be true. No way. Why are you doing this to me? It is some kind of warped joke, isn't it? It is not possible. This couldn't have happened." Charlie insists that he is not joking. A flicker of hope starts to spring forth inside her. She fervently wants to believe him. But disbelief wedges its way back into Yvonne's mind. After all, only yesterday she had resigned herself to her fate; she had been forced to accept bankruptcy. "No. No," she declares, shaking her head back to reality.

Charlie is smiling insisting that it is true. Charlie opens up his arms ready to give the emotional server a bear hug. "It could happen. It has happened. It has happened to you!" "Really, Charlie, you really mean it?" Her voice quivering as she asks again.

"Yes, yes, yes!"

With that, her doubts are resolved. Yes! She suddenly finds herself dancing, swirling through the tables of customers, contemplating her new life, a life forever changed by Charlie's free gift. A little coffee shop in New York is the scene of unexpected, overwhelming, hard-to-believe joy.

Now let me take you to another scene of unexpected, overwhelming, hard-to-believe joy. It is found in the last chapter of the gospel of John. The faith of

Jesus' disciples had been wobbling between disbelief and joy. He was crucified, dead, and buried. That was for certain. Then came the events of Easter morning. It was so staggering, so hard to believe. Did the greatest miracle of all really happen? Or could our minds have been playing tricks on us?

The disciples had been fishing all night and caught nothing. A stranger on the shore encouraged them to cast their nets on the other side. Why? They were professionals. They had fished this lake most of their adult life. But what did they have to lose? They cast their nets on the other side and they immediately caught 153 fish. As soon as the astonished John saw what had happened, he announced, "It is the Lord!" For the next forty days they walked, talked, and ate with the resurrected and living Lord. Yes. It really happened.

Jesus lives. Someone desperately sensing their need, the bankruptcy of their hope, hears with wonder the glorious message of God's gift of eternal life. The God of the universe loves them Can it be true? Oh yes! It is true. When Yvonne finally accepted Charlie's message she said, "Why? You didn't have to give me this gift. Why are you doing this?" Charlie's reply is classic: "Because a promise is a promise." God, why did you do this? "I promised to send a Savior to rescue my children from sin, death, and the Devil. A promise is a promise."

"God does not show favoritism..."

Acts 10:34

Dodie Gadient, a schoolteacher for thirteen years, decided to travel across America to see the sights she had taught about. One afternoon on Interstate 5 in Southern California, a water pump blew out in her RV. She was tired, scared, and alone. There was a lot of traffic but no one seemed interested in helping. She prayed, "Please God, send an angel to help me—preferably one with some mechanical skills."

Within minutes a huge Harley roared up. An enormous fellow sporting long hair and a bushy beard jumped off his cycle with a definite air of confidence. He took a brief look under the hood and then flagged down a truck with a tow bar, which pulled Dodie's recreational vehicle off to the side of the road where he went to work on the water pump.

The intimidated schoolteacher was too dumbfounded to talk, especially when she saw the words on his jacket: Hells Angels. Finally he said, "OK, lady, it ought to work fine now." She mustered up the courage to humbly say, "Thank you." As he climbed back up on his Harley, he looked her in the eye and left her with this parting comment: "Remember, you can't judge a book by its cover."

It's possible that when you pray for an angel, you may need to be very specific. It could be a Hells Angel.

Tall and short, fat and thin, young and old, black and white, full beard and clean shaven, male and female, God's children come in a variety of colors and shapes.

At an unexpected time in my childhood I learned a powerful lesson that literally shaped my whole life. Some friends of my parents had planned a special wedding anniversary celebration for them. Relatives, neighbors, and members from the church had been invited. Invitations had also been sent to some of my mother's coworkers at Lockheed—people I heard much about but had never met. Mother had often mentioned Esther, Charlie, Marian, and Cosetta and all responded yes to the RSVP.

My brother and I were dressed in our Sunday best as we prepared to welcome our guests. The doorbell rang and a smiling stranger introduced herself as Marian, who worked on the assembly line with my mother. She had a hardy handshake and a distinct Polish accent. Somehow she didn't look or talk like we had imagined. Visitor number two gently bowed, held out his hand and announced that he was Charlie, "your mother's friend and coworker." There was another knock on the door and soon we met Esther, who greeted us with a charming, "Buenos dias." Shortly thereafter we ushered in a gracious African-American lady who happily informed us that her name was Cosetta and she was honored to be included in this wonderful celebration.

It was an important lesson for two young boys to learn. You see, Mother never referred to these coworkers as "Charlie, my Chinese friend," or "my Mexican coworker, Esther." They were simply her friends. If only everybody had an example like that in their childhood. God loves people in all sizes, shapes, and colors and doesn't show favoritism.

A college professor from Eastern University in Philadelphia was walking along an avenue when he came upon a homeless person, dirty from head to toe, with an enormous beard with rotted food stuck in various parts of it. He was holding in his hand a cup of coffee. He called out, "Hey, mister! This is good coffee. You want a taste?" He seemed to be sincere in his generosity, and so wanting to be nice, the professor took a sip, thanked him and then added, "You're a generous man." To which the bum replied, "If God gives you something good you ought to share it."

The teacher thought for a moment that he was being set up. Nevertheless, he asked, "Is there anything I can do for you?" preparing to hand him five bucks. "Sure is," the homeless man declared. "Give me a hug." His immediate thought was that he would much rather give him five bucks, but he gave him a hug anyway and discovered the vagrant wasn't going to let him go, at least not anytime soon. People walked by, staring at the two of them hugging. The professor said he was getting embarrassed when a thought came over him. Jesus said to him, "I'm the bum you are hugging on our city street in Philadelphia." Indeed, in many surprising ways Jesus chooses to make himself known to us through people that are very different from ourselves.

Alexander Mackenzie is a Canadian hero. An early fur trader and explorer, he accomplished an outstanding feat when he led an expedition across Canada from Fort Chipewyan in northern Alberta to the Pacific Ocean. His amazing journey was completed in 1793, eleven years before Lewis and Clark began their famous expedition to the West. Mackenzie's earlier attempt in 1789, however, had been a major disappointment. He and his men had as their goal a discovery of a water route to the Pacific. The valiant team followed a mighty river (later named "the Mackenzie") with high hopes. They oftentimes found themselves paddling furiously amid great danger. With sadness, they discovered it did not empty into the Pacific but instead into the Arctic Ocean. In his diary, Mackenzie called it the "River of Disappointment."

All of us at times need to learn how to handle our own rivers of disappointment: at home, with our friends, with our job. I like the line expressed by a comedian when he quipped, "I was looking for a self-help CD out there. I ordered one called *How to Handle Disappointment*. I opened the box and, guess what, it was empty."

When it comes to disappointment, tune into what happened to David Marston, former U.S. Attorney for Pennsylvania under President Jimmy Carter. In response to a direct summons from the president, Marston braved the worst snowstorm in years to get to Washington, D.C. All flights were canceled so the barrister boarded a train which derailed outside Baltimore. Not one to take a presidential summons lightly, he pressed on to the capitol by bus. When the bedraggled civil servant finally arrived at the Justice Department, he was told his interview with Carter would be his last–he was about to be fired. The Chief of State felt it would be more considerate to do it personally rather than by letter. Talk about a river of disappointment. The dismissed executive said he laughed in order to keep from crying.

We all know what it is like to be disappointed. Pastor Crawford Flanders had a sign on his desk during the first five years in the ordained ministry, that read: "Win the World for Christ." Five years went by and he replaced the placard with one that declared: "Win Five for Christ." After ten years he changed it to: "Don't Lose Too Many." Life can oftentimes be hard with disappointment just around the corner.

Edith Lillian Young was inspired to write the song lyrics: "Disappointment–His appointment, change one little letter then I see that the thwarting of my purpose is God's better choice for me." Dietrich Bonhoeffer, another Christian leader, and martyr who was hanged by the Nazis at the conclusion of World War II, stated,

"In view of our supreme purpose, the present difficulties and disappointments are trivial."

Hamilton Whaley was a prosperous lawyer in Tampa, Florida. From his own story which appeared in *Guideposts* magazine, he was happily married, father of five healthy children, and owned a very comfortable home in a beautiful upscale community. He was making more money than he ever dreamed of. He was a full partner in one of the leading law firms in the state, a vast organization with seventy attorneys. He was also a member of a growing church and was quite content with his life.

Then he was in an auto accident. It could have been very serious–the car was totaled– but he was quite fortunate in that he suffered only minor injuries. However, the next morning his telephone started ringing. "Mrs. Whaley," a sympathetic voice uttered, "I just read in the County Bar Association Newsletter about your husband's death. I want to express my regrets." His wife was dumbfounded as calls continued throughout the day. Printed on the first page in large, black, bold type was his death notice. Attorney Whaley for a time almost seemed to enjoy joking about it. Then that feeling started to change and he became more and more bothered by it. What if it had been true? What was his legacy to show that his life had truly made a difference? He was facing his own river of disappointment as he reflected upon his lifelong achievements.

He decided to give up his law practice. He and his wife made the decision to become house parents at the oldest orphanage in America, The Bethesda Home for Boys in Savannah, Georgia. The couple was responsible for the lives of twenty boys, ages five to seventeen. They found their calling and their purpose. Both husband and wife declared with a great deal of satisfaction that they were convinced they were where God wanted them to be. Hamilton said, "We are living a life that began, instead of ending, with my obituary." It took a ride down the river of disappointment for the Whaleys to discover their reason for being. Have you discovered yours?

Each one of us has a great high calling from Jesus to make our life count. We dare not be like the hunting dog whose owner took him out into the woods. The hound scented a deer and followed it for a while, then switched to the trail of a jack rabbit, but quickly turned aside to flush out a covey of quail. When his owner finally caught up with him, he was barking down a gopher hole. Some of you may be at this moment paddling down your river of disappointment, feeling like the disciples on Good Friday, but God's children know that Easter is coming.

"While we were yet sinners
Christ died for us."

Romans 5:8

Centuries ago, a beloved monk informed his congregation that his evening message would be on the theme "God Loves You." His faithful flock returned at dusk looking forward to hearing more about God's amazing love for them. They sat in their pews waiting patiently for the friar to arrive. There were no lights in the chapel and it had now grown dark.

Finally, he made his appearance and advanced up to the altar where there was a large crucifix. A candle was lighted. He never uttered a word as he moved toward the cross. The venerable man of God held out the candle close to the feet of the crucified Jesus. All could see the nail fastened to the feet of God's Son. In slow motion he moved the light up to the wounded side of the sacrificed One where the Roman soldier had thrust his spear. He held it there for several moments so that all could see it. Then in death-like quiet, the somber brother moved the taper up to the nail-pierced hands of the Savior–to the left hand and then to the right hand. From there he proceeded to move his flickering candle to the face of Jesus where he held it close to the bleeding head crowned with thorns. There the Franciscan stood, holding it steady while all reverently pondered what they were witnessing. "Amen," proclaimed the priest as he blew out the candle. The sermon on the love of God was ended. The people, profoundly moved, headed for home. Christ's death on the cross turned an ancient symbol of torture, suffering, and death into a symbol of life, hope, and love.

The tale has been told of a rebellious teenage daughter who seemed to delight in breaking her mother's heart. She was dabbling in drugs and alcohol, hanging out with bad company, careless and indifferent about her schooling, ignoring her mother's pleas and pain. It reached its zenith when the police called from the juvenile detention center to report that she had been arrested for drunk driving. The mother drove downtown, bailed out her daughter, and the two headed home in silence. No words were spoken until the next day when the mother handed her sullen child a small wrapped gift box. The girl nonchalantly opened the present and was exasperated by what she saw. There was nothing in the box but a small stone. She rolled her eyes and with a note of disgust she sighed, "So what's with this silly little rock?" Her mother replied, "Please read the card with it." She did, looked up, mother and daughter made eye contact, then a flood of tears burst forth. The card stated: "This rock is more than a million years old. That is how long it will take before I give up on you." Agape love. Unconditional love. A love that continues no matter what. It is God's love available for all but thrust on no one.

In 1830, George Wilson, an American traitor involved in several shootings, was sentenced to death. He was to be hanged. President Andrew Jackson, in an act of mercy, granted a formal pardon to Wilson. It was written and signed with the president's signature and imprinted with the presidential seal. A courier traveled to the federal penitentiary and hand-delivered the document to the warden. The jailer immediately made his way to the condemned man's cell. "I have wonderful news! The president of the United States has granted you a full pardon. Just sign your acceptance and you're a free man." However, in a decision that shocked the country, Wilson refused the pardon. Now what? It went back to the courts where Chief Justice John Marshall declared that a pardon was of no value if not accepted, therefore the original sentence would need to be carried out.

All of us, like George Wilson, find ourselves on death row as the Scriptures declare: "All have sinned... the wages of sin is death." It's utterly hopeless until Christ appears. He has paid the penalty; we are offered a pardon. It is not forced on anyone. We have a choice: we can accept the pardon and go free or reject it and remain a hopeless captive. If the pardon is accepted, then every day is lived in the awareness that it is Jesus' love for me that has set me free and by his grace I will strive to make the most of each day in a God-honoring way.

"God works for the good of those who love him..."

Romans 8:28

A Chinese parable tells of an old man who lived with his son in an abandoned fort. One night the elderly gentleman's horse, the only one he had, wandered away. His neighbors all came to say how sorry they were for the misfortune. He replied, "How do you know this is ill fortune?" A week later the horse came home, bringing with him a whole herd of wild horses. The neighbors came again, helped him capture the wild horses, and congratulated him on his good fortune.

As the days went on the sage's son began to ride the horses. One day he was thrown and wound up with a badly broken leg. The neighbors appeared once more to tell him how sorry they were for his bad luck but the man asked, "How do you know it is bad luck?" In less than a week along came a territorial warlord conscripting all the able-bodied young men for his private little army. The youth, however, with a broken leg, missed the draft. Soon his neighbors came to rejoice with him in his good luck. The story ends here but it obviously could go on some more. May it not be that the sorrow, heartache, or disappointment we suffer today will turn out to be a blessing tomorrow?

A ship was wrecked at sea. The lone survivor found himself on an uninhabited island. He was able to scrounge around for food to help him keep alive. After a while he managed to build a hut where he stored a few items that he had salvaged from the wreck. Every day he scanned the horizon for any ships that might be passing that way. One day he spotted a frigate, ran to the shore, frantically waving an orange blanket. But the vessel kept moving steadily away until it was out of sight.

Brokenhearted, the marooned sailor returned to his shack only to find his little dwelling in flames. In anguish both at the failure of the boat to see him and the destruction of his shed, he crumbled to the ground in utter despair and wept until he fell asleep. As he opened his eyes later, he discovered a frigate had dropped anchor off his little island. It was the same one that passed nearby the day before. Explained the captain, "We saw your smoke signal."

What may seem like defeat today could very well turn out tomorrow to be a divine incident in God's master plan. After all, He has promised that all things will work out for good to those who love Him (See Romans 8). Think of Joseph, whose story is found in the book of Genesis. As a teenager, he was sold by his jealous brothers into slavery. With intelligence and integrity, he served his owner, Potiphar, a wealthy businessman. He was falsely accused by the owner's wife of a crime he did not commit and was imprisoned for several years. He continued living a life of courage and virtue and eventually was freed from prison and became a prince in Egypt, second in power only to Pharaoh himself. His unbreakable faith and wisdom were used in such an extraordinary way that it was through his wise leadership that literally hundreds of thousands of lives were saved. When he was reunited with his brothers, he shook them to the core when he forgave them, declaring, "What you did you intended for evil but God intended it for good." And so often that is the case.

Or think of Good Friday. Jesus was betrayed, mocked, scourged, spit upon, and nailed to a cross to suffer and die. It certainly looked like the ultimate victory of evil. The very Son of God had been crucified, executed in the cruelest of ways. The cross was an instrument of punishment, hatred, and death. Then came Easter morning with the greatest news ever heard: "He is not here. He is risen!" The resurrection of Jesus represents eternal victory over death, our greatest enemy. The cross was forever transformed into a symbol of love, hope, and life.

In many cases, an explanation for ill fortune, heartache, or tragedy will show up in the morning, or in a week, a month, or a year and all things will be made clear to us. But there may be other times when we'll have to wait until we reach heaven's gates where the Lord himself will explain what it all meant. Suffice it to say that although there are times when the wrong seems oft so strong, God is the ruler yet. All that happens to us may not be good, of course, we all know that. Our God has never promised us that our lives would be a bed of roses but He has pledged to bring good out of every experience of life for all who love Him and He has assured us that He will never leave us or forsake us. He keeps His promises.

A young man was sent to Spain by his company to work in a new plant. He accepted the assignment because it would enable him to earn enough to marry his longtime sweetheart. Their plan was to pool their resources and put a down payment on a house when he returned. As the lonely weeks went by, she began expressing doubts that he was being true to her. After all, Spain is populated with many beautiful women. Her beloved declared that he was paying absolutely no attention to the local girls. "I admit," he wrote, "that sometimes I am tempted but I fight it. I'm keeping myself for you."

In the next mail her boyfriend received a package. It contained a note and a harmonica. "I'm sending this to you," his fiancée wrote, "so you can take your mind off these pretty girls." Her sweetheart wrote back that he was practicing on the mouth organ every night and thinking only of her. When the traveling suitor returned home to the states, the object of his affection was waiting at the airport. As he rushed forward to embrace her, she held up a restraining hand and stated firmly, "Hold on. First I want to hear you play that harmonica."

This may sound like a Valentine's Day story but it really is about lips and hearts. St. Paul wrote, "If you confess with your mouth that Jesus is Lord and believe in your hearts that God raised him from the dead you will be saved." Believe in our hearts and confess with our lips. What does it mean to confess and believe?

In World War II one of the boldest and most dramatic decisions in all naval warfare was made by Admiral Marc Mitscher in the Battle of the Philippine Sea. Late in the afternoon of June 20, 1944, Mitscher had dispatched a near nightfall bombing mission against the fleeing Japanese fleet. It was pitch dark when the first of the flyers began returning to their carriers. However, the fleet was under strict wartime blackout regulations, the pilot's fuel supplies were running dangerously low, and the carriers were nearly invisible.

Admiral Mitscher took a calculated risk. He ordered the blackout be ended and the lights turned on! One returning aviator described the scene this way, "It was a glorious sight–like a Hollywood premier, Chinese New Year, Fourth of July celebration all rolled into one." For two hours the planes, guided by the light, landed safely. Eighty pilots found their way home.

To a community where there still are many in spiritual darkness, we need to boldly dedicate ourselves to turning on the lights. If God is to be known in this country it will be because there are those whose light is shining as they are confessing with their lips and lives that Jesus is Lord. Our words don't have to be polished or eloquent. Only real and from the heart.

National president of the Fellowship of Christian Athletes, James Jeffries, was one of the most articulate and dynamic Christian inspirational speakers of his time. In many ways, his son, Neal, was a lot like his dad. He was a strongly built athlete, good-looking and deeply committed to Jesus.

But there was one respect in which Neal Jeffries was as different from his father as night and day. For while James was an exciting, charismatic public speaker, Neal was afflicted with a severe stutter. He was quite shy, although he was a thoughtful, wise, and intelligent young man. Surprisingly he was chosen to be one of the presenters at the FCA national convention. Over one thousand young athletes were in attendance as Neal stepped onto the platform and began to speak. Many in the audience didn't know about the young man's speech impediment and some of them thought his performance was a joke, part of a skit, so they started to laugh.

Neal, however, continued his testimony. It took him twenty minutes to say what most of us could have said in five minutes. Yet at the conclusion of his message something amazing happened. He offered an invitation to his listeners to delay no longer but to seize this hour and give their lives to Christ. From every corner of the room, inspired young people got out of the chairs and walked forward. Never had any FCA conference had such a powerful response. Neal certainly was not loqua-cious—far from it—but he was passionate and his passion stirred the souls of those whose lives would never be the same.

God doesn't call all of us to be eloquent. However, He calls all of us to let our lights shine.In Wauconda, Illinois (population 6,500) two large lighted crosses were placed on the top of the city water tower annually for over forty years. Sometime back the city council received the threat of a lawsuit if the crosses ever again appeared on the water tower. But the people decided that they had a right to put up whatever they wanted on their own property. So all over that little community lighted crosses sprang up. The small town had never dazzled like that before. The lights of Wauconda were visible from the interstate. The brightness could be viewed from 100 miles away! It was almost as bright as day in Wauconda, Illinois because the people decided to turn on the lights. If we profess with our lips that Jesus is Lord and believe it in our hearts we'll be turning on the lights.

> *"May the God of hope fill you*
> *with all joy and peace..."*
>
> Romans 15:13

One of the great pieces of music that help us celebrate our two most wonderful holy days, Christmas and Easter, is George Frederick Handel's magnificent work, *Messiah*. This amazing artist's life history is a living parable of the meaning of Christian hope. Handel, after some brief periods of popularity, had been reduced to a pauper with hardly a nickel to his name. It is reported that he felt so defeated that he would wander aimlessly along the darkened streets of London, convinced that he was without a friend in the world. To add to his despair, he suffered a partial stroke which impaired one entire side of his body. It was at this low time in his life that he was given a manuscript by a friend named Charles Jennens, who wanted Handel to compose a score for his new work. Somehow a spark was lit in this musical genius' heart. He worked feverishly and, in less than a month had produced that wondrous piece of music, *Messiah,* which has thrilled audiences for over three hundred years.

Hope is the message I want you to receive right now. Why? Because I suspect that even now someone can identify with Charlie Brown in the following tale which was taken from the Charles Schulz's *Peanuts* cartoon: Lucy is addressing Charlie Brown while standing with her hands on her hips and bellows, "You, Charlie Brown, are a foul ball in the line drive of life! You are the shadow of your own goal posts! You are a miscue! You are three putts on the 18th green! You are a 7/10 split in the tenth frame! You are a love-set! You have dropped a rod and reel in the lake of life! You are a missed free throw, a shanked nine iron and a called third strike! Do you understand? Have I made myself clear!?" Unfortunately, she has made herself very, very clear.

There comes a time when even the most confident and the most competent of us sense that our resources are not enough. There will certainly be those times when we discover that we are in desperate need of some kind of light or hope that seems so elusive. Sometimes it may even seem like evil is in command, but never lose sight of the truth: "Although the wrong seems oft so strong, God is the ruler yet." These are the words in Maltbie Babcock's hymn, "This Is My Father's World."

It is hard to believe that only six or seven generations ago, slavery was the accepted practice in much of our country. The battle to free this land from that evil scourge began long before the Civil War. It was dragged out and sometimes appeared to be a hopeless battle. During one particular period, an especially dark cloud hung over the entire movement to free slaves. There seemed to be no way of deliverance. Frederick Douglass, an African American writer and gifted orator of the abolitionist movement, was addressing a crowded meeting, vividly depicting the terrible condition. Everything was against his people. One political party had gone on record approving slavery; the other proposed not to abolish it but only to restrict it in some places. The Supreme Court had its say and declared that black people had no rights. Douglass drew a picture of his race writhing under the lash of the overseer, trampled upon by evil and vicious men. As he went on describing this utter hopelessness, a great horror of darkness appeared to settle upon his audience. Everything, every event that was happening, was not for good but for evil. It seemed as if the entire race was doomed.

Just at that instant, when the cloud was most heavy over the despairing crowd, there arose in the front seat an old black woman. Her name was Sojourner Truth. She had given herself that name. Far and wide she was known and respected as a women's rights activist and prophetess. Every eye was on her. Frederick Douglass paused in his oration. Reaching out toward him with a long bony finger, Sojourner Truth cried out, "Frederick, is God dead?" One historian has written that her words were a "lightening flash in the midst of oppressive darkness." The cloud began to break, and hope returned with the idea of a personal and loving God, a compassionate Father who will never leave us and has promised us a hopeful future. Martin Luther King, Jr. once said, "We must accept finite disappointment, but we must never lose infinite hope."

The story has been told of an Asian king who once owned a magnificent, nearly perfect diamond. It was the pride of his kingdom. Under mysterious circumstances, however it was damaged. Its beauty was marred by a long, hair-like scratch. The king was heartbroken and offered an enormous reward to anyone who would repair his diamond. No one came forward. The most skilled diamond cutter feared failure. Then an artist stepped forward. "The great flaw shall be its glory," he declared. He kept it in his possession for several weeks and then returned it to the king. The monarch held his breath as he unwrapped his precious stone. Perhaps the craftsman's efforts were such that now his gem was worthless. With great caution, he opened the package, and gasped. The engraver had turned the hair-like flaw into the stem of a rose. It was incredible, more beautiful that he could ever have imagined. That is the story of the cross. A symbol of evil, shame, and death transformed into a beacon of love, hope, and life. We join with George Handel in singing, "And he shall reign for ever and ever..."

"The time is short..."

I Corinthians 7:29

Business leaders from across the country were present as Dr. David Cowen, Director of the American Time Management Institute, began his presentation by placing a large jar next to the podium. With much care he inserted several big rocks into the container until it could hold no more. "Is it full now?" he asked those in attendance.

"Yes" was the most common response.

"Not yet," declared the presenter as he added a box full of pebbles. "Nothing more can be placed in the jar, right?"

The majority agreed with that conclusion.

The speaker smiled, shook his head, and poured a bucket full of sand into the mouth of the bottle. "This time we have certainly reached our limit, have we not?"

Of course, it had reached its capacity, they thought. Not so.

The time management expert poured a glass of water into the receptacle. Several times the bottle seemed to be full and yet he managed to add more. He then asked, "So what was the point of this demonstration?"

Several reported that the lesson they learned was that no matter how busy you may think you are it is possible to still fit in more.

"Wrong!" was the leader's resounding conclusion. "The point is this: unless all the big rocks go in first, they will never fit. So, what are your big rocks? For me, it is God, my marriage, and my children. If we don't manage our time someone will do it for us."

The following story appeared in *Newsweek* magazine. A sleeper dreamed that he came to an impressive building, something like a bank yet not a bank, because the brass marker advertised "Time for Sale." There he saw a pathetic sufferer, breathless and pale, painfully pull himself up the stairs like a victim of some dread disease. "My doctor told me I was five years too late in coming to see him," he told the teller. "I'll buy those five years now and save my life."

An older gentleman shuffled his way up to the clerk and explained, "When it was too late, I discovered that I had been given great natural gifts that I failed to develop and use. Sell me ten years so I can be the man I could have been."

Up the walkway came a distraught woman who declared, "My company manager told me that next month I can have a big promotion if I'm prepared to take it. But I'm not ready. I have not taken advantage of opportunities that were offered to me. I need to purchase two years of time in order to qualify for the job."

They continued to come–a steady procession. The ill, hopeless, despondent, worried, unhappy, they all left rejoicing, for each had what was desperately wanted—TIME.

Charles Spezzano, founder of Psychology of Vision, summarized the meaning of the dream in these words, "You don't really pay for things with money. You pay for them with time. In five years, you claim, 'I'll have enough put away to buy that dream vacation house. Then I'll slow down.' That means that cottage will cost you five years of your life. Translate the dollar value of your house, automobile, or anything else into time and then ask yourself if it's still worth it. That phrase spending your time is not a mere metaphor. It is how life works."

What follows is an ancient tale that never grows old and still speaks to us today. A certain lord kept a fool or jester in his house as many great men did in olden times for their amusement. This lord gave a staff to his fool and told him to keep it until he met a greater fool than himself, and if he ever met such a person, a greater fool, he should give him the staff. In the years that followed, the simpleton encountered many other dullards but in his heart of hearts he sensed that he had yet to meet a greater fool than himself.

One morning the fool came to see his lordship and was told that his master was very ill. Concerned, he asked, "Master, what is happening to you?"

"I'm soon going on a long journey," came the reply.

"When will you come back? Next month?"

"No," muttered the ruler, "I will never return."

His alarmed servant questioned, "What provisions have you made for your journey?"

The dying man answered, "None at all."

"You mean you are going away, never to return, and have made no provisions before your departure? No plans? Master, take my staff for I am not guilty of any such folly as you. Surely you are a greater fool than I am."

What time is it? One day closer to the last day. God help us all to make the most of the time.

> *"When you are tempted He*
> *will provide a way out..."*
>
> I Corinthians 10:13

I was a high school student taking an advanced math class. Mrs. Lisa Ball, soon to retire, was our teacher. Several of her students were masters at cheating. I watched how creative some of my classmates were in how they circumvented honesty. At times I found myself envious of them. Earl entered the classroom with his shoelaces untied. Sooner or later he would lift up his foot, presumably to tie his laces, but in fact this was a ruse to allow him to see the bottom of his shoes where his cheat notes were written. Willie always wore long sleeves, even on warm days, so he could slip answers under his cuffs. Then there were a couple whose names I've forgotten so I'll just call them Jack and Jill. Jack always sat behind Jill who had long, flowing hair. Hidden away on the back of her neck was a cheat sheet. It seemed as if most of the class was cheating, or so I thought. The pressure to do likewise was enormous.

So there I sat, ready for the final exam which would be worth half our term grade and my mind was an absolute blank. I could not seem to recall anything that I had studied. I was feeling desperate, thinking I had to pass this test. Guess what? Esther was sitting in front of me. She was the smartest girl in class and completed the test in less than twenty minutes. Then she lifted up that precious answer sheet to review what she had written. Wow! What a lucky break! I could see her paper. I wrote as fast as I could and with great relief had soon copied most of her answers. Now I rationalized–who is really going to be hurt by this? Nobody. The bright young lady will get an "A" whether I copy her paper or not. Actually, this would make Mrs. Ball look good. If I got a high grade it would be positive evidence that she was an effective teacher.

"When you finish your exam," Mrs. Ball instructed, "please bring it up front and place it on my desk." I had decided I'd wait a bit, not make it look too easy. Maybe I should also give a couple of wrong answers, I thought, just in case Mrs. Ball suspected anything. The minutes ticked by. I got out of my seat with my test papers in my hands, and walked up to the teacher's desk. She made eye contact; I hesitated, then dropped my exam sheets in the wastebasket and headed for the door. Mrs. Ball immediately called out my name and asked me to wait for a minute after the class was over.

Soon the classroom was empty. She made it clear: "Your exam in the wastebasket means you get a zero today." I nodded that I understood. Then she added, "I have been watching you," she started to smile, "and although you failed this written exam you just passed a much higher exam." She stood up, reached out, and squeezed my hand.

On sober reflection I recognize that I was about to break a lot of commandments. The first commandment–putting my self-interest above God's plan; the last commandment–coveting that which I had no right to have; and commandments in between–stealing, by taking that which I had not earned, and lying, by presenting someone else's work as my own. Each time we give in to temptation it makes us weaker and more vulnerable to the next enticement. Each time we resist it strengthens our spiritual muscles and prepares us to recognize and overcome the allure of the Tempter.

There is a P.S. that I want to include in my story. A week later I received my report card and was startled by the passing grade I had received from Mrs. Ball. I stopped by her office and said, pointing to my report card, "I don't understand this grade." She gently placed her hand on my shoulder. "I couldn't bring myself to flunk someone I'm so proud of. Accept it as a gift and bring something good out of it." I thanked her for this act of grace. It was one of those brief, perhaps defining moments of my life.

Generally, temptation slips up on us before we recognize the seriousness of it. Ah, we think, I can quit anytime I want to. If that is really true, then do it now. Right now! This minute! A Hollywood star of a previous generation, Lauren Bacall, described how she became romantically involved with Humphrey Bogart, a married co-star. They were in almost daily contact during the filming of several movies. Bacall recalled, "Bogie and I got to know each other really well and had lots of laughs and fun together. Our relationship got closer and stronger without our even knowing it." Her last comment is so telling: "without our even knowing it." Such is the powerful but oftentimes subtle and gradual pull of temptation. The church reformer, Martin Luther, is credited with the following quote: "Temptations, of course, cannot be avoided, but because we cannot prevent the birds from flying over our heads, there is no need that we should let them nest in our hair."

"The most excellent way…"

I Corinthians 12:31

One day, at a particularly quiet moment in the normally noisy newsroom where he worked, young H. L. Mencken shouted at the top of his lungs, "It's coming in the doors!" Needless to say, everyone stopped and looked in his direction. "It's up to the bottom of our desks!" he shouted as he leaped to his feet. "It's up to the seats of our chairs!" he screamed as he jumped unto his chair.

"What are you talking about?" asked one of his bewildered colleagues.

"It's up to the top of our desks!" hollered Mencken as he sprang on top of his desk. "What are you yelling about?" rang a chorus of shouts.

"MEDIOCRITY! We are drowning in mediocrity!" he bellowed over and over again, ran to the doors, made his exit, and never returned.

Mencken may not have been far off. We are drowning in a sea of mediocrity. Think of how really few role models there are for our young people. How many politicians can we truly admire without any reservations? We can flip through hundreds of channels on our TV and are fortunate if we are able to find something that is really good to watch. Mediocrity everywhere you look. That is why the words of St. Paul come as such sweet music to our ears: "I will show you a more excellent way." He shows us the way of love.

Love indeed is the answer to most of the problems we face. All persons want to love and need to be loved: the ninety-year-old and the newborn, men and women, boys and girls, black and white, prisoner and free, rich and poor, pretty and not-so-pretty. All need love. Life becomes unbearable for one who believes that he/she is not loved. Albert Schweitzer, one of the world's best known medical missionaries, was once asked to name the greatest person in the world. The good doctor replied, "The greatest person in the world is some unknown individual in some obscure corner of the earth who at this very hour has gone in love to another person in need."

I read of an ex-Marine in San Francisco who was exceedingly despondent and determined to end his life by jumping off the Golden Gate Bridge as scores of others have done. He was actually out heading toward the bridge when he was approached by a man walking his dog. The amiable fellow smiled and in a pleasant tone said, "Good evening, neighbor," and went his way. The would-be suicide victim later stated that a smile and a word from a stranger was enough to convince him that there yet may be hope and prevented him from making the fatal decision to end his life. The more excellent way, the way of love, is the way of kindness.

I suspect that is why the whole world has such respect for Mother Teresa. Steadfast in her belief that dying people deserved to be treated with dignity, she left the security of a comfortable teaching position and went into the streets of Kolkata looking for dying people. She dragged them into a deserted old temple that she had been given, cleaned, and put to use. There she loved and cared for terminally ill people. "Everybody at least deserves to have someone love them while they are dying." Some amazing things happened. Some of the terminally ill patients she took in even felt so much love that they received a surge of hope and stopped dying. Love is the only excellence that matters.

Karen was a member of Panther Creek Methodist Church in Morrisville, Tennessee and the mother of a three-year-old son, Michael. Like any good mother, when Karen discovered that a second baby was on the way, she did all she could to help the little fellow be prepared for the arrival of a sibling. Before long, he was told that he was going to have a baby sister. He asked if he could sing to his sister and every day he would get close to his mommy's tummy and sing to the unborn baby.

The day came when baby sister arrived, but there were major complications and she was in serious condition. The newborn was immediately transferred to the neonatal ICU in Knoxville. The days went by and the infant child grew weaker and weaker. The doctor declared, "There is very little hope. Prepare for the worst." Michael kept begging his parents to see his sister and sing to her. Another week went by, death seemed to be drawing near, but Michael kept hounding his Mom and Dad. He longed to sing to his sister, but, of course, children are never allowed to visit in the ICU. Finally, Karen made up her mind—she wrapped Michael up in a surgical gown and brought him in. He resembled a walking laundry bag. "Get that child out of here now!" the head nurse ordered. Karen, mild-mannered and somewhat shy, said defiantly, "He is not leaving until he sings to his sister."

Michael looked at his tiny sibling losing the battle to live and, in the pure-hearted voice of a three-year-old, he sang, "You are my sunshine..." Instantly the baby responded. Her pulse rate became calm and steady. KEEP ON SINGING, MICHAEL. "You never know dear, how much I love you..." Her strained breathing became as smooth as the purr of a kitten. KEEP ON SINGING, MICHAEL. "I dreamed I held you in my arms..." The infant relaxed, and healing rest seemed to sweep over her. KEEP ON SINGING, MICHAEL. The hard-nosed nurse started to cry, "Please don't take my sunshine away." Funeral plans were scrapped. The very next day, a healthy baby girl went home with her family. The stunned medical staff exclaimed they had witnessed a miracle. The apostle Paul wrote, "I will show you a more excellent way."

"If I have not love, I gain nothing."

I Corinthians 13:3

A few months ago a newspaper in a small town in Michigan was celebrating its golden anniversary, fifty years of publishing, by duplicating stories and advertisements from some of its early editions. There was much that was interesting and fascinating in the "personal ads." There was also that which was sobering and sad. A husband and wife ran an advertisement in which they offered to give all that they possessed for news leading to the recovery of their daughter, who had vanished. As proof of their good faith, they offered an inventory of all they owned. It was not a long list: a cottage home and furniture valued at $2,400, $334 in a bank account, the father's silver watch, and the mother's wedding ring. They would surrender all that they had for the restoration to the arms of their beloved daughter. For love no price was too great to pay, no sacrifice worth counting.

Scripture seldom tries to define love; instead, it shows us how it works. It points us to Jesus on the cross and cries out: "See the sacrifice. He has taken your place. That's love." Real love is modest and willing to serve. It is secure in the knowledge that it is involved in a relationship that will never end. A babysitter was working in a home where there were three small children. Teasingly, she asked the four-year-old girl which child her mother loved the most. The thoughtful little one responded in a beautiful way: "She loves Johnny the most because he was her first child. And she loves Jimmy the most because he was her last child. And she loves me the most because I'm the only girl." Wow! Now there is a young lady with a deep, profound understanding of love.

"Love," writes St. Paul in his first letter to the Corinthians, "rejoices in the right." It is sometimes amazing to see how children will blossom when there is someone there to share in their little victories. And there is a child in every heart, isn't there? It was said of a beloved old Scottish preacher at his death, "Now there is no one left in our town to appreciate and rejoice in the triumphs of ordinary folk." That tells us a whole lot about the effectiveness of that pastor's ministry. He was a lover rejoicing in the right. Love in its highest form is always self-sacrificing.

One of the most beautiful examples of such love took place in a hospital room. It seemed that a frail, six-year-old girl was about to have emergency surgery. She had a very rare type of blood and would need a donor. This crisis occurred over a half century ago when there was not a mechanism in place to locate on short notice the proper blood type. The only available source was that of her ten-year-old brother. He was asked if he would be willing to donate his blood to his sister. His eyes grew misty, his breathing came in sudden, anxious spurts. He relaxed a bit and said softly, "Yes."

Both children were brought into the operating room and the surgical process got underway. Afterwards the boy inquired, "Is my sister all right now?"

With a big smile on his face, the surgeon responded with a cheerful heart, "I'm quite certain that she is going to be just fine."

The boy pondered what he had just been told and asked, "Then why am I still alive?" "What do you mean? Why are you still alive? Did you think that you would be giving all your blood to your sister and that you would die?"

"Yes," he whispered.

The astonished physician stood there staring at his little patient's brother. He wiped a tear from his eye as he blurted out, "My Lord, I have never ever witnessed love like this."

"Death has been swallowed up in victory."

I Corinthians 15:54

Have you ever heard of Harry Houdini? He died in 1926. His claim to fame was that he was the world's greatest magician and escape artist. He laughed at locks and chains. It seemed as if there was nothing that could hold him. It was said that he was as slippery as an eel and had as many lives as a cat.

He would be sealed in coffins and somehow escape. He was placed in a boiler which was secured with rivets and he was able to slip out. They handcuffed him with ten pairs of handcuffs but—no problem—he was quickly free. Police locked him up in a maximum security cell. To their utter amazement, he was soon gone. They sewed him in a canvas bag. Somehow he broke out. Finally, in October of 1926, death laid its clammy hands on Harry Houdini and he could not escape.

He told his wife when he was talking about death, "If there is any way out I will find it. If there is any way out I will find you and make contact on the anniversary of my death." After Harry's death, his wife kept a light burning at the bottom of his portrait. After ten years she turned out the light. Houdini, the greatest escape artist the world has ever known, could find no escape from death.

Death laid its hands on Jesus Christ also. He was crucified, dead, and buried in a rock-hewn tomb. But on the third day he rose up from the dead. Grave clothes were left behind and he walked through the walls of the tomb. The grave was now empty. Our greatest enemy–death–had been conquered.

Remember the Easter story when Simon Peter entered the tomb and found the linen wrappings lying there and the face cloth which had been on Jesus' head, rolled up in a place by itself (read about it in the gospel of John, chapter 20).

What did Jesus do for an occupation before he started his public ministry? He was a carpenter. Brandon Park reminds us that carpenters had an interesting custom. When they would go to someone's home to build what was requested, they concluded the workday in the following manner: The craftsman took a towel, splashed some water over himself, and thus cleansed the sawdust off his hands and face. Following that, he took the towel, folded it in half, carefully folded it in half again. He then placed the towel on top of the finished piece, whether it be a table, chair, or cabinet. When the family got home they would see the newly finished project and the folded towel on top of the work. They recognized that the carpenter had left a silent signature–a reminder that the job was finished.

When Peter stepped inside that empty tomb and saw the face cloth of Jesus folded and laying by itself, he knew that Jesus was leaving a silent reminder that the job was finished. The penalty for our sins had been paid in full. Christ's resurrection means that we never need fear death again.

Danny Thomas tells the story of his father's last illness. His father realized that he was very near to the end of his life. One thing he wanted, above all else, was that his family should be with him at this time. They all responded to his call. He had a personal visit, a sacred time, with each of them. He asked that they all join hands and gather around his bedside. He slowly moved his head around the circle and his moist eyes made contact with theirs. Then Danny Thomas saw his father close his eyes and softly whisper a prayer, "God damn death."

Please don't get hung up on his use of a four-letter word. In the providence of God, the resurrection victory of Jesus is a response to that prayer. For in the cross, the burial, the stone that was rolled away, the empty tomb, the resurrection of our Lord—isn't that exactly what God has done? "Death is swallowed up in victory," shouts the apostle Paul. God has damned death.

My grandfather was engaged to my grandmother for seven years. They were married less than a year when she died. Her death came just a few days after giving birth to my father. My grandfather Paul wrote the following to me: "Your grandmother's sister, Louisa, was sitting on a chair near her bed. I was on the other side holding her hand. She earnestly spoke to her sister in a calm, clear voice seeking a promise from her that she would care for the baby. Her weeping sister made such a pledge. Then she turned her eyes toward me. A tear was rolling down her cheek—the only tear I ever saw her shed—as she softly spoke, 'I love you, Paul. Thank you for loving me.' She closed her eyes just as the doctor stepped in the room. He said, 'There she goes.' Suddenly the room was filled with light. I heard the distant sound of a trumpet and then a chorus of angels singing, 'Here she comes. Here she comes.' "

Death is swallowed up in victory. Robert Lowry, in 1874, wrote these inspiring words:

"Up from the grave he arose with a mighty triumph o'er his foes. He arose a victor from the dark domain and he lives forever with his saints to reign. He arose! He arose! Hallelujah! Christ arose!"

"Where, O Death, is your sting?"

I Corinthians 15:55

Larry Jones, former pastor of St. Michael's Lutheran Church in rural western Minnesota, was sitting at his desk struggling to come up with a powerful and memorable way to present the message of Easter to his little flock. Then he had an idea.

On Easter Sunday the service started with the choir processing down the center aisle joyously singing, "Christ the Lord is risen today!" They had just finished when the minister started walking down the aisle wearing a rubber apron over his robe and carrying in his arms a lamb that could not have been more than five or six weeks old. The sanctuary was filled to overflowing with people wearing curious smiles on their faces, wondering what he was up to now. He reached the altar, stripped it clean, and carefully placed a water basin in the center. He then reached under the altar and drew out a huge knife. He placed the lamb in the basin and pushed back the lamb's neck. He raised the knife as if in preparation to slice open the little lamb's throat. Parishioners gasped, parents covered the eyes of little children. Someone cried out, "No! Don't do it!" He held his position for a long time then slowly put the knife away as a collective sigh went up from the congregation. The preacher cradled the lamb in his arms, smiled, and stated, "Aren't you glad we don't have to do this anymore?"

Twenty centuries have passed since lambs were brought to the house of worship to be slaughtered in the belief that in so doing, an angry God would forgive their sins. Two thousand years ago the Lamb of God was slaughtered on our behalf. And on that most beautiful of mornings God said, "No more." No more slaughter and death. The ultimate price has been paid. Aren't you glad we don't have to do this ever again?

One of the most fascinating stories that I remember from my European history class was the tale of how the word of Wellington's victory over Napoleon reached England. News of the history-making battle came by sailing vessel to the south coast and by semaphore wig-wagged overland to London. Atop Winchester Cathedral the flag code started to spell out the eagerly awaited dispatch: W-E-L-L-I-N-G-T-O-N D-E-F-E-A-T-E-D... Then a dense fog came rolling in and settled over the land. The semaphore could no longer be seen and the sad, heartbreaking report swept the city. The entire English nation was plunged into gloom and despair. Wellington defeated!

But eventually the fog lifted and again the signals became visible, spelling out the complete message: "Wellington defeated the ENEMY!" Now the tidings were all the more glorious because of the preceding gloom. Like wildfire, the joyous word spread across the nation–Wellington defeated the enemy.

On that first Good Friday, the sinless Son of God willingly gave himself for the sins of the whole world. Jesus hanging on the cruel cross cried out, "Father, forgive them...into your hands I commit my spirit," and He died. To anyone who was there, Calvary meant one thing– Jesus defeated. But Sunday was coming and the stone was rolled from the tomb as angels announced, "He is not here. He is risen!" Jesus won, death defeated.

A father and his young son were traveling down a country road on an afternoon in spring when suddenly a bee flew in through an open window. The child was deathly allergic to bee stings and cried out in panic and fear as the bee buzzed around inside their Toyota. Seeing the horror on his boy's face, the father reached out and caught the bee in his bare hand and kept his fist clenched. Slowly he opened his hand and once again the bee began to buzz its menacing sounds. The terrified little fellow started to cry. The father answered in a soothing tone, "The bee can't harm you. It no longer has a stinger. See? The stinger is in Daddy's hand. It cannot hurt you." The empty tomb is our Father's way of saying to us, "Peace, my child. I have removed the sting of death. It cannot hurt you."

> *"God comforts us so that we
> can comfort others..."*
>
> II Corinthians 1:4

Cheepie the parakeet never saw it coming. One second he was peacefully perched in his cage, then suddenly he was sucked in, washed up, and blown over. The problem started when Cheepie's owner decided to clean the tiny bird's cage with a vacuum cleaner. She removed the attachment from the end of the hose and stuck it in the little feathered friend's cage. The phone rang, so she turned to pick it up. She barely said hello when–swoop– Cheepie got sucked in. His owner gasped, put down the phone, turned off the vacuum, and opened the bag. The poor battered creature was still alive but stunned.

Since he was covered in dust and soot, she grabbed him and raced to the bathroom, turned on the faucet, and held the pathetic songbird under the running water. Then, realizing that he was soaked and shivering, she did what any sympathetic pet owner would do: she grabbed her hair dryer and blasted the diminutive critter with hot air. Poor Cheepie never knew what hit him.

A few days after the harrowing experience, the reporter who had initially written about the trauma contacted Cheepie's owner to see how the parakeet was recovering. "Well," she replied, "Cheepie doesn't sing much anymore. He just sits and stares." It is not hard to see why. Sucked in, washed up, blown over–that is enough to steal the song from anyone's heart.

Having the song taken out of our hearts because of a sudden trial can leave us identifying with Cheepie. It may leave us just sitting and staring into space. But it is during or after such troubling times that we are most able to help those around us who are hurting, struggling, or in need of a compassionate listener. America's most beloved president, Abraham Lincoln, expressed a wonderful truth in these words: "To ease another's heartache is to forget one's own."

Six young athletes were slated to compete against each other in the 100-yard dash in Seattle, Washington. They eagerly awaited the sound of the starter's pistol and then took off running as fast as they could. At about the halfway point, the leading runner stumbled and fell, scraping some skin off his knees. The other five sprinters all stopped, helped him up, brushed him off, made sure that he was OK, joined hands, and finished the race together in a dead heat.

None of the judges could tell which finisher won the blue ribbon; their tears blurred their vision. No one who was present that day ever forgot the demonstration of compassion. The crowd stood and cheered for a full ten minutes. These young men were competing in the

Special Olympics and showed the world that they cared more for a fallen comrade than winning a race. There is more to living the Christian life than running the race and finishing it. Sometimes it's very Christ-like to stop along the way and help someone who has fallen.

Ludwig van Beethoven, world famous composer, was not known for his social graces. Because of his deafness, he found conversation difficult. However, one day he received word of the tragic death of a friend's son. Filled with grief, he hurried to the house. He had no words of comfort to offer but he saw a piano in the room. For the next half hour this great musician sat there pouring out his heart in the most eloquent way that he could. He finished playing, hugged his friend, and made his exit. With a voice filled with emotion, the deceased's father remarked that no one else's visit had meant so much.

"The Spirit who calls out, 'Abba, Father.'"

Galatians 4:6

A teacher was telling the story of Jonah to her first grade Vacation Bible School class. She then led them in a discussion about how they would manage to escape if they were swallowed like Jonah. "I'd start a fire in the big fish's stomach and he'd cough me out," announced an exuberant student, perhaps remembering the scene from Pinocchio. "I'd stomp on his tongue until he might spit me out," responded a toughie wearing a Superman shirt. The suggestions grew wilder by the minute. Then a thoughtful little girl spoke up, "I'd call my daddy and wait till he got me out!" Now there is a blessed young lady. She has learned to trust her father.

It is not easy being a good father nor is it a piece of cake to be a good mother. Every home from time to time has tensions. Two explorers in central Africa were comparing their stories. "I am a man of action," declared the bearded adventurer. "Modern life was too stuffy and predictable for me. I wanted to experience new excitement, horizons and dangers. I craved to see nature in the raw. That's why I came out here. What about you?"

"I came," quietly stated his companion, "because my son is taking saxophone lessons."

Family life always has its tensions even in the best of homes. Every Christian father's constant prayer is that their children will catch a glimpse of the Heavenly Father through their earthly father. A dad had promised to take his two young sons to the circus. The anticipation and excitement was almost more than they could bear. The day had arrived; it was going to be so much fun, maybe even the best day of their young lives. Then the phone rang. It was an important business call. Dad was asked to come to work on his day off as his expertise was needed. His boys were on the verge of tears as they braced themselves for bitter disappointment. Then the startled children heard Dad say, "I'm sorry. It will not be possible for me to come in this morning."

When he came back to the breakfast table, his wife was smiling. "Ben, the circus will be coming back, you know."

"Yes, I know that, but childhood doesn't." Daddies are entrusted with the task of making memories for their children.

Poet John Greenleaf Whittier wrote, "For all the sad words of tongue or pen, the saddest are these: 'It might have been.' " Now is the time to demonstrate love, because tomorrow the baby won't be rocked, the toddler won't be asking why, the child won't need help with schoolwork, teenagers won't be wanting your counsel. The time to give time is today. Susanna Wesley, mother of nineteen children, most of whom lived wonderful

Christian lives, somehow or other managed to spend one hour a week with each individual child. She stated simply, "You can't express love without spending time."

No amount of professional success can compensate for failure in the home. Robert Leroe remembers years ago, when his children were quite young, his son asked him to read a story from a book which was too long to read in one sitting. After completing two chapters, he put the book down and stated, "Well, maybe later we can find out what happens." Then he heard a soft voice, "Mom already read me the whole story twice." What did the child really want? To hear a story repeated or to spend some time with his dad? Kids crave and deserve our time. It has been said before but we'll say it again: love is often spelled T-I-M-E.

Such a dad would surely have the respect of his children. Craig Wilson was from such a home. At age eleven he went to visit his cousin in another city. He became acquainted with boys in the neighborhood and spent a lot of time playing with them. One day his new friends planned to do something that his father taught him not to do. He shook his head indicating that he would not be participating in this questionable activity. One of the tough guys taunted him, "What's the matter? Are you afraid?"

"Yes, I'm afraid of my dad."

"Hey, don't worry about your old man. He's miles away and he'll never know about it."

"I know that but he trusts me and I don't want to do anything that will disappoint him or hurt him."

Nobody said another word. They were probably condemned that they didn't have that type of relationship with their own father.

John Drescher, author, husband, father of five children, and now a senior citizen, wrote a book which he titled *If I Were Starting My Family Again*. In the first chapter, he notes that he would love his wife more. He elaborated: "I would be more free to let my children know how much I loved their mother. For example: I would whisper loving words about her in the ears of my children. I would say complimentary things about her in public. I would better realize that nothing gives a child a greater sense of joy and security as seeing parents loving each other."

In the following chapter he added: "I would laugh more with my children. I would be on the lookout for humor in experiences that we shared. Homes seldom crumble where laughter is common. I would listen more. I would strive to refrain from using words of impatience and I would be quicker to offer words of praise and encouragement." This author would add: "I would thank God for them in my prayers, prayers that were prayed in their presence."

"Your love for all the saints..."

Ephesians 1:15

A decade ago a group of Christians from the U.S. visited war-torn Nicaragua. While there, a young man in the group was killed by terrorists. This left the team confused and full of questions. On the next Sunday a memorial service was held. During the celebration of Holy Communion the congregation was silent. Then someone called out a name. In one voice all responded, "Presente!" Another name was loudly proclaimed. Once again everyone chimed in, "Presente!" At least twenty names were shouted out and each time "Presente!" echoed through the church. Finally it dawned on Ron DelPene, the pastor leading the group, that all the names were those of persons who had died. From that moment on, he joyfully joined in crying out "Presente!"

"Presente!" is used by schoolchildren to answer roll call. At the Lord's Table, "Presente" means "present with us." Shouting "Presente!" in this service was a way of proclaiming the reality of the communion of saints. Although all those persons named were deceased, their presence and influence was still felt.

I received an invitation to be guest speaker at a congregation in downtown Cleveland, Ohio. It was one of the oldest churches in the state. The banquet, at which I was asked to give an inspirational address, was held in the church's basement. I noticed as I reached the lectern that I was standing on a slab of stone that was quite different from the rest of the floor around it. Later on I asked about that unusual floor marker. I was told that it was the grave of the founding pastor. I was stunned. Then I reflected–in a sense isn't that what we are always doing in the church? We are standing on the shoulders of those faithful saints who have paved the way for us.

Pastor Matt Smuts told me of a widow in his congregation who for over fifty years had been married to a medical doctor. He was a wonderful man of God who had taught Sunday school for decades. After her husband died, his wife was usually the first one present on Sunday mornings. She would often come a half hour early and sit quietly in her usual place in the sanctuary. One Lord's Day the preacher stopped, smiled, and asked her why she was always such an early bird. "Well, Pastor," she softly replied, "I like to sit here for a few minutes before the service with Doc, the way we used to."

Was she some kind of neurotic, grieving woman? Of course not. We know what she meant and she was right. Love is eternal and we are never closer to our departed loved ones than when we're in the presence of Jesus. I think of the saints that have preceded me, "that blessed communion who now in glory shine..." and I see joyous faces. I hear again well-remembered voices. I recall the things they said in a spirit of love and are still echoing today. I see the glowing faces of those whose victory is won.

Nicolas Berdyaev in his book, *The Destiny of Man*, wrote these thoughtful and memorable words: "Our attitude toward all people would be more Christ-like if we regarded them as though they were dying and determined our relation to them in the light of their death and our own. A person who is dying calls forth a special sort of feeling. Our attitude to them is at once softened and lifted to a higher place. We then can feel compassion for people whom we do not even love. But, every person is dying. We are terminal cases from the moment of birth. I, too, am dying and dare not forget about death but remember that I am daily preparing for eternal life."

An ancient manuscript has been found that was written to a colleague by a Roman citizen who lived in the first century. He shared with his friend about a new religion that was having extraordinary success in the ancient world. Here is an excerpt from that letter: "If any righteous man among the followers of Jesus passes from this world, they rejoice and offer thanks to God as they escort his body with songs and thanksgiving, as if he were setting off from one place and going to a better place nearby." Oh yes, yes, yes. Amen to that.

"Fathers, do not exasperate your children..."

Ephesians 6:4

A fourteen-year-old girl, her eyes filled with tears, asked if she could speak to her pastor for a few minutes. The minister nodded as they headed for the privacy of his office. They were barely seated when she started to cry. After gaining some composure, she blurted out the pain that she felt in her heart. Her mother had asked her to take the fresh laundry out of the dryer, fold what needed to be folded, and then put it all away in its proper dresser drawer. She was placing socks and underwear in her father's chest of drawers when she stumbled upon some hidden pornography. The distraught counselee described it as shocking and revolting. The tears continued to come as she declared, "I look at my dad now and the respect is all gone."

A week passed and another young teenage girl asked for an appointment with the same pastor. She commented that her friend had told her about the pornography that her father had tried to conceal in his clothes drawer. This led her to do something really foolish when she got home. She waited until she was certain that no one was in the house and then went into her parents' bedroom and started rummaging through all her father's personal belongings to see if she could find any incriminating items. At this point in her story her eyes brimmed with tears.

"I discovered a journal, a book like a diary, tucked away behind his pajamas. My heart seemed to skip a beat. I opened it. On nearly every page he had thanked God for his children, listing us by name, and prayed that he would be a wise and godly father." The young lady burst into tears. Blessed tears of joy.

I have in my office a copy of a Norman Rockwell painting. In my estimation, it is a classic. Mother, son, and daughter are dressed in Sunday best as they leave the house to attend worship services. Dad is wearing his pajamas and bathrobe, sitting in his favorite chair, reading the extra thick newspaper. I'm afraid that if we did a follow-up on this Rockwell masterpiece it would be of Mom going to church by herself. It is almost impossible to overestimate a father's influence upon his children, for better or for worse.

Samuel Coleridge, the gifted English poet of two centuries ago, exhibited his God-given wisdom in the following manner: He was having an interesting conversation with a gentleman who stated flatly that he did not believe in giving his children any religious instruction. His theory was that the young child's mind should not be prejudiced in any direction. It is not unlike what many of us continue to hear today: "Wait until children get older and then let them decide if they want some religion to be part of their lives."

Coleridge didn't say anything at the time but later on asked his friend if he would like to see his garden. His visitor responded in the affirmative. He opened the gate and into the backyard they went. Nothing was growing there except weeds. The astonished guest looked at Coleridge with a confused expression. "This is not a garden. This is merely a field of weeds."

"Well, you see," answered his host, "I certainly did not want to infringe on the liberty of the garden in any way. I wanted to give the garden a chance to express itself and choose its own production."

How this relates to the raising of children should be obvious to all.

A young father, Larry Edwards, found himself with too many commitments in too few days. It seemed like he was always in a hurry. After dinner one evening, his five-year-old daughter wanted to tell her daddy about something important that happened to her at school. She began in a big hurry, "I want to tell you something and I'll say it really fast." Realizing her frustration, Larry assured her that she didn't have to tell him really fast. She could say it slowly. The little girl's dad said that he will never forget her response: "Then listen slowly." Dad, Mom, all the rest of us: that is powerful advice.

> *"But in humility consider others*
> *better than yourselves."*
>
> Philippians 2:3

Samuel Morris, a young man from Liberia, Africa, had become a Christian and came to this country where he enrolled in seminary with the intention of becoming an ordained pastor. The president was the one responsible for making room assignments for all incoming students. So when President Reade asked Morris if he had a preference for a room he replied, "If there is a room no one else wants please give that one to me." Reade was startled by that answer. He stated later that he had assigned rooms to over one thousand young men, all fine Christians, but Samuel Morris was the first and only one who ever responded that way.

Humility is one of the most forgotten and yet among the greatest of all virtues. It is often misunderstood. It is not groveling in the dust or beating oneself over the head while crying out, "I am nothing." Humility is best seen in Jesus Christ, who humbled himself and became obedient, even to death on the cross.

Humility is hard to attain. The moment we think it is ours, it is gone. Did you hear of the coed who was given a gold pin for being the most humble student on campus? It was taken away the next day because she wore it. Furthermore, have you ever thought about the fact that only the smallest birds sing? You've never heard a note from an eagle, turkey or ostrich. But you have enjoyed the melodious sounds of the parakeet, canary, and the cockatiel. The sweetest music comes from Christians who are small in their own eyes.

The story has been told about the funeral of Charlemagne, one of the greatest of all Western European rulers. The mighty funeral procession came to the cathedral, only to have the gate barred by the bishop, a representative of God. "Who comes?" shouted the bishop.

The proud escorts answered, "Charlemagne, Lord and King of the Holy Roman Empire!" The bishop replied, "I don't know him. Who comes?"

The heralds, a bit shaken, replied, "Charles the Great, a good and honest man."

Again, the bishop answered, "I don't know him. Who comes?"

Now completely crushed, the chastened guards replied, "Charles, a sinner who trusts in Jesus Christ as Lord."

The bishop answered, "Ah, him I know. Enter in."

Humility is a very elusive virtue. It has been said that we have yet to see the amount of good that could be accomplished if we just went about doing it, not caring who got credit for the fine things that were done. C.S. Lewis once said, "True humility is not thinking less of yourself; it is thinking of yourself less."

Art Kolsti, pastor of Pilgrim Church in Massachu-setts, was an eyewitness to the following scene which took place in a veteran's hospital near his city. The pa-tients in the ward were men without arms and legs, veterans with bodies forever broken. Every now and then celebrities visited this sector of the institution. It was good public relations. The announcement over the loudspeaker informed them that the visitor on this par-ticular day would be a clergyman, a bishop. Someone murmured, "Guess what guys? Rev. Celebrity will be here today. Wanna bet he tells us to keep our chin up?"

The bishop came later that day. He quietly went from bed to bed and didn't offer any trite cliches or sug-gest unlikely achievements to the hopelessly disabled. He remembered not to try to shake hands with an arm-less man. Then someone said, "Hey, padre, how about a speech?" So he spoke. It was a good sermon, graphic and sincere. But with the added sense that every good speaker has, the bishop knew they were listening just because they were a captive audience. But he went on with passion, sharing the good news about Jesus the wounded, Jesus the crucified. He explained then how God identifies with each one of them. Again, he was aware that they were listening because they had no other choice. A bed is a bed and they couldn't get up. Before leaving, the man of God prayed a prayer from the heart but he recognized that as far as they were concerned, it was just another visit.

As he was leaving, he passed the door and then sud-denly walked back as if he'd forgotten something. The fact is, he had remembered something. He stood before the men and began to disrobe. That's right—the bishop started undressing. Off came his coat and tie, falling to the floor. He peeled off his shirt and undershirt. The patients were spellbound, for they saw how painful each motion was. Then he took off his shoes, socks, and trousers. And everyone saw plainly that each part of his maimed and deformed body was strapped together by an intricate system of braces, pulleys, and wires. He stood there for a moment and with painstaking care turned around. Then, with great effort, he managed to put his clothes back on. There was absolute total silence throughout the ward—a deep sense of kinship. He then raised his hand in blessing and left. A powerful reminder of the God who comes among us.

He was one of the greatest soldiers of his era. He lived at a time when his country needed great soldiers. Yet his past so discouraged him that he almost never became the leader that his country needed. Hiram was born to a father who was harsh and cold and often reminded him how weak and puny he was while shaking his head from side to side and murmuring, "Failure, failure." His mother was not a source of emotional comfort for him either; she was cold, reserved, and seldom smiled. He was always small for his age and grew up sad and ashamed that he was not the leader his father expected him to be.

At seventeen he was pushed by his parents into the U.S. Military Academy. Hiram was 5'1" and tipped the scales at 120 pounds. He hated the school and lived in constant fear that he would flunk out. But he dared not buck his father's decision. In fact, when the academy listed his name incorrectly, the young soldier was too timid even to get the wrong righted. He went through the rest of his life with the error uncorrected.

Through a mighty effort he managed to graduate, albeit in the bottom half of his class. After marrying and attaining the rank of captain, he left the military and tried several civilian jobs. The Civil War was looming so he decided to reenlist. Initially he struggled to even find someone who would interview him. At last, word came that more officers were needed for the war effort and the rest is history. The diminutive man labeled by his father as a failure was named Hiram Ulysses Grant, leader of the victorious Union Army and later president of the United States.

Yogi Berra was right: "It ain't over till it's over." There are far too many people resigned to live as failures, as rejects, as disappointments to themselves, to their families, and perhaps to God. It need not be that way! It is not too late to make a new beginning. God has a marvelous plan for each of us.

Did you hear about the man whose death was erroneously reported in the obituary column of a local newspaper? Much enraged, he called the editor and told him in the words of Mark Twain that the news of his death "had been greatly exaggerated." He insisted that a retraction be published the very next day. The editor replied, "I'm sorry but it is the long-standing policy of The Gazette to never retract something that we have published. But I tell you what I will do. Tomorrow I'll print your name in the list of new births so you can start all over again."

St. Paul wrote, "But one thing I do, forgetting what lies behind and straining forward to what lies ahead I press on toward the goal for the prize of the upward call of God in Christ Jesus." Our initial clue is found in the first phrase: "But one thing I do..." Not many things, but one thing! If you and I were to hire a consultant to look into our lives and advise us how our life can be more God-pleasing and productive, what he might say to us is: "You are trying to do too many things at once." The Quakers have a saying for those of us who spread ourselves too thin, "You cannot be crucified on every cross."

In her book *A Practical Guide to Prayer*, Dorothy Haskin writes about a noted concert violinist who was asked the secret of her mastery of the violin. The artist answered the question with two words: "Planned neglect." Then she explained, "There are many things that used to demand my time. When I went to my room after breakfast, I made my bed, cleaned my room, vacuumed and did whatever I could to make it spic and span. When I had finished everything, then I turned to my violin. This daily pattern prevented me from accomplishing what I should on the violin. So I changed several things. I deliberately planned to neglect everything else until my practice period was complete. That program of planned neglect is the secret to my life. You can't do everything." Most of us need to focus on the few things that really matter and forget about the rest.

It is amazing how much better life works when we are focused. Dr. David Yonggi Cho, a Christian pastor in Korea, shared a story about a man who walked for four days to reach a mission station. There he recited without a mistake the entire Sermon on the Mount. The missionary was delighted but felt compelled to warn the man that just memorizing the Scripture was not enough; it was necessary to practice the words and not only commit them to memory. The man's face lit up with a happy smile. "That is the way I learned it. I tried to simply memorize the words but they wouldn't stick so I hit upon a plan: I would learn a verse and quickly do what it said. Then I discovered it would stick." So we remember these words: "But one thing I do..."

"Children, obey your parents in everything..."

Colossians 3:20

His name was Ben. He grew up in a poor section of Detroit. His mother married his father when she was only thirteen years old. The marriage didn't last, and soon Sonya Copeland Carson found herself struggling as a single mother with two young sons. She took on two, sometimes even three, cleaning jobs to support her family.

Ben wanted almost more than anything to fit in with the other kids. One year, silk Italian shirts were the popular items at school. Ben pleaded with his mother to buy him one of these cool shirts, so she made him a deal: for one week he would be in charge of the family finances. She would turn over to him all the money and every bill. Once he paid off the necessities, he could keep the leftover money for himself and buy whatever he wanted. He had never been more excited in all his life. He had a vision of Benjamin Solomon attired in garb that would be so impressive to his peers. But he learned at the end of the week that there was no money left over. Not a cent. Zero.

As he reflected back on that day he learned such respect for his mother. Ben, who had never been a motivated student, went from a self-described "dumbest student in the class" to one of the very best students. Why? He was determined to do everything in his power to make this special lady proud of him. Sonya had high expectations for her sons. She expected them to be obedient and to give their very best. She was the most powerful example in Ben's life and led him to believe he could "go anywhere in the world, be anybody, do anything..."

Ben is now known as Dr. Ben Carson, one of the world's leading neurosurgeons, a powerful man of God and, as I write this, a candidate for president of the United States. His mother, devout follower of Jesus Christ, passed along the following advice for all parents: "Pray for your children, give them unconditional love, encourage them and teach them to obey."

One Sunday morning in June, I was at worship and listening as Pastor Greg Hoffmann was preaching. He told a story about a mischievous little girl who seldom obeyed her parents. But they never really demanded obedience, and even smiled at some of her stubborn defiance, thinking her actions were cute. They seemed to find some sort of satisfaction in referring to her as a "free spirit."

The day came when the preschooler managed to open the front gate and headed in the direction of a busy boulevard. Her terrified parents screamed at her to stop. She turned, hesitated for a moment, laughed, and ran ahead. The child was struck by an SUV as she darted into the roadway. There she lay, critically injured.

It never should have happened. "Parents," St. Paul admonished us in his letter to the Ephesians, "teach your children to obey."

For whatever reason I was thinking about that sermon while spending my usual Thursday afternoon visit with Andrew, my two-and-a-half-year-old grandson. We had been playing games in the Sabre Springs Park— swings, slides, sandbox, all were there for us to enjoy. We were on our way home when we saw a rabbit scurry by and into the bushes. "Grandpa, where did he go?" I responded, "I guess he went home. He must live near here." Now the little fellow's curiosity had been aroused. "Let's see if we can find his house." So we left the sidewalk and started up the side of the brush-covered hill. He was excited and trotting along four or five steps in front of me. Then, by the grace of God, I heard the rattle. There in front of us was a diamondback rattlesnake, coiled and ready to strike. Little Andrew, of course, had no reason to be afraid. I shouted, "Andrew! Stop! Bad snake!" He halted in his tracks, put his hands in the air and, now frightened, ran back to me. I picked up that precious little person and slowly backed away as we watched the rattler slither into the weeds. While hugging him, I thanked the Lord that my grandson was from a home where his parents had taught him to obey.

Dr. Joyce Brothers, well-known psychologist and columnist, wrote articles for *Good Housekeeping* magazine for over forty years. I have in my files an article that she wrote about children's behavior and the importance of being taught to obey. Dr. Brothers participated in a study involving almost 2,000 fifth graders. Some were raised by strict parents, while others were growing up in permissive homes. The investigation produced some surprising results: The children who had been taught to obey were most often high achievers, had healthy self-esteem, and were socially well adjusted. They were happier and far more content than the undisciplined young people. Furthermore, they loved and respected the adults who made and enforced the rules they lived by. I'll add this to Joyce Brothers' treatise: Parents, discipline and encouragement should come in equal parts.

"Give thanks in all circumstances..."

I Thessalonians 5:18

There is an Israeli folktale about a Persian king named Shah Abbas the Great who wanted to truly know his people. At night he would often dress himself as a monk and visit the poor section of town to better understand how the peasants lived. One day the disguised monarch came to a simple hut where he met a cobbler. The cobbler was barely able to support himself but praised God from the depths of his heart every morning. The Shah was impressed but then did something strange: he passed a law announcing that no one could repair shoes without a very costly permit. Since the cobbler could no longer afford to earn his way, he started drawing water and delivering it to his neighbors. He prayed, "Blessed be God, day by day."

A short time later, the king decreed that no one could draw water. Then he returned that night–still in disguise–for a visit with the ever-grateful commoner. "Blessed be God, day by day," was how the ruler was welcomed. That day the ex-cobbler had chopped wood in exchange for his daily bread.

Early the next morning, the sovereign ordered all wood choppers to join the king's guard and each was given a shiny steel sword. But now the commoner had no money to buy food, so he sold his steel sword and made himself a sword out of wood. He kept it in his sheath so no one would know. That night the camouflaged emperor paid another visit to the godly serf who told him what he had done. His astonished guest responded, "But what if there is a call for a weapon inspection?" His host shrugged his shoulders and declared, "Blessed be God, day by day."

Shortly after sunrise, the captain ordered the cobbler to execute a prisoner. The poor soul had never harmed another person and couldn't do it now. He grasped the handle of his sheathed sword and boldly proclaimed, "Almighty God, it is known to you that I am not a murderer. If this captive is guilty, let my sword be steel but if he is innocent let the blade be turned to wood." He pulled his wooden sword from his scabbard and displayed it before the amazed guards. Shah Abbas hugged the humble shoe repair subject and explained to him his deception of the past few nights. Then he named him to be the chief court advisor and in a joyous tone proclaimed, "Blessed be God, day by day."

Have you noticed that true thankfulness has little to do with one's circumstances? Gratitude—or lack of it—reveals more about a person's character than just about anything else. During World War II, a young man was drafted into the U.S. military and was stationed at an army camp near the Mojave Desert. His bride of a few months went to live there to be near her husband. He was gone most of the time and the newly transplanted wife soon grew to hate just about everything in her surroundings.

She was renting a miserable little shack; the temperature some days neared 120 degrees. She had no friends and her closest neighbors were Spanish-speaking people with whom she could not communicate. She complained the hot wind never ceased from blowing. There was sand in her clothes, her hair, and her food. She finally got so fed up she wrote her parents stating that she couldn't stand it anymore; she would rather be in prison. Her father answered her letter with just two lines: "Two men looked out from prison bars, one saw the mud, the other saw the stars."

She felt ashamed of herself. She resolved to look for what was good about her situation. She became friendly with her neighbors who responded in kind. She took an interest in cactus plants and shrubs. She even made an effort to learn all she could about prairie dogs. She discovered how beautiful desert sunsets could be. What happened? Her environment had not changed, but she had. Christ in us enables us to see the "stars" no matter what our circumstances may be.

"Godliness with contentment is great gain."

I Timothy 6:6

Some 350 years before the time of Christ, a man later known as Alexander the Great was born. At age fourteen he complained that his father, Philip of Macedonia, had accomplished so much that there was nothing left for him to do. He decided at age twenty to conquer the world. By the time he reached thirty he had fulfilled all his dreams and ruled the civilized world. It is said at that point that the "King of the Universe" sat down and wept because there apparently were no more worlds to conquer.

Our society is filled with Alexanders. Competent, innovative, hard-working people who set out goals, convinced that once they realize these dreams they will attain happiness. And so they get the promotion they were yearning for, they purchase their dream home, there is even a new bass boat in dry dock. They now have in their possession all they have hoped for and sought after and yet find themselves frustrated and empty.

Then there is the Hollywood actress who has more money than she knows what to do with. The beauty queen is covered with make-up, flaunting her extravagant wardrobe and her diamond jewelry. A smile is pasted on her face as she attends the Academy Awards escorted by her fourth husband. In her heart remains the haunting question: "Am I truly happy now?" Or the well-known CEO with a garage full of exotic autos, a multimillion dollar beachfront villa, and his own Learjet. Now are you content?

How about the guy sitting next to you in the barber shop? You know he has a hectic work schedule–literally two jobs–in order to vacation in Hawaii, pay his country club dues, and make payments on his house with a view. I wonder how happy he is? What about the average middle-class American? Nice house, dependable vehicle, steady employment, gadgets galore, and more food on the table than most people on Earth have. Is he/she satisfied, content, happy, thankful? All too often that question brings a negative answer.

Poet, Rudyard Kipling, commencement speaker at a Canadian university, cautioned graduates not to care too much for riches, power, or fame. He advised, "Some day you will meet a person of such stature that he will care for none of these things and then you will realize how poor you are."

The tale has been told of a tax collector who visited the home of a humble preacher in rural America in order to assess the value of his property and determine the amount of his taxes. "Oh, I'm a rich man," declared the minister.

"Is that right?" was the response from the official as he pulled out a note pad and his favorite fountain pen. "I'm ready now. Tell me exactly what you possess."

"First of all, I have a Savior who is preparing a mansion for me in heaven."

That was not at all what the assessor thought he would hear. "Ah...OK. What else?"

"I have a marvelous loving wife and the Bible tells me that such a woman is far more precious than jewels."

"Anything else?"

"Oh yes. My health and my wonderful children."

One more time the somewhat exasperated inquisitor requested, "Is there more?" "Contentment and peace of mind. That about covers it."

The bureaucrat closed his book, put his pen away and concluded, "You are indeed a rich man and not one bit of it is subject to taxation."

There is hardly anything in all this world that will reveal the character of men and women better than how they spend their money. Every day there are those whose life draws to a close, who go to where their treasures are–laid up for them in heaven. And there are also those who, when they leave this life, leave all their treasures behind. It was Jesus who said, "Why do you work for that which perishes...spend your energy for that which endures which I will give you."

> *"The love of money is the root*
> *of all kinds of evil."*

I Timothy 6:10

I n a Colorado Historical Society meeting, a story was told of a pioneer preacher who had accompanied gold miners to the gold fields. His intention was good. He built a little chapel and tried to meet the spiritual needs of all the prospectors. But before long he, too, caught the gold fever and was devoting much of his time in searching for that precious metal. Early one morning while feverishly panning for gold, it suddenly dawned on him that this was Sunday morning, the Lord's Day. So absorbed was the parson in searching for riches, he had even forgotten to open the chapel doors. The stunned minister realized what was happening to him and, with confession on his lips, he climbed up on a high peak, opened the handkerchief which contained his treasured gold dust, then shook the cloth and let the winds cleanse it. There is certainly no disgrace in working hard to better ourselves but the Colorado preacher had become obsessed with the desire to become rich, and recognized the danger he was in. In subtle ways that we cannot even imagine, the love of money has the potential to grasp us in a vice-like grip.

Have you heard the story of an eagle sitting on a frozen limb? A hunter once observed an eagle alighting on an ice-crested limb, floating in a river and rushing toward a waterfall. At any moment the eagle could have turned loose of its icy perch and soared into the sky, but it was confident, careless, and relaxed. It stayed in that position too long; its talons froze onto the limb and it could not let go. For a while the eagle had the limb, but now the limb had the eagle and carried the majestic bird over the falls to its death. There is a point in our drive for a better life when we must make a decision about the role of money in our lives. Do we have it or does it have us?

In R.C. Sproul's book *Objections Answered*, he writes about a young Jewish boy growing up in Germany in the 1830s who had a profound sense of admiration for his father. The life of the family revolved around the religious practices of their faith. His father, son of a rabbi, faithfully led them to the synagogue and was meticulous in his observance of the Sabbath.

In his teen years, however, his family moved to another village in Germany. This town had no synagogue, only a Lutheran church. The life of the community revolved around that church and almost all of the most influential people in the area belonged to it. Suddenly the head of the household announced to his wife and children that they would give up their Jewish traditions and become Lutherans. When the stunned family asked why, they were told matter-of-factly because it would be good for business. The teenager was bewildered, confused, and angered. Eventually an intense bitterness took over his life and plagued him as long as he lived.

Later he left Germany and went to England. There, after much study, he composed a book in which he introduced a whole new worldview and started a movement that changed the history of the world. In his literary masterpiece, millions have read and studied it, he described religion as "the opiate of the people." One of his goals was to convince his readers to live a life of atheism. His name? Karl Marx, founder of the communist movement. Since that time, the story of our planet has been severely affected because a father let his values become twisted. Money became his god. He held onto the limb too long. No, that is not accurate. It was the limb–his love of money–that had him.

Jesus himself had little interest in money but he had a whole lot to say about it. He spoke often about wealth and possessions because he knew that our attitude toward them was an accurate gauge of our character and our sense of values. Our Lord reminded us that our dollars could be a curse or a blessing. He taught us that the love of money is the root of all kinds of evil but that the right use of it could expand the kingdom of God and be a God-pleasing benefit to a hurting world.

> *"We have all had human fathers*
> *who disciplined us..."*
>
> Hebrews 12:9

It was my first trip to Donovan State Prison in San Diego. High walls, guard towers, razor wire fences combined to make this a dark and foreboding institution housing over four thousand prisoners. Some, convicted of minor crimes, were there for a couple of years. Others, such as murderer Sirhan Sirhan, are serving life sentences. Oh, I had not been arrested. I was there to visit a friend who would spend the next nine years behind bars. He was glad to see me but was very distraught, fearful, and depressed.

A month later I returned and was relieved to see that he was in a much more positive frame of mind. What had changed? With enthusiasm, he responded that he had met one of the volunteer prison chaplains and now he felt like he had a friend on the inside. As I prepared to leave after an enjoyable half hour together, he suggested that I stop by the chapel on my way out and get acquainted with Chaplain Jack. "You will like him," was his parting comment. The chapel was not exactly what I expected it to be. On the outside it looked nothing like a church. The facility at one time had been a storage room. Everything was painted white—the entire interior, ceiling, chairs, bookcase, desk, everything. The four walls were blank except for a bulletin board with some faded memos attached. And, of course, no windows.

From the back of the room came a welcoming voice, "You are now in the Church on the Rock. I'm Chaplain Jack. Welcome." Jack was probably in his late fifties, shaggy salt and pepper beard, wearing khakis and a western style shirt. He put down his guitar as he reached out a glad hand. I introduced myself and we chatted for a while about our mutual friend. "He just showed up one Sunday and mentioned that he loved to play the guitar. That was good news. I need some relief and would be glad to utilize his talent."

"Jack," I inquired, "who comes to these services?"

"Anybody who wants to is welcome—convicted drug dealers, rapists, some lifers, all kinds, ages eighteen to eighty. Hispanics, Asians, whites, and blacks. And, by the way, this is the only place in the entire prison where you will find guys from all different races socializing with each other. Otherwise this is a segregated society, not by policy but by personal choice. This can be a very dangerous place so you stick to your own kind for your own protection."

That was certainly an eye-opener for me but, sadly, it did make some sense. It had been an exciting, interesting, and informative visit. I thanked my new friend for his hospitality, and started to make my exit when I came up with an idea which I thought I'd bounce off the chaplain.

"Mother's Day is just around the corner. Could I get you a hundred cards that you would make available for the men to send to their moms on her day?"

The pastor to prisoners smiled. "That is generous of you. Thank you."

The cards were sent in and a few weeks later I received a note from Jack: "Every card was picked up at last Sunday's chapel service. We probably could have used another dozen or so." Of course I felt very good about that and immediately went out and bought a similar number of Father's Day cards. The chapel leader accepted the cards with little enthusiasm and mumbled, "Thanks." I was disappointed in his response. There didn't seem to be much appreciation for my donation.

The week after Father's Day I was back at the chapel and startled to see most of my cards sitting on the desk. Shrugging his shoulders and with a look of sadness Chaplain Jack explained, "You left one hundred cards. Eleven were picked up." I obviously had a bewildered look on my face as my unasked question was answered. "Why all these leftover cards? Because the vast majority of these inmates have no one to send a card to. One of the main reasons most of them are here is because of a rotten relationship with their father or no relationship at all. To be sure, you have some exceptions but they are few and far between."

This was all news to me as I listened in stunned silence.

"Did you ever hear the story about the elephant herd and the white rhinos at a national park in South Africa?"

I confessed that I had not heard the tale and wondered what it had to do with our previous conversation.

Then he related the following account: The game managers at Kruger National Park had to figure out what to do with their elephant herd. It had grown well beyond the ability of the park to sustain it. They decided to transfer some of the herd to another game park. A couple of years went by. Some of the young, male elephants, now teenagers, started attacking white rhinos, an endangered species. Sometimes they became very vicious, chasing them a great distance and then stomping them to death—all for no apparent reason.

Park rangers felt they had no choice but to cull some of the worst offenders. They removed four or five of them when someone came up with a bright idea. They brought back some of the mature male elephants. Maybe these bigger and stronger males could bring the adolescents under control. The big bulls quickly established the natural hierarchy and reduced the violent behavior of the young bulls. The young males started following the big daddies around, yielding to their authority and learning from them proper elephant conduct. The violence and the assaults on the white rhinos ended.

It was a powerful story. The point was obvious to me. Young males, both wild animals and human beings, need dads.

A book on the required reading list when I was a college student was Edward Gibbon's *The History of the Decline and Fall of the Roman Empire*. He summarized by listing five basic reasons for the fall of the mighty dominion. First on this illustrious historian's list was the disintegration of the family and home: infidelity, divorce, and the ignoring of wedding vows. Next, the wild spending of public money resulting in higher and higher taxes. Third, the mad craze for pleasure: entertainment each year becoming more exciting and more brutal. Fourth, the building of a gigantic military complex when the real enemy was within. Finally, the decay of religion in which faith faded into mere form and meaningless rituals.

There is no way we can look at that picture of years gone by without looking at today. What are our priorities? What really matters to me? What do I truly treasure? What am I hoping for?

Winston Churchill, writing about Lawrence of Arabia, pointed out that his power lay in his distain for most of the common pleasures and comforts of life. He noted that the world actually looks with some awe on the person who appears unconcerned and indifferent to riches, power, and fame. The world feels a certain apprehension about such a person because here is someone who is outside its jurisdiction and they don't know what to make of it.

Some years ago I listened to an audio tape in which James Dobson shared with us the thoughts that went through his head after he had received word that his father, someone he loved with all his heart, was dying. He boarded a plane and headed for his father's bedside. His memory floated back to a treasured time from his early teen years. He and his dad had gone deep into the woods at the crack of dawn. In complete silence they had taken a place behind a log and together watched as forest creatures appeared and the woods came alive. That precious memory, and others like it, triggered something inside of him so that more than anything he wanted to be like that man and wanted his father's values to be his values. He concluded by asking, "When the day comes that my children and your children reflect back on their father, what memories will they uncover?"

I remember years ago when my children were young and we were romping along a beach, laughing and tossing a Frisbee, when one of my sons observed, "Dad, we're making memories, aren't we?" Oh yes. God help us to take the time to make special memories.

The story has been told of a Christian missionary who was on a bus traveling across central India. It was a typical contraption that appeared to be held together by bubble gum and piano wires. As you can well imagine, it was packed not only with human cargo but with packages, boxes, and several domesticated animals. Sitting across the aisle from the young American was a very tired native whose neatly wrapped package sat on the luggage rack over his head. The senior citizen wanted to yield to the sleepiness that was threatening to overtake him but he couldn't, for fear someone might take his package. The bus rattled on and the old fellow dozed from time to time. He was often jolted awake with a sense of fear that his package might be stolen.

This went on for several hours. He snapped out of one of his momentary catnaps and, to his dismay, realized that he had been robbed. Then he relaxed, leaned back, and fell into a long and peaceful sleep. He was now relieved of that which had caused his anxiety and so was able to enjoy being unburdened. I wonder how many of us are feeling tremendous stress because we have one eye continually fixed on our package? Have we forgotten our Heavenly Father's admonition not to worry, for He cares for us?

My colleague, Pastor Greg Hoffmann, shared the following story penned by some unknown author. It is about a rich landowner named Carl who often rode around his vast estate so he could congratulate himself on his great wealth. One day while traveling across his spacious acreage on his favorite horse, he saw Hans, an old tenant farmer. He was sitting under a tree as Carl rode by.

When the noble asked Hans what he was doing, he replied, "I was thanking God for my food," holding his black bread and cheese.

Carl protested, "If that's all I had to eat I wouldn't feel like giving thanks."

Hans smiled. "I'm grateful. God has given me everything I need."

The old farmer added, "It is strange that you should come by today because I had a dream last night. In my dream a voice told me that the richest man in the valley will die tonight. I don't know what it means but I thought I ought to tell you."

Carl sneered, "Dreams are nonsense," and galloped away, but he could not forget Hans' words. He was obviously the richest man in the valley, so he called for his doctor that evening. He told the physician about Hans' dream. After a thorough examination, he was assured that he was as strong and healthy as a horse. No way was he going to die anytime soon.

Nevertheless, the doctor stayed with Carl and they played cards through the night. Carl apologized as the sun was rising on a new day for being so upset over a silly dream. Later that morning a messenger arrived at Carl's door. "What is it?" he demanded. "It's about old Hans. He died last night in his sleep."

*"Some have entertained angels
without knowing it."*

Hebrews 13:2

We adopted Gus, our English bulldog, when he was two months old. He was the runt of the litter and never weighed more than thirty-five pounds. He was part of our family when my wife and I moved from Cleveland, Ohio to Compton, California where I had accepted a call to pastor a congregation in this racially changing suburb of Los Angeles. This was to be our home for the next seven years and it is where our two sons were born.

It seemed as if no one in our new community had actually seen a live bulldog, so there was a certain mystic about him which I cultivated. We had been there less than a year when the FBI labeled Compton as "America's most dangerous city." Juvenile gangs, the Bloods and the Crips, made their presence known. Illegal drugs could be purchased anywhere and anytime. The public schools were listed as the worst in the state and some law enforcement officers had been busted for corruption.

One evening I was out on our front lawn playing tug of war with Gus who was at the other end of a six-foot rope hanging on with amazing tenacity. A group of six or seven teen males were loudly jostling with each other. They slowed down and with caution approached us in an effort to get a closer look at what we were doing. Gus had a vice-like grip and was not about to let go of his end of the rope. I started to swing it, raising it higher and higher until it was six feet off the ground, whirling around my head. Gus was flying in circles as the young toughs stared in awe. "Man! Does that dog ever have strong jaws!" exclaimed an astonished gang member. I added, "Can you imagine what would happen if he latched onto someone's arm or leg? It would be as brutal as a bear trap." The word soon spread, "No messing with that preacher. He has a killer dog." Gus had become our guardian angel.

Infestation of crime continued to run rampant through our town. Our next-door neighbors were burglarized, a woman living on our block was raped, a friend mugged, a parishioner's child was struck by a stray bullet, our church vandalized many times. It was not an easy or safe place to do ministry but we sensed that this is where God wanted us to be at the time. Each day as I would leave home, prayers for our family's protection were prayed and Gus was gently admonished to stay alert. He seemed to understand. There was a certain sense of security and peace for us in knowing that our "guardian angel" was on duty.

It was summertime and about eight o'clock in the evening. I mentioned to my wife that I'd left some materials at the church that I needed. It was only a block away so I would be gone no more than fifteen or twenty minutes. Marcia suggested that I take Gus with me. He had received no outside exercise that day. Still, this was something we almost never did. His place was at home with the family when I was gone. But following my spouse's surprising suggestion, Gus and I trotted off together.

The entry to my office faced a busy boulevard. I pulled out my keys, unlocked the door, flipped on the light switch, and walked in. In somewhat of a hurry, I neglected to lock the door behind me but headed straight for my desk. I sat down and searched through my desk drawers for those elusive notes. Gus was content to be at my feet. Suddenly the door flung open. A crazed, profanity-spewing drug addict burst in the room. He laughed, brazenly waved a knife, and threatened to cut me into many pieces. I leaped to my feet, frantically looking for something with which to defend myself. I could find nothing. Escape would be impossible as he was standing in the doorway which was the only exit from the room. I prayed, "Lord, I don't know what to do. Help me!"

Gus had not made his presence known. Now he got up, casually walked around the desk, and stood between me and the knife-wielding would-be attacker. Gus didn't bark, he never even moved. My guardian angel stood there and stared at my adversary. The deranged junkie with his mouth wide open stared in horror at the sight of Gus, "No! No! No!" The lunatic grew hysterical. He staggered backwards, knocking over a chair. Gus remained motionless and silent. Now in absolute panic, my would-be assailant, totally disoriented, tripped and fell while scrambling to get out of the door. The knife fell from his hand. Shrieking in terror, he stumbled down the steps and disappeared into the darkness.

What had happened? How could a thirty-five pound non-aggressive dog cause such fear? I believe God used a drug-induced hallucination to cause him to see in Gus not a little pug-faced pet but a ferocious 500-pound lion about to eat him for lunch.

In the New Testament book of Hebrews, chapter 13, we read, "Do not forget to entertain strangers for by so doing some people have entertained angels without knowing it." That Bible passage speaks to us. Strange as it may sound, could it be that through Gus we were entertaining our guardian angel and not even knowing it?

"But each one is tempted..."

James 1:14

D r. Kenneth McFarland was superintendent of schools many years ago. He had under his supervision the Coffeyville Community College in Coffeyville, Kansas. It was the day before their annual commencement. A young lady came into his office. He recognized her as one who was about to graduate as an honor student. She was a very pleasant, pretty woman named Nancy Hollingsworth. Nancy related her own personal, fascinating story.

Her father was killed shortly after she was born. Her mother struggled as an assembler in a factory to raise her and her two older brothers. Ms. Hollingsworth's only other relative was her Uncle Ben. He had a serious drinking problem which resulted in losing several jobs and serving time in jail for a DUI.

One night while Tommy, Jimmy, and Nancy were still quite small their beloved mother suffered a fatal heart attack. The sobbing, grief-stricken children looked to Uncle Ben and cried, "Now what is going to happen to us?" His response: "I love each one of you and I'll go down to the courthouse and ask for custody of you. Next I'll get on my knees every night and ask God to help me raise you right."

With a voice filled with emotion and her eyes sparkling, she exclaimed that was exactly what he did. "Each time alcohol tempted him he would declare, 'You are from Satan. Jesus, Jesus, Jesus help me.' His prayer was answered and temptation resisted. He never touched liquor and never again missed a day of work. Jim is now in medical school. Tom is a graduate student at MIT and I've just received a full scholarship to the university where I'll complete my training to be a teacher. Uncle Ben has been to every one of our graduations but he won't sit in the parents' section. He feels that would show disrespect for Mom. I would be ever so grateful if you'd say something about Uncle Ben at commencement."

So, Dr. McFarland told the story. At the conclusion, the entire assembly stood and applauded the dedication, commitment, tenacity, and love of a recovering alcoholic who became a Christ-like father figure to three hurting children.

We resist temptation best when we are committed to something so important, so lasting, of such great value that we will not allow ourselves to be dragged down by that which we know in our hearts is contrary to God's Will. Our Lord has promised us that His grace will be enough to meet all our needs. Resisting temptation puts us into a position of strength. When we give in we become weaker and more vulnerable. Conversely, when we withstand the Tempter we get stronger and are better equipped to recognize and reject the next enticement that comes our way.

Paul Harvey told the following story: It was 1864. A Bowery bum with a slashed throat was brought into Bellevue Hospital in New York City. The victim was unable to recover from his injury because his body had been weakened by the excessive use of alcohol. He had a high fever and was in obvious pain. The pathetic soul had lost a great deal of blood and was suffering from malnutrition. The stranger survived about a week until he died. He was thirty-eight. There was a bit of irony in finding exactly thirty-eight cents in his pocket. As the narrative unfolded, however, they discovered that this was not just another Bowery bum. This homeless street person had been well-known all over America, famous for his songs. He had charmed us with "Oh! Susanna," "Jeanie with the Light Brown Hair," "My Old Kentucky Home," and scores of others. His name was Stephen Foster. On a cold wintry night in New York City, he died, leaving behind the legacy of a wasted life.

You can be sure that this beloved and popular song-writer never intended to have his life end as it did. Nobody ever does. The Tempter never tries to lead us astray by saying, "Come here and I will show you something evil and ugly." Of course not. Satan is much too clever for that. Instead he charms us with, "I am about to show you something pleasurable and exciting, a new thrill for you. You deserve this happy opportunity."

In 1853, Robert Allen was campaigning against Abraham Lincoln for a place in the Illinois legislature. Allen had few moral scruples and attempted to pull a crafty political trick on his opponent. He claimed to have proof of corruption on the part of Lincoln, but he announced that he would not smear the opposing candidate by releasing the evidence to the public. Brilliant and ugly at the same time–attacking your rival's character while appearing to be a man of high moral values yourself!

But "Honest Abe" was too sharp to fall for Allen's trick. He had nothing to hide. So he requested that Allen release any damaging information that he might have and to do it now. After all, if Allen knew of some dishonest actions that would keep him from properly leading the people, he would be "a traitor to his country" by concealing the evidence.

When we have nothing to hide, we have nothing to fear. A momentary lapse in our values can leave lifetime scars. It has happened to those who are smarter and more successful than we are. Our Lord knows the weakness of our flesh and thus has taught us to pray (and to pray often): "Lead us not into temptation... deliver us from the evil one."

*"Pure religion is this: to look
after orphans..."*

James 1:27

It was Easter Sunday afternoon and time for our semi-annual all-church picnic. The celebration featured a potluck meal to be shared by everyone. The barbecue grill was lit where soon hundreds of hot dogs and hamburgers would be grilled. An Easter egg hunt for the younger children was high on the agenda. All others were invited to participate in a Frisbee toss, softball games, or various other activities. There was wholesome fun and enjoyable conversation which contributed to a great day.

I was sitting on a lawn chair chatting with Lisa and Steve, a delightful couple and the parents of two pre-schoolers. I soon learned that they were sponsors of a young orphan in India cared for by the United Evangelical Mission. They confessed with amazement that the homeless child would receive food, clothing, shelter, and schooling for a dollar a day. Their enthusiasm was contagious. For only a dollar a day we, too, could help provide hope and life for one of God's helpless little children.

The very next day we contacted UEM and expressed our desire to sponsor a child. Soon we received a photo and biography of nine-year-old Ashwini. We signed the sponsorship form. Both my wife and I felt very good about our decision to provide care for this child.

A year later I was in attendance at a church leaders' conference at the Town and Country Convention Center in San Diego. While looking through a listing of recently published books by Christian authors, my attention was drawn to a small pamphlet with a focus on deceit and fraud in nonprofit organizations. One chapter targeted a popular scam which would grab the reader's attention through the presentation of a suffering child in a Third World country. It was a ploy intended to touch our heartstrings. What followed was a plea: "You can give life to a desperate, innocent child."

So, how did this scam work? In some cases, no such waif existed. An image was just pulled off the internet and some crook was pocketing the dollars received and then forging a thank-you note from the non-existent orphan. An even more widespread scam depicted a parentless child in dire need of help. Hundreds of un-suspecting benevolent souls faithfully provided a dollar a day to sponsor the same child! The con artist would spend a dollar for the juvenile's care and keep the other $199 for his own purposes. Was it possible that I, too, was being tricked? Was there actually a real person, Ashwini, benefiting from our gifts or were our checks finding their way into some shyster's bank account? I needed to know the answer.

I contacted UEM and stated that I would like to meet Ashwini in person. "How can arrangements be made for this to happen?" The answer to my question came as a pleasant surprise. "God bless you. That's wonderful. Perhaps the best way would be for you to join a short-term mission team that will be going in February." I soon had my India visa and booked travel arrangements to Bangalore via Frankfort, Germany, where I would meet members of the mission team. All went as planned and after twenty-three hours of flight time, traveling halfway around the world, at 3:00 a.m. we arrived at our destination. John Peter, our Indian host, along with some of his aides was there to meet us and escort us to our hotel.

Two days later we traveled by van to the United Children's Home in the heart of this congested metropolis of eleven million residents. Three old buildings, one a former warehouse, had been rented and with great care converted into a residential school. The core curriculum was reading, math, science, English, and Bible.

Over one hundred children greeted us with shouts of welcome and songs of joy. Countless flower petals were strewn on our pathway. Plastic chairs had been set up under an awning for the guests while all the students were seated on the ground. The principal, a humble man of God, invited each of us to share a word of greeting. "No translator is needed. All our youth speak and understand English."

When my turn came, I related my story of why I was there. I concluded, "I hope Ashwini is a real person. Ashwini, are you here?"

Cheers rang out and a hundred hands started clapping as a petite, smiling young lady stood up and headed down the aisle and reached out to take my hand.

"Ashwini, you are real."

"Yes," came the happy response, "I'm a real person."

With a bit of hesitancy I asked, "May I give you a hug?"

She opened her arms wide, an action that was met with the roaring approval of the assembly.

The structured portion of our time together was soon ending, with scores of children crowding around us, shouting questions and comments.

"Do you know my sponsors, Tom and Maggie Smith from Dallas?"

"Dick and Linda Swenson are in Wisconsin."

"My sponsors, Ben and Leah, live in Florida."

What followed were many earnest prayers of thanks for all the sponsors.

Ashwini took me by the hand and proudly showed me her underlined Bible and homework papers (all marked with passing grades). She explained that when her father was murdered he left behind a widow with three children who had no marketable skills. Soon they were beggars living on the streets. A Christian friend suggested they contact UEM. They were informed that Ashwini and her younger sister could stay at the orphanage as soon as sponsors had been found. "We prayed really hard and here I am," she said. Our conversation continued as she introduced me to several of her friends, one of whom responded, "Ashwini is the finest

Christian in the whole school."

The time came to head back to the hotel. I was still clutching her hand as I confessed, "India will never be the same. Now when I remember this fascinating country I will think of my Indian daughter who lives here." This precious young lady stood on her tiptoes and gave me a kiss on my cheek. She squeezed my hand and declared, "It's like having a daddy again." My heart melted.

Father Barry Foster, a priest in Dublin, Ireland, parked his Toyota close to the church. His little fox terrier was lying on the rear seat and could not be seen by anyone outside the vehicle. The genial priest stepped out into the street and then turned to lock the door with his usual parting command to his pet, "Stay!" Then he repeated it to an apparently empty car. An elderly woman was watching the performance with amused interest. Grinning, she suggested, "Why don't you just put it in park and set your hand brake?"

To the mind of the unbeliever, prayer is the equal of watching someone say, "Stay!" to their automobile, fully expecting it to obey. To such a person, prayer is an exercise in futility that may be an accurate description of prayers that are contrary to God's will.

An example of this is the account of a six-year-old who was ignoring his mother's orders and was playing ball in the house. He smashed a treasured glass bowl into many pieces. The scared little guy, now in a panic, picked up all the pieces and hid them in a drawer. Anguished and trembling with fear, he came up with a plan of action. He remembered a Sunday school teacher reading to them from the Bible a message that God was an "ever present help in time of need." He was in big trouble and this was a real time of need. He decided he would spend the rest of the day in prayer. He would plead with God for a miracle. He bargained that he would do anything for God if only the bowl could be made new.

Then next morning he opened the drawer, hoping against hope that his prayer had been answered. But that was not to be. He groaned out loud. The bowl was still in ruins. He would have to face his punishment while his faith in prayer was left in shambles.

The lad, now nearly fifty years old, grumbles, "When people pray nothing happens." As far as his understanding of prayer is concerned, this poor fellow never grew up. He is still a disobedient little boy calling on God to do a magic trick that would get him out of a tight spot. God can surely do the impossible but he seldom answers that kind of prayer.

Illegitimate prayers would also include the student who goofs off all semester and then pulls an all-nighter while asking his Creator to intervene in order to help him pass his finals and then announces that prayer is a worthless waste of time. Another illustration might be that of the thirteen-year-old girl who informs her parents in a voice of contempt that she was never going to pray again. Why? Because for the last week she had beseeched the Lord to turn her into a gorgeous blonde but nothing happened.

All of us, I'm sure, can look back at some prayers we prayed and now thank God that His answer was delayed or was no. Our Lord, of course, sees all the future. We can only see today. So it is that a loving Father sometimes will say no to that which we are requesting today because He sees everything in the light of eternity.

A child wanted a bicycle and wanted it now. His mother told him it was not something they could afford. Then she added, "Why don't you go to your room and bring your request to the Holy Mother?" On his desk was a statue of the Virgin Mary, so he wrote a prayer and set it under the image. It read, "I want a bicycle soon. Please." For three nights he followed that same evening ritual. The fourth evening he took the statue down, wrapped it in a blanket, and tucked it into his dresser drawer. He then jammed some other things in front of it and slammed the drawer. He got out his prayer paper and added, "Dear Lord Jesus...if you ever want to see your mother again..."

Lyrics from an old Garth Brooks song sum it up perfectly: "Remember when you're talking to the man upstairs that just because He doesn't answer doesn't mean He don't care. Some of God's greatest gifts are unanswered prayers." Waiting for an answer to prayer isn't always easy but it's usually good for us. Our Father knows what we need and when it's best for us to receive it.

On a cold day at twilight a ragged, unkempt man shuffled into a little music shop on a side street in London. Clutched under his arm was an old violin. The shop was owned by a Mr. Betts, a kind elderly gentleman. The weary visitor said, "I'm hungry and need something to eat. Please take this violin and give me some money so I can buy some food." The shopkeeper already had a stack of violins on his shelf. He really didn't need another one, but he was a compassionate soul and pushed across the counter five English pounds (about ten American dollars). The famished stranger gratefully accepted it and hobbled out into the darkness.

The benevolent store owner was a musician as well as a businessman and so out of curiosity, he took a bow and drew it across the strings of this old violin. The result was a wondrous tone, so beautiful that it startled him. Astonished, he took a light and stared intently into the inside of the violin. There he saw, carved into the wood according to the master's custom, the magic name, "Antonio Stradivari" and the date "1704". Betts knew at once that this was an extremely valuable instrument. The attics of Europe had been ransacked for over 200 years looking for just such a priceless gem. He bought it for a measly ten dollars.

He dashed out into the street to find the indigent stranger, but he had disappeared completely into the London fog. Mr. Betts spent several days trying to locate the vanished vagrant. Eventually he sold the instrument for $100,000 (a Stradivarius recently sold at auction for over $3 million). The penniless, destitute peasant never realized what he possessed. He lived in poverty, on life's edge because he did not recognize what he had.

In the same way, the identical words might be said of you and me. We possess, each one of us, the power to live beautiful, productive, God-pleasing lives. Yet too often we settle for a fearful, exhausting, weak, and unsatisfying existence when it is so unnecessary. We need to ask ourselves what we have done with the talents, gifts, and abilities that God has built into us. Henry van Dyke once said, "Use the gifts you have. The woods would be very silent if the only birds that sang well were those that sang the very best."

Katherine Elliott, author of children's books, wrote, "When I was about ten years old Grandma received a gift of perfume in a bottle that fascinated me. Made of green pottery with a long slender neck and a square bottom. It looked like pictures I had seen of ancient ware. I begged Grandma to open it. 'No,' she declared, 'I'm going to save it for later.' When I was thirty-three Grandma gave the perfume to me saying, 'Let's see how long you can keep it without opening it.' One day when I picked up the perfume bottle I was shocked to discover that it was empty, although still sealed. Turning it over I could see why. The bottom of the bottle had never been glazed and thus the perfume had slowly evaporated. How sad that no one ever enjoyed the perfume, not Grandma or anyone else. How disappointing for the gift giver. Then it struck me that I frequently treat God's gifts to me the same way, not using them because of shyness, selfishness, or just plain laziness. Failing to use our gifts disappoints God and we deny others the opportunity to enjoy God's blessings with us." It is amazing what we can do when we open ourselves up to Him and use the gifts–all of the gifts–that we have.

Some years ago a local TV station carried a program where a sophisticated violinist played some rather difficult numbers. When he finished his concert, the audience broke into genuine applause. Then, as he was taking his bows, a workman clad in overalls came walking out on the stage carrying an ordinary carpenter's saw. The initial reaction of the audience was that the janitor had made some mistake and should never have been on the stage, however, he quietly handed the saw to the musician and stepped aside. The master placed one end of the instrument on the floor, drew his bow across it and started to play.

It was ridiculous to see this star performer in a tuxedo drawing a bow across an old saw blade. People started to snicker. Gradually the laughter died down and the music lovers listened as marvelous sounds started to come out of the old cutting tool. Finally, without comment, the violinist concluded what he was playing and

handed the saw back to the workman. The theatergo-
ers sat in stunned silence for a moment before bursting
into thunderous applause. What a reminder it was to
all what the Master can do with a commonplace instrument. It causes us to wonder what amazing blessings
can be distributed when we place our abilities and gifts
in the Master's hand.

"Let us love one another for
love comes from God"

I John 4:7

A young lady once read a novel, found it to be of only mild interest, and put it aside. Probably not something that she would ever pick up again. In the course of time, she started dating a really nice fellow and sensed that she was falling in love with him. One evening she casually mentioned to him that she had a paperback at home written by an author with the same name as his and then commented what a coincidence that was. "Maybe not," he responded, "I've done a little writing and the book you described is one of mine." That night she stayed up until the wee hours of the morning rereading the adventure story. This time she found something of interest on nearly every page. What had turned such a seemingly dull book into such an inspiring one? The answer: she was in love with the author. And so it is as we grow in love for the author we find the truths of the Bible to be more and more vital, relevant, and life-changing. It is our Father's personal letter sent to His beloved children.

As a little girl, Alice Gray discovered a great secret from her grandparents. Ever since she could remember they had played a mysterious little game. They would leave the letters SHMILY around the house for each other. Grandfather would write little notes with the letters SHMILY in the steam on the bathroom mirror so Grandmother would see it when she took her morning shower. Grandmother would tuck little notes in the cupboard or cereal box with SHMILY written on them. Over the years they seemed to see who could find the most creative ways to leave a SHMILY note for the other.

When Grandmother lost her seven-year battle with cancer, her casket was wreathed with a huge garland of white roses and painted on a yellow ribbon around the bouquet were the letters SHMILY. SHMILY was the thing that held their marriage together, the thing that sustained them in life and death. What does SHMILY mean? SEE HOW MUCH I LOVE YOU! The greatest mystery of all is why God loves us. He knows my every thought, sees each one of my actions, hears each word I utter, and still loves me. Why? That is a great puzzle.

Do you remember the story once told of Karl Barth, the brilliant Swiss theologian who lived about six decades ago? He was invited in his semi-retirement years to give a theological dissertation at Princeton Theological Seminary. Faculty, staff, and students turned out in mass; the auditorium was filled to overflowing. Students in this elite institution were ready with pen and notepad in hand, eager to keep track of every word from the lips of this distinguished professor. Indeed, he did present a very learned and scholarly discourse and received loud and sustained applause when he finished. Then the moderator announced that the esteemed doctor had graciously consented to field a question or two from the audience. One excited student raised his had, jumped to his feet, and boldly asked, "Dr. Barth, what is the greatest truth that you've discovered in all your studies?" The students held their breaths, poised and ready to mark down his every word.

The aged mentor, now in his 80s, with a shock of grey hair covering his head, slowly walked up to the microphone, faced this august student body and then proclaimed, "Jesus loves me this I know for the Bible tells me so." With that he sat down. A truth, a mystery so profound that the brightest minds cannot probe its depth, yet so simple that little children can sing it with joy.

Pat Watson described God's love for us as an illogical love. It simply does not make any sense. He told of the love that his little daughter had for a cheap rag doll. It was her pathetic plaything that helped him see God's unreasonable love for us. Watson reminds us that some things are loved because they are valuable but other things are valuable because they are loved. So it is with God's groundless love for us. We are truly his rag dolls and are valuable because we are loved.

Officer Tori Matthews of the Southern California Humane Society received an emergency call–a boy's pet iguana had been scared up a tree by a neighbor's Chihuahua. It then fell from the pine tree into a swimming pool where it sank like a brick. Officer Matthews came with her net. She dove into the water, emerging seconds later with the pet's limp body. "Well," she thought to herself, "you do CPR on a person and even on a dog. Why not an iguana?" She put her lips to the iguana's.

"Now that I look back on it," she reports with a smile, "it was a pretty ugly animal to be kissing but the last thing I wanted to do was tell that little fellow that his iguana was dead." The lizard responded to her efforts and is expected to make a full recovery.

I tip my hat to Officer Matthews. She went way beyond the call of duty. "While we were dead in our transgressions Christ died for us..." writes St. Paul in his letter to the Ephesians. In simple terms, we might say that because of His love for us Christ has resuscitated an iguana—and we are that iguana.

"Perfect love drives out fear."

I John 4:18

Chursh School caters to learning-disabled children. At a fund-raising dinner, the father of a student delivered a never-to-be-forgotten message.

"Where is the perfection in my son Shaya?" he demanded. "Everything God does he does well with perfection. But my son cannot understand things as other children do. It is not possible for him to remember facts and figures so where is God's perfection?" The audience was shocked and disturbed by the father's question. He continued, "I believe that when God brings a child like this into the world the perfection that he seeks is the way people react to this special child."

What followed was this beautiful story: One Saturday morning, Shaya and his dad were walking through the park where they saw a group of boys playing baseball. Shaya very much wanted to join them but his father hesitated. Would the other boys let him play or would they laugh at him and reject him? Dad was surprised and delighted that the ballplayers allowed Shaya to join the game. It was obvious that poor Shaya had zero athletic skills so most of the time was spent on the bench.

The game reached the final inning with a tie score. Then something amazing happened. The team captain announced that it was Shaya's turn to bat. The pitcher, seeing this small uncoordinated kid, stepped forward a few feet and softly tossed the ball. He swung the bat and missed it by a country mile. The captain stepped up behind him and placed his hands over Shaya's. Together they managed to hit the next pitch where the ball slowly rolled toward the pitcher. For some reason he couldn't seem to pick it up. "Run to first," shouted his father, "run to first!" The little fellow ran as fast as his legs would carry him. The pitcher grabbed the ball and threw way over the head of the first baseman. His teammates were screaming, "Run to second! Run to second!" He was less than halfway there when the fielder grabbed the ball but sensing what the pitcher's intention was, he tossed it over the second baseman's head. Now the whole team was hollering, "Run to third! Run to third!" He reached third just in time to see the ball go bouncing by the third baseman. Now it seemed as if everyone was cheering at the top of their lungs, "Run home! Run home!" A joyful little Shaya scored the winning run. He received a hero's welcome as the team lifted him in the air and treated him like a conquering hero.

"That day," the father stated in a voice barely above a whisper while tears streaked his cheeks, "was a day when we reached the level of God's perfection." God's perfection is found in people who care.

"His name was Kenny," Max Lucado writes, "and he'd just returned with his family from Disneyworld where he saw a sight that he knew he would never forget. He and his family were visiting in Cinderella's castle. It was packed with kids and parents. In what seemed like only a few seconds, all the children dashed to one side. Had it been a boat it would have tipped over. Cinderella had entered. She was a perfect princess, a very attractive young lady with each hair in place, flawless skin and a beaming smile. She stood waist deep in a garden of children, each wanting to touch and be touched. For some reason Kenny glanced toward the other side of the castle. It was vacant except for a boy of about eight years old. His age was hard to determine because his body was so badly disfigured: small and squatty with a deformed face. He stood in silence holding the hand of his older brother.

It was quite obvious what he wanted and that was to be with the other children. He wanted what they desired—to call her name and maybe touch her. You could almost feel his fear, fear of another rejection, perhaps being taunted or mocked. Wouldn't it be wonderful if Cinderella would go to him?

Guess what? She did! She noticed the lonely child. She moved in his direction politely but firmly inching her way through the crowd, then she broke free. She walked in a straight line right to him. She knelt down at eye level with the stunned little fellow and placed a kiss on his face. God's perfection is found in people who care.

"We love because he first loved us."

I John 4:19

Psychologist Philip Crane tells of a wife who came into his office full of bitterness toward her husband. "I not only want to get out of this marriage but I want to get even. Before I divorce the lout I want to hurt him as much as he has hurt me," the bitter woman fumed.

Crane suggested an ingenious plan: "Go home and act as if you really loved your husband. Tell him with emotion and conviction how much he and your marriage mean to you. Praise your partner and thank him for every decent thing he does. Go out of your way to be kind and loving. Make believe that you love him from the depths of your heart. Then after you have him convinced that you cannot live without him, drop the bomb. Announce that you are getting a divorce. You know that is truly going to hurt him."

With revenge in her eyes and a smirk on her face, she cried out, "Yes. Oh yes. That is beautiful! This is going to feel so good." It was with great enthusiasm that she followed through on all the counselor's suggestions. The oh-so-sweet wife showed him forgiveness and patience, kindness, admiration, and love.

Some time passed and she missed her next appointment with Dr. Crane. So he called her and asked, "Have you filed for divorce yet?"

"Divorce?!" she exclaimed. "Never. I have discovered what a great guy he is, how much I love him and how fortunate I am to be his wife."

Francis Desales, towering man of God, wrote centuries ago, "You learn to speak by speaking, to study by studying, to run by running, to work by working; and just so you learn to love by loving." We are able to love because we have been loved. It is the knowledge of God's love for us that penetrates our fears and creates within us the courage to love.

Pastor Quentin Morrow made the following observation: "I have spent long hours in the hospital intensive care waiting room, watching with anguished people, listening to urgent questions. Will my husband make it? Will my child ever walk again? How can I live without my companion of thirty years?"

The ICU waiting room is different from any other place in the world because the people sitting there are different. They can't do enough for each other. They are polite and considerate. The distinctions of race, age, and class fade away. A person is a father first, a black man second. The garbage collector loves his wife as much as the university professor. It is here where the world changes. Vanity and pretense vanish. Seemingly the entire universe is focused on the doctor's next report. Everyone knows that loving someone is what life is about.

Can we imagine how very different our days would be if we realized that our everyday life is in fact the crucible of the intensive care waiting room? Knowing that we are loved enables us to love. It cannot be bought, begged, stolen, demanded or commanded. Love is freely given or it is not love.

In *Memories of a Traveling Preacher,* the unknown author writes about witnessing a slave auction in Louisiana in 1850. A beautiful biracial girl was soon to be sold to the highest bidder. As expected, the bids ran high until only two potential buyers remained. One was loud, drinking, swearing, and obviously lusting after the slave girl. The other was quiet, calm, sober, with a look of determination about him. The young mulatto stared out at her would-be owners with eyes that seemed to be crackling with hatred. In the end the bidding got so high that the lascivious drunkard eventually offered up his horse for sale. Even so, it would not be enough. He had been outbid. Cursing and shaking his fist at his opponent, he stomped away.

Proud, contemptuous, and with eyes still glaring with contempt, the hapless woman was roughly pushed over to her new owner. A slave had no rights. She was now his property. He carefully read his ownership papers and then signed his name on the bottom. The high bidder placed the papers in her trembling hands and said with conviction, "You are no man's property. I bought you in order to set you free." She could not comprehend what he had just told her. In disbelief she searched his eyes. This time, now with a smile on his face, he repeated those way-too-good-to-be-true words, "I bought you in order to set you free." The suddenly liberated young woman started to sob as she knelt before her benefactor, wrapping her arms around his knees. "Sir," she begged. "Please sir, I want to go with you and serve you the rest of my life."

Nothing could buy from her or force from her that love, loyalty, and respect. But through an unselfish act of kindness and love, it was freely given. The apostle John wrote in his first epistle, chapter four: "Dear friends, let us love one another for love comes from God. There is no fear in love for love casts out fear."

"I know... of your service and perseverance..."

Revelation 2:19

Attorney Edward Bennett Williams once spoke humorously of what he called the Zeke Bonura theory of chance. Bonura was a clumsy first baseman for the Chicago White Sox baseball team back in the mid 1930s. Each year he strived to end the season with the best fielding average in the American League. He did so by recognizing an obscure MLB rule: you cannot be charged with an error unless you touch the ball. Hence, Mr. Bonura avoided touching anything that looked the least bit difficult. "This," claimed Williams, "is a rule that has been respected by most politicians of our century. If it is the least bit difficult then leave it alone." Anyone who attempts to do anything significant is going to mess up sometime. God-fearing people understand that and will not let setbacks keep them from service. Venerable Benjamin Franklin mused, "We are old too soon and wise too late."

Some time ago, a rather unusual announcement was repeated over the radio. The announcer described several scenes in the progressive history of a certain person. Scene one showed a proud papa. The father boldly proclaimed that it was a boy, his name would be Stanley, and some day he could be president of the United States. In the next scene, Stanley was getting married. The father of the bride said to Stanley, "Oh, I know you had your heart set on going to medical school but I'm delighted that you have chosen to join me in the purse manufacturing business." In the third scene, Stanley and his wife were on an expensive round-the-world cruise. He obviously had been successful in the purse-making business and made lots of money. The final scene depicted Stanley's minister preaching his funeral sermon. The preacher quipped, "Stanley was much loved by all here at Shady Nook Rest Home. He was the best gin rummy player in this retirement center. Few people knew that he also had the lowest cholesterol count of anyone here." The radio announcer concluded, "Isn't it sad to live your whole life and never make a ripple in the water and never rock the boat? Join the Peace Corps."

Billy Sunday, great Christian evangelist of the early 20th century, put it this way: "More people fail through lack of purpose than through lack of talent or ability." Norman Vincent Peale, author of the best-selling *Power of Positive Thinking*, shared the story of the very early Kentucky frontier. The year was 1782. About one fifth of the pathetically small community had died of disease or been killed by Indians. There were not enough hands to do the simplest job. Each adult was extremely valuable and each child a burden.

The spiritual leader of this colony was Rev. Joe Craig, better known for his frank approach to problems than for his preaching ability. He was called to the bedside of a dying woman to hear her last words. He had a brief prayer with her and then in a commanding tone said, "Hannah, if you die today and leave all these kids to be raised by someone else with things the way they are now, it will be the meanest thing you ever did in your life!" What he said made her furious; she sat up with a look of defiance on her face and the fever left her. She read the riot act to him and, in no uncertain terms, let the minister know what she thought of him. In his frankness he had restored her courage and her will to live.

The following poem was written by Amy Carmichael, who served as a Christian missionary in India for fifty-five years where she suffered pain, persecution, and illness which would haunt her for the rest of her life.

Hast thou no scar?
No hidden scar on foot, or side, or hand?
I hear thee sung as mighty in the land;
I hear them hail thy bright, ascendant star.
Hast thou no scar?

Hast thou no wound?
Yet I was wounded by the archers; spent,
Leaned Me against a tree to die; and rent
By ravening beasts that compassed Me, I swooned.
Hast thou no wound?

No wound? No scar?
Yet, as the Master shall the servant be,
And pierced are the feet that follow Me.
But thine are whole; can he have followed far
Who hast no wound or scar?

Quintus Fabius Maximus was a Roman general and dictator during what has been described as the worst crisis in Roman history. The notorious Hannibal and his vast army were threatening to destroy Rome. Maximus was deliberating at his staff headquarters about how to handle a difficult position. One of his officers suggested how it could be done and added, "It will only cost the lives of a few good men." The general replied, "Are you willing to be one of the few?" Looking for a life of significance, purpose and meaning? Listen to the words of Jesus: "Deny yourself, take up your cross and follow me."

"There will be no more death or mourning..."

Revelation 21:4

It was Monday morning. I was in my office at the church when I was informed that I had a phone call. It was from a woman who had been a visitor yesterday at one of our worship services. She introduced herself as Jeanne and asked if she could make an appointment for some one-on-one conversation. I agreed and a date and time was placed on the calendar.

A few days later, a smiling stranger walked in, thanked me for agreeing to meet with her and commented on how meaningful she found the Sunday service to be. The pleasant lady further identified herself as a thirty-eight-year-old homemaker, wife to Todd, and mother of four children. She went on to say some nice things about our church and the gracious hospitality that she had felt. I was encouraged by her kind words but in the back of my mind I was thinking, "We've not yet discussed the main reason you wanted this meeting." As if able to read my mind, she took a deep breath and explained, "I'm here to ask a favor of you. Would you be available to officiate at my funeral?" I'm sure the startled expression on my face was evidence that I wasn't expecting that response. Gaining my composure, I asked if there was some reason to believe that this would take place in the near future. "Yes," she said matter-of-factly, "cancer has invaded just about every part of my body. There is no treatment that can arrest its progress. It's terminal. Oh, at first I was angry, then went into a state of denial, from there to pleading with God to save me from this ugly disease. Now I've accepted that it is inevitable so I'm making final plans."

With calmness in her voice, the cancer victim outlined the following scenario for me: For the next few Sundays, she planned to be present with her husband and would sit on the north side of the chancel near the organ. She added that the day would soon be coming when her ravaged body would require a wheelchair. As her condition grew worse, she would be assigned a room at Mercy Hospital but when the end drew very near, she would go back to her own home for one final visit. Her doctor and her family had been reminded of her request.

For the next three weeks, Jeanne and her husband attended the traditional service sitting near the organ. On the fourth Sunday, I noticed they parked in the disabled parking section and Jeanne entered the sanctuary in a wheelchair. A few weeks later, Todd called to inform me his beloved was at Mercy Hospital. This courageous lady was propped up in her bed when I entered her room. In front of her was a box with a half dozen indulgent pastries. She welcomed me, pointed to the doughnuts and, with a twinkle in her eye, explained, "When you know you're soon going to die you no longer need to worry about your figure." Our time together included a prayer for the conquest of cancer and peace for each member of her family. With words of gratitude she accepted a large print Bible since her illness had also attacked her vision. On our next visit I asked if there were some particular passages of Scripture she would want read. She replied, "Read the promises and then underline them for me." Two days later we met again. "I've been writing letters. I'm just about finished. Will you please read them at my memorial service?" I assured her that her surprising appeal would be honored.

Wednesday morning a call came from her husband, "You need not make the trip to Mercy today. Jeanne is now home." The next day's trip was to her San Diego residence. This dauntless sufferer had requested that her bed be placed out in the living room so she could remain in the center of family life. She was in a very weakened physical condition but was still mentally sharp. "What's going through your mind these days, Jeanne?" She pondered the question and then, in a soft voice barely above a whisper, I heard these words: "I'm at peace– ready to go now." That night the Lord sent forth his angels to escort her to her heavenly home.

Per her wishes, mostly hymns of Easter were sung at her funeral. At the conclusion of the homily, it was announced that Jeanne had written some personal notes that she wanted read at this time. This wife and mother had prepared a message for each of her children, thanking God for them, for the joy of being their mother, and cited some special virtue she saw in each one. It was powerful and very moving, a mother's legacy for her children.

The final letter was a thank you farewell to her husband, extolling many admirable qualities. She closed by writing, "Honey, I only have one regret…" I thought, *'Oh, no! I should have read this in advance. This is not the spot for something negative.* But I found that my concern was unwarranted as I continued reading: "Is that I'm checking out on you so soon but I had no control over my departure time. I thank God for our love, which even my passing cannot end. Thanks everyone for loving me. You are much loved. Now you are all invited to our house where I want you to party hearty." C.S. Lewis reminds us: "Our Father refreshes us on the journey with some pleasant inns, but will not encourage us to mistake them for home."

"There will be no more night."

Revelation 22:5

A young woman tells of losing her mother whom she called her dearest friend. Cancer had taken her life. She remembered her mother as always supportive of her: clapping loudest at her school plays, holding a box of tissues while listening to her first heartache, comforting her in her college days, and praying for her her entire life.

When her mother's illness was diagnosed, the woman's sister had a new baby and her brother had recently married his childhood sweetheart and moved out of state, so it fell on her, the twenty-seven-year-old middle child with no entanglements, to take care of her mother. She counted it an honor.

Now she sat at her mother's funeral. The hurt was intense. She found it hard to breathe. "What now, Lord?" she asked as she sat alone on the hard pew, grieving. Her brother and sister had families but she had no one. Her place had been with her mother: preparing her meals, taking her to doctor's appointments, and having evening devotions together. Now her mother was gone and she was all by herself.

She was sitting isolated on her pew when she heard hurried footsteps moving along the carpeted floor. An exasperated young man looked around briefly and then sat down next to her. His eyes were brimming with tears. He folded his hands. "I'm sorry," he whispered to her, "that I am so late." After several eulogies he leaned over and asked, "Why do they keep calling her Margaret when her name was Mary?"

"Oh," the woman replied, "she was always called Margaret, never called Mary." She wondered who in the world was this total stranger who continued to interrupt her grieving with his tears and sniffling. Why didn't he sit somewhere else?

"No," he insisted in a loud whisper, "her name is Mary Peters." Now several people were glancing their way, probably wondering why they didn't be more quiet.

"This isn't Mary Peters. Her name is Margaret and she is my mother."

With a stunned look of confusion on his face he stammered, "Isn't this the Lutheran Church?"

"No," she said, "that is across the street. You're at the wrong funeral."

The solemnness of the occasion mixed with the realization of the man's mistake just bubbled up inside the woman and came out as laughter. Embarrassed, she cupped her hands over her face hoping it would be interpreted as sobs. Now it seemed as if just about everyone at the service was looking at her and the uncomfortable misguided young man sitting next to her. He was now covering his face and trying to stifle laughter. She smiled, convinced her mother was looking down from heaven and snickering, too. After the final amen, they dashed out together and into the parking lot. "I do believe that we are the talk of the town," he commented with a grin. He announced that his name was Rick and since he'd missed his aunt's funeral he hoped she would accept an invitation to have a cup of coffee with him. She responded with a warm smile, "Why not?"

That began a lifelong journey. A year later they were married at the church where Rick was an associate pastor. This time they both arrived at the same church right on time. She recalls, "In my time of sorrow God gave me laughter. In place of loneliness, our Father gave me love. This past June we celebrated our twenty-second wedding anniversary. In the middle of a long, dark night Jesus gave me hope."

The middle of the night can be dark and lonely but St. Peter reminds us in his first epistle that we have been called out of darkness into His wonderful light. Poet Colin Sterne, in his hymn, "We've a Story to Tell to the Nations," writes that "the darkness shall turn to dawning, and the dawning to noonday bright; and Christ's great kingdom shall come on earth, the kingdom of love and light." The apostle John, inspired by the Holy Spirit, gave us this description of heaven in the last chapter of the Bible, Revelation 22:5: "There will be no more night...for the Lord God will give them light."

Epilogue

"I'd rather see a sermon than hear one any day; I'd rather one should walk with me than merely tell the way: the eye's a better pupil and more willing than the ear, fine counsel is confusing, but example's always clear."

– Edgar A. Guest

Biography

J erald Borgie is an ordained Lutheran pastor who has served congregations in Ohio and California. He and his wife, Marcia, reside in San Diego. They have two married sons and five grandchildren. He is also the author of *Chapel Chats For Children (of all ages)*.

CPSIA information can be obtained
at www.ICGtesting.com
Printed in the USA
FSOW02n1743041116
26993FS